The Digital Humanities

The Digital Humanities is a comprehensive introduction and practical guide to how humanists use the digital to conduct research, organize materials, analyze and publish findings. It summarizes the turn toward the digital that is reinventing every aspect of the humanities among scholars, libraries, publishers, administrators and the public. Beginning with some definitions and a brief historical survey of the humanities, the book examines how humanists work, what they study, how humanists and their research have been impacted by the digital and how, in turn, they shape it. It surveys digital humanities tools and their functions, the digital humanists' environments and the outcomes and reception of their work. The book pays particular attention to both theoretical underpinnings and practical considerations for embarking on digital humanities projects. It places the digital humanities firmly within the historical traditions of the humanities and in the contexts of current academic and scholarly life.

Eileen Gardiner is cofounder and copublisher of Italica Press. She has served as director of ACLS Humanities E-Book, executive director of The Medieval Academy of America and coeditor of *Speculum: A Journal of Medieval Studies*. She is author of *Visions of Heaven and Hell before Dante*, *Medieval Visions of Heaven and Hell*, *The Pilgrim's Way to St. Patrick's Purgatory* and *Hell-on-Line*, a website on the infernal otherworld in various traditions.

Ronald G. Musto is cofounder and copublisher of Italica Press. He has served as director of ACLS Humanities E-Book, coexecutive director of The Medieval Academy of America and editor of *Speculum: A Journal of Medieval Studies*. He has taught at New York University, Duke University and Columbia University and has held American Academy in Rome, National Endowment for the Humanities and Mellon Foundation fellowships. He has published nine books and various articles, including *Apocalypse in Rome* and *Renaissance Society and Culture* (coedited with John Monfasani).

The Digital Humanities

A Primer for Students and Scholars

Eileen Gardiner
and
Ronald G. Musto

CAMBRIDGE
UNIVERSITY PRESS

32 Avenue of the Americas, New York NY 10013-2473, USA

Cambridge University Press is part of the University of Cambridge.

It furthers the University's mission by disseminating knowledge in the pursuit of education, learning and research at the highest international levels of excellence.

www.cambridge.org
Information on this title: www.cambridge.org/9781107601024

© Eileen Gardiner and Ronald G. Musto 2015

First published 2015

A catalogue record for this publication is available from the British Library

Library of Congress Cataloguing in Publication data
Gardiner, Eileen.
The digital humanities : a primer for students and scholars / Eileen Gardiner (Italica Press), Ronald G. Musto (Italica Press).
pages cm
Includes bibliographical references and index.
ISBN 978-1-107-01319-3 (hardback) –
ISBN 978-1-107-60102-4 (paperback)
1. Humanities – Data processing. 2. Humanities – Research. 3. Humanities – Methodology. 4. Humanities – Study and teaching. 5. Humanists – Intellectual life. 6. Digital media. 7. Digital communications. 8. Information storage and retrieval systems – Humanities. I. Musto, Ronald G. II. Title.
AZ105.G37 2015
025.06′0013–dc23   2015003103

ISBN 978-1-107-60102-4 Paperback

Contents

Illustrations

Preface and Acknowledgments

The following book grew out of a 2010 Fulbright Fellowship proposal by Eileen Gardiner for teaching digital humanities to undergraduates and graduate students at the National University of Ireland, Galway. The proposal was successful, but another challenge presented itself – taking on the executive directorship of the Medieval Academy of America – so that pedagogical plan was transformed into a book that we hope will guide and benefit more than the original several dozen students.

This book also derives significantly from our many years as both scholars and publishers. In 1993, at our own Italica Press, we had published some of the first e-books for scholars, including *The Marvels of Rome for the Macintosh*, an early digital (HyperCard) edition of the celebrated medieval guide to the city, one of the earliest electronic books produced.[1] We also draw on our twelve years at the American Council of Learned Societies (ACLS) where we took over leadership of an electronic publishing project shortly after it was funded by the Andrew W. Mellon Foundation. The ACLS History E-Book Project, later ACLS Humanities E-Book (HEB), was a forward-looking project in 1999, with the goal of publishing approximately eighty-five new digital monographs in history, adding a substantial digital backlist, incorporating the insights from the digital realm and pushing the boundaries of scholarly communication in the humanities. When we left HEB in 2011, it had published nearly four thousand e-books, including a large backlist of print-first titles converted into digital format and more than one hundred new titles that ranged from born-digital projects to enhanced digital monographs featuring sound, image libraries, video, virtual reality, archival databases and other external resources.

During our time at ACLS, we had the opportunity to add to our own publishing experiences by engaging with scholars from a variety of humanities disciplines who were pioneers in the emerging field of what only later would begin to be called the "digital humanities." This experience and the people we collaborated with on this project provided us with a perspective on the digital humanities that combined the views of the various stakeholders in a then-emerging enterprise. Twelve years at ACLS also served as an informal apprenticeship for two humanities PhDs in the issues of higher-ed, scholarly communication, university presses, libraries and learned societies. Issues of hiring, tenure and promotion (HTP) seemed to permeate all aspects of scholarly communication, and these issues are raised throughout the book. We attempted to transfer this experience to our positions as executive directors of the Medieval Academy of America and editors of its scholarly journal, *Speculum.* With the insights gained over these years, we therefore now set out to do a "little book" on the digital humanities to guide those trying to understand what is involved in this new direction for the scholarly and academic humanities community.

As the reader will see throughout this book, we use the plural form for "digital humanities," because we take a nonprescriptive, non-ideological approach to our topic, allowing numerous definitions and approaches and avoiding any airtight demarcations by theoretical frame, department, field, area of expertise, mission, skill base or individual status. We also avoid the acronym "DH" with its assertive administrative connotations of specialized departments, programs and funding channels: our approach certainly addresses these issues but is far more comprehensive of various definitions and approaches. Throughout this discussion of digital humanities, there also persists the constant presence of the historical humanities. But this book is not an elegy for a lost, first age of humanism, and its authors certainly shared in the creative excitement of the first two decades of the digital. This book is therefore as much about the current state of the humanities in our culture as it is about the digital: the fates of both seem inextricably linked at this point. It is also an attempt to reach out beyond the academy to the general public in order to help explain the current status of the humanities in our society.

It seems particularly appropriate that this book should appear at this point. Over the past two decades, the digital humanities have matured to the point where everyone knows something about them, but only a few would offer a clear-cut definition, and even fewer really know what they entail through experience or praxis. Many remain intimidated by the term and its acronym – put off by ideological and exclusive approaches and attempts to narrow down a "field" to a relatively small cadre of theorists. But the fact is that most of us do "digital humanities" much of the time in our basic research, with our daily tools of scholarly communication, in our writing and revision, in our final published work and in its assessment.

It is also a good time to write about this topic because the speed of developments appears to have slowed down considerably from the pace of the past decade. Technology is plateauing and no longer "disruptive," and the insights of Clayton M. Christiansen's *The Innovators Dilemma*[2] have been well absorbed by humanists. Initial experimental gains are being scaled, consolidated and made sustainable; alliances are broadening; and the subject itself has become less of a shifting seismic plate. By now so many humanities scholars have engaged in successful projects that there are solid examples – of successes and failures – that others can clearly copy and learn from, if not engage with directly. We have tried here to step back from a mere journalism of new projects and approaches to reflect on how this maturing process is working and what its long-term characteristics might be.

Again, this book is essentially a "primer," a small handbook, that we hope will be a clear and practical guide to explain what the digital humanities are, beginning with some definitions and a brief historical survey of the humanities. The book moves from there to how humanists work, what they work on, how humanists and their work have been impacted by the digital and how, in turn, they are shaping the digital. It presents a survey of digital humanities tools and how humanists use them, with examples of projects. The book then examines the way the digital impacts the way we work, the environments that we work in and the outcome of our work: its format and its place in the realm of scholarly communication within the community of scholars and scholarship. Throughout we pay attention to the theoretical underpinnings of the digital humanities: many of these foundations lie in the historical, literary, linguistic, gender and materiality turns of the past several decades. Some have emerged newly under the impact of our cyber-driven work and lives.

We wrote this book in full knowledge that by now most humanists, their colleagues in the social and physical sciences and the broader public have all been exposed to the products of the humanities in their traditional and digital forms in an overwhelming array of examples: everything from the scholarly monograph, journal article and lectures delivered at the Modern Language Association's annual meeting, to the History Channel; the medievalist high drama of *Game of Thrones*; to music, TV and film reviews; to art exhibits and performances; to poetry, drama, fiction and nonfiction books; to biblical archaeology and American Civil War magazines: all are the products of humanists at work throughout American society. Every time we see an animation or virtual-reality reconstruction of a battle, see a gladiatorial contest in the movies or on TV, build or explore an ancient city on our computers, hear on NPR about a new treasure trove discovered under the high seas or watch on cable TV a frightening exploration of heaven and hell, we have already been exposed to the work of digital humanists and their colleagues in computer technologies. Writing about the digital humanities is therefore both very easy – it is an intrinsic part of our culture now – and also very difficult, precisely because it has become part of the air we breathe, the water we swim in, the fabric of our lives. To explain in carefully formulated and rigorous terms what is all around us – and what therefore seems so obvious – may be one of the hardest tasks of humanists. It is something akin to explaining to someone who never considered the fact before, that everything we touch, see or use in our daily lives is the product of some designer's mind and hand; that every major building we pass through, work, live or entertain ourselves in is the product of a team of architects who consider every detail from retaining walls to ceiling tiles to light sockets; or that every page of a history book we read is not simply something picked up from a world already there but a carefully and deliberately constructed model created by the skill and hard work of the humanists in their midst.

As we will explain in the following chapters, the humanities have a long, ancient and venerable tradition in our culture: shaping our perceptions of our present world and forming our understanding of its past and the relationships between the two. Now in the digital age and with the ubiquity of digital forms, it becomes even more necessary to take a fresh perspective on how humanists accomplish this by using the newest of technologies, just as they once did using the technologies of the manuscript book, the printing press, the photograph or the vinyl record.[3]

We hope that this book will provide a rich sense of all these thoughts and activities. We have attempted to engage them through a variety of sometimes overlapping approaches, and we do not expect everyone to read every chapter or to start at the beginning and work through every page. For a book of this size, covering so many topics required a great deal of compression and brevity, with a few carefully chosen examples, with all URLs accessed in late January 2015. There have been so many books, articles, conferences and lectures covering the digital humanities, expressing such a wide range of opinion and research findings, that one of our main tasks here has been to synthesize many of the discussions and issues without, we hope, oversimplifying or eliminating too much nuance. We are sorry if we could not cover all important exemplars and approaches in the space allotted. Each of these topics should and has received far greater attention than we could give them here. But we do hope that our approach has brought them together clearly and comprehensibly.

Everyone sets out to write the book that will answer their own questions, and we wanted here to explore the world of digital humanities in order to take stock after fifteen years to determine whether it fulfills the promise that it seemed to hold out in 1999. We came to the end of the book with the insight that Vincent Mosco offers in his *The Digital Sublime*:⁴ that despite all the almost millennial claims that America usually makes for each of its new technologies – whether the railroad, the telegraph or telephone, electricity, the radio, movies, TV, the fax or the computer – new technologies ultimately transform the way we live and the way we think not through their most dazzling new displays, but when they have become commonplace and broadly accepted, even perhaps banal and mundane – when everyone is using them without thinking twice. It was, after all, not Edison's electronic wonder shows that transformed America but his light bulbs. The computer and the digital world have transformed the way we work, but they are now such a part of that work that we seldom think about them twice. There are exemplary, high-end applications that only a few use, or have any use for, but most humanists use far more mundane tools frequently and learn new ones every day. It is not the virtual reality walk-through that has changed the way we work but the word processing program and the PDF, not the data mining tool or the million-pixel image but the simple database and the JPEG, not the stand-alone pyramid of data, interpretation and comment but the aggregation of digitized journals and monographs that have altered our research methods and agendas. While the Appendix offers a simple taxonomy of digital tools organized by function, it also presents a compelling second narrative of the advanced work humanists have been conducting across the disciplines. And while most humanists continue to use a limited suite of tools, largely determined by discipline and research agenda, the Appendix will demonstrate the degree to which humanists have both embraced the digital and made it their own. The digital humanities may no longer appear spectacular to most of us – a wonder show of individual virtuosity – yet they have been transformative in the everyday way in which scholars research, organize, analyze and present their work. Have they brought about this transformation in the ways that we expected? Perhaps not yet, or perhaps they already have, and we are not yet fully aware of it.

As the following chapters will make clear, we approach this topic from the viewpoint of traditional humanist scholars, where the methods and historical perspectives of the humanities take precedence over considerations of humanities computing. However, we also view the phenomenon from outside any disciplinary or methodological stance, making neither an apologia for continuing the work of the humanities as they stood two decades ago nor seeking any movement from within the computer and IT worlds to reconfigure humanities studies and disciplines into subdisciplines for a special core of cutting-edge researchers and theorists. We hope that our experience of the praxis of digital humanities has allowed us to avoid either extreme here and to judiciously lead the reader through a complex and intriguing topic. True to humanistic method, our purpose is to probe and to ask ever new questions from developing solutions.

We would like to thank several individuals for generously sharing ideas, insights, concerns and hopes. Seeing the projects of, and engaging in conversations with, Edward Ayres, Kevin Guthrie, Kate Wittenberg, John Unsworth and James J. O'Donnell opened our eyes to the possibilities then in the making. Working with the dozens of directors of the learned societies that make up the ACLS – including Arnita Jones and Robert Townsend of the American Historical Association, John Monfasani of the Renaissance Society of America, Lee Formwalt of the Organization of American Historians, Amy Newhall of the Middle East Studies Association and Susan Ball of the College Art Association – we gathered perspective on the issues and problems facing humanists and the promise of solutions that the digital offered. Carol Mandel, Deanna Marcum, Ann Okerson and James Neal, among many others, provided the university library's perspectives; Lynne Withey, Jennifer Crewe, Peter Dimock, Niko Pfund, Steve Maikowski, James Jordan and Rufus Neal, also among many others, offered the university press perspective; and our partners at the University of Michigan Libraries, particularly John Wilken and Maria Bonn, opened doors to new concepts and technologies. Several lengthy interviews and conversations with John B. Thompson in preparation for his *Books in the Digital Age*[5] helped us formulate our own ideas and place them into larger and more rigorous contexts. We would also like to thank Richard Superti for his close and observant reading of the manuscript.

Our editor at Cambridge University Press, Beatrice Rehl, took up our proposal for this book with enthusiasm, guided it through its peer review and afforded us a great deal of leeway as our outstanding professional commitments delayed the manuscript's completion. Our two groups of anonymous peer reviewers have helped form and improve this book in important ways. We would like to thank all the ACLS Humanities E-Book authors who worked with us on exciting new projects over almost twelve years at ACLS, from Joshua Brown to Burr Litchfield and Bernard Frischer to Benjamin Kohl. We would like to thank Donald J. Waters of the Andrew W. Mellon Foundation and Steven C. Wheatley of ACLS for their support throughout our days at ACLS Humanities E-Book. Nina Gielen, now managing editor at HEB, was able to transform many of our editorial and publishing ideas into robust and sustainable digital realities. And we would particularly like to thank John H. D'Arms, a friend for more than thirty years, who offered us the challenge.

Introduction to the Digital Humanities

DEFINITIONS

What are the "digital humanities"? Ask a physicist to define *gravity*, and she will most likely first reply with a brief textual description about forces and masses in the universe and then present a formula. Ask an economist to define *poverty*, and he might refer you to the U.S. Census Bureau's lists of scales, rates and other metrics. But ask a humanist to define *peace*, and she will turn first to the dictionary and then to a brief historical survey of how the word evolved, from what languages and therefore from what historical contexts and developments. She might then proceed to construct a narrative based on available written records. She would do these two things because the humanist, unlike the physical or social scientist, deals not with the objects and forces of the natural world or with large abstractions like social groups and economic trends but with language, its origins, constructions, development and perception over time. The very core of humanistic study is to seek out origins and to interpret how we use language – including the language of the visual arts, music and architecture – to understand the world that humans have created. All humanistic study begins and ends with language, its meaning and its ability to bring the past alive.

How then do we understand the *digital humanities* – a term widely used in administrative, scholarly, library and information technology (IT) circles but rarely defined in any specific way? What exactly do these partners – the digital and the humanities – have to do with one another? Many people look at the marriage and come away with very different impressions, all from their own perspectives. One can analyze the term's exact meanings from several different points of view, conditioned by historical and contemporary thinking and practice. Many have very firm opinions on what they consider a closed case; others have yet to deter-mine some of the most fundamental questions around that term.

For example, what were, are and will be the humanities in Western, and now world, culture? What is the role of the digital within the acad-emy, in scholarly communication and in the humanistic disciplines as a whole? Are the digital humanities a series of practical approaches? Are they a specific theoretical frame that is nuanced within each disciplinary approach? Are they a distinct discipline with its own set of standards, dis-tinguished researchers, hierarchies and rules of engagement? Are they a set of ad hoc working arrangements between traditional humanists in various disciplines and IT departments or teams on campuses and in research centers?

Or even more far-reaching, is the term *digital humanities* a redundancy? That is, are the humanities, like all contemporary scientific research and teaching, already digital to all important extents and purposes? Or – an even more vexed question for professional humanists – has the arrival of the digital forever changed the way humanists work, in the way they gather data and evidence or even in the very questions that humanists and the humanistic disciplines are now capable of posing? Is technology determinative? What role does the solitary scholar – the centuries-old model of the humanist since Petrarch – have in a digital environment that is increasingly collaborative, data-driven, report-oriented, ephem-eral, "social" and unmediated?

Some quickly dismiss such questions and concerns with what was essentially the response of the Prince of Salina in Lampedusa's *The Leopard*: "Everything must change so that everything will remain the same." That is, we could easily fit the digital revolution into a set of historically determined metaphors and similes: the digital revolution is Gutenberg updated, the changes in the digital book are "like" the changes from the scroll to the codex or from the codex to the printed book, the rapid social and economic changes brought about by the World Wide Web are "like" the rapid changes brought about by print in the fifteenth century. And so on.

But twenty years after the digital revolution was born, we may no lon-ger be able to rely on comfortable metaphor and simile: something has fundamentally changed in the way the digital accesses, preserves, aggregates and disaggregates, presents, privileges and reflects back upon scholarship that may leave old categories behind and change the way even Petrarchan humanists think, do research, author, publish and inter-act with their own communities. To examine these changes, we should, like all good humanists, turn back to history: the recent and relatively brief history of the digital and the far longer history of the humanities themselves.

Over the years, and particularly over the past decade, humanities scholars have collaborated with computer scientists to build tools that facilitated the work of the digital humanities. However, scholars generally date the beginnings of this collaboration to 1949 when Roberto Busa, an Italian Jesuit and theologian, approached Thomas J. Watson, founder of IBM, seeking help in indexing the works of Thomas Aquinas. Busa was successful, but he was not alone in seeking to harness computing power to the work of humanistic scholarship. Nor were search engines and word counts his aim: that was a "doctrinal interpretation" of Aquinas's theology and moral philosophy. The digital was a means to the qualitative improvement of the humanist's moral goal.[1] In the process, however, Busa and Watson demonstrated that the search-and-sort functions of the computer were compelling tools for certain aspects of research. Storage and retrieval appealed equally so. From that time the worlds of the humanities and of computing were intertwined first in experimentation and then in efforts at creating a sustainable infrastructure for humanities scholarship.

The intersection of the humanities and the digital created an environment in which the humanities became subject to new approaches that raised issues about the nature of the humanities while also opening up new research methods. The array of platforms, applications, techniques and tools, all developed under the rubric of "digital," have been dramatically changing the way that humanists work, how they do research, gather information, organize, analyze and interpret it and disseminate findings. How does the digital affect this basic work? While some believe that the digital is fundamentally changing the work of the humanist, others continue to believe that the digital merely helps humanists to work better. Some even believe that the digital may be undermining the fundamental nature of this work. Many humanists tend to view the digital humanities as a methodology that brings the tools and power of computing to bear on the traditional work of the humanities. Computer scientists tend to view the digital humanities as the study of how electronic form affects the disciplines in which it is used and what these disciplines have to contribute to our knowledge of computing.

Let us therefore start with some basic definitions. A chapter in the recent *Debates in the Digital Humanities*[2] offers twenty-one definitions culled from a far longer online list; this is a provocation as part of the "debates" around digital humanities. But let us try to settle on something less controversial from a standard source. The first thing worth noting is that we begin our research online; the second is that a Google Search offers none of the standard dictionary entries one expects. The Dictionary.com, Merriam-Webster and Free Online Dictionary entries are missing from their usual prominent placement. Instead, the Wikipedia article on "Digital Humanities"[3] offers the following, categorical definition:

> Digital Humanities is an area of research and teaching at the intersection of computing and the disciplines of the humanities. Developing from the fields of humanities computing, humanistic computing, and digital humanities praxis, digital humanities embraces a variety of topics, from curating online collections to data mining large cultural data sets. Digital humanities (often abbreviated DH) currently incorporates both digitized and born-digital materials and combines the methodologies from traditional humanities disciplines (such as history, philosophy, linguistics, literature, art, archaeology, music, and cultural studies) and social sciences with tools provided by computing (such as data visualization, information retrieval, data mining, statistics, text mining, digital mapping) and digital publishing.

By contrast Anne Burdick and her coauthors provide a far more open-ended, inclusive definition in their book *Digital_Humanities:*

> [Digital humanities] asks what it means to be a human being in the networked information age and to participate in fluid communities of practice, asking and answering research questions that cannot be reduced to a single genre, medium, discipline, or institution. . . . It is a global, trans-historical, and transmedia approach to knowledge and meaning-making.[4]

The sharp contrast between the two approaches demonstrates the contested nature of the term, and perhaps this is the result of the fact that while humanists and computer scientists are in dialog here, each with their own distinct perspective, the digital element of the definition underlies both. Perhaps this will be resolved eventually by reestablishing the digital humanities and humanities computing as two different areas, each with its own perspective: the former (digital humanities) as a methodology; and the latter (humanities computing) as a field of study or a discipline. However, the question would then arise as to whether humanities computing were a humanistic, a social science or technological/scientific discipline. Our perspective in these pages, however, is not with humanities computing, but with the digital humanities, with harnessing computing power to facilitate, improve, expand and perhaps even change the way humanists work. Our focus remains that of the humanist and the humanities with deep historical roots and outlooks.

How then should we proceed to create a working definition that will facilitate and guide the following book? The two definitions in the preceding texts do offer a realistic assessment of the current state of humanities computing and some useful insights. But if we give credence to our first definition, is the digital hurting the humanities by drawing scholars away from the traditional work of humanists and turning them into number crunchers or bell-and-whistle builders? Some believe that the digital is dramatically improving the work of humanists; that the digital can make scholars think and work better, or at least differently, as is vaguely implied by the second definition in the above text. It is true that the digital expands the amount of material that one can access and process in any given amount of time. The digital can also connect things with powerful search capabilities. Scholars can enhance the efficiency of their work with tools for organizing and mining materials. Writing and editing are facilitated in the digital realm. As Roberto Busa first asked, do these changes reconstitute the way scholars work or are they merely helping scholars do what they would normally do, but more quickly and efficiently? Are the digital humanities changing the way humanist scholars think? Is there a body of evidence that anything so fundamental is already changing, or do the humanities remain at the early stages of the digital era?

If we examine the question in broader context: can we believe the "digital futurists," those who claim ground-shifting capabilities for the digital? Have old ways of research, writing and publication been supplanted as the digital alters all historical relationships and models? Are such traditional forms as monograph and article publishing, textual editing and image archiving too minor to be encompassed by their visions of the digital? Or may such narrow definitions and prophesies of ineluctable change actually inhibit the adoption and acceptance of the digital by intimidating potential users, reviewers and administrators? Some may fear that their disciplines will be overtaken by digerati, whose work will outstrip anything that traditional humanists can accomplish. Instead of accepting the accessible tools that can work for anyone, the futurists project a techno-future filled with astounding wonder shows, to which, by comparison, all other efforts pale. What is the point of using a few architectural photos of the Château de Fontainebleau captured by a digital SLR if the futurists present NASA technology–derived million-pixel images of one of its garden sculptures? Why continue to edit texts using traditional philological methods when digital text mining can serve up all possible variants for any text? Instead of celebrating what is now done on a daily basis by so many humanists, has the promise of an unknown future made potential adopters hesitant to take their first steps or to claim the recognition for their own achievements and those of their colleagues for what they are?

To re-pose the question raised by the first two definitions above from the perspective of funding agencies and grant applicants: Are digital humanities projects worth doing only if subsidized by a $2 million grant from the Mellon Foundation or the National Science Foundation? Have foundations that have funded high-end digital work supported the creation of a class of high-end academic and humanistic futurists, prophets and superstars to the neglect of most working humanists? Have large grants that have gained access to media and public relations on and off campus raised the ante for those engaged in the small and particular of traditional scholarly work and further accelerated the marginalization of the historically oriented humanities from both the academic campus and American life in general? We aim to explore such questions as well. And while the major task – and the one that will occupy most of this small volume – will be to examine both the impact of the digital on the humanities and the influence of humanists on the digital, we should first discuss the nature and historical development of the humanities themselves.

To begin, it will be useful to briefly distinguish what we mean by the term *humanities* and its relative, *humanism*. By "humanism," we do not mean the *Merriam-Webster's Dictionary* definition 3 of the term: "a doctrine, attitude, or way of life centered on human interests or values; especially: a philosophy that usually rejects supernaturalism and stresses an individual's dignity and worth and capacity for self-realization through reason." Nor do we mean definition 2: "humanitarianism"; nor even fully definition 1: "a. devotion to the humanities: literary culture" or "b. the revival of classical letters, individualistic and critical spirit, and emphasis on secular concerns characteristic of the Renaissance."

Rather, throughout this book, we will focus on the historically conditioned and contextualized meanings of the terms studied and clarified over the past two generations by scholars of the Renaissance. We will attempt to find historical analogies and precedents for digital humanities theory and practice throughout these chapters, making apt historical comparisons (in true humanist fashion), until the analogy is stretched to the breaking point by modern phenomenon. When this occurs, we will then ask how and why our new realities are different from our historical precedents and what questions these breaks pose for our attempts to define the digital humanities and the humanities in general in the digital age. Our methodology is nothing new, even for examining the digital: James J. O'Donnell used it masterfully in his *Avatars of the Word*,[5] and much early digital theory constantly referenced the ages of manuscript and print.

Our working definition of the humanities and of humanists has been established by Paul Oskar Kristeller[6] and three generations of colleagues and students. Essentially these historians sought the origins of humanism and the humanities first in the intellectual culture of late medieval France and then primarily of Italy and in one set of the standard seven liberal arts of the Middle Ages – the *trivium* (grammar, rhetoric and logic) – and only later and more peripherally in the *quadrivium* (arithmetic, geometry, music and astronomy).

These scholars also focused on the contrast between humanism and the education of the Italian business classes in the later Middle Ages. This business-class education was strongly practical, emphasizing literacy in the vernacular, in basic business math, in secular literature (romances and violent adventures) and popular religion (saints' and other celebrities' biographies and spiritual self-help) and the rhetorical and grammatical skills involved in public speaking and creating legislation, legal documents and private contracts and accounts. In short this was the equivalent of our modern career-oriented, practical college education, which has in fact largely displaced traditional humanities concentrations on college campuses over the past generation.

By the late thirteenth and early fourteenth century, however, beginning in the free communes of northern Italy and then spreading to central Italy, most especially Florence, a different subset of this curriculum began to be emphasized, especially under the influence of Francesco Petrarch. Throughout his long and varied career (b. 1304–d. 1374) this poet, classical scholar and man of letters set off to consciously rediscover and then imitate the works and the spirit of his ancient Roman models, especially Cicero. He rejected the medieval Latin of the universities and the contemporary urban professional classes – the doctors, lawyers and theologians trained at Italy's and France's universities – and began to attempt to write in a new, pure Latin style in imitation of the ancients. He did so not from any esoteric, elitist or formalistic love of good writing for its own sake – how one text or textual tradition might influence

another, how one writer's style might form the model for another's –
but for deeply moral and spiritual purposes: the wisdom and learning
inherent in the texts themselves. Like Dante before him, Petrarch saw
the world around him as decadent and corrupt, its secular and religious leadership mired in power politics, personal ambition and spiritual emptiness. He therefore looked back to the ancient world for its
pure expression of moral life in the letters of Cicero, for example, and
in the works of the early Christian writers like Augustine. He was the
first to formulate our idea of the period between the fall of Rome and
his own time as the "middle ages," a period of decline and darkness. For
Petrarch the learning of the ancient world was both a personal solace
and a means to reform and renew the world by changing people's minds
and then their actions: by clearly understanding the writing, and hence
the thought of the great ancients, we could come to imitate them. But
the key lay not in religious observances or politics but in language and
thought.

He soon gained a brilliant circle of followers and admirers, including
Cola di Rienzo, Giovanni Boccaccio, Coluccio Salutati and, in a later
generation, Leonardo Bruni and many others, who by the early fifteenth
century had begun to consciously focus on a set of skills and activities
that would soon distinguish them from their academic peers at Europe's
great universities: the philosophers, theologians or lawyers (canon and
Roman). Instead, the first humanists focused on what they saw as the
key to Petrarch's revival of antiquity: grammar and rhetoric, including
what today we would call philology. In addition to these they studied
and wrote poetry, history and moral philosophy, rejecting the logic and
dialectic philosophy of the medieval schoolmen, the Scholastics. While
their focus lay in language, they valued the result of proper understanding: public moral action and ethical life.

Our analysis is necessarily somewhat simplified here, and the humanists should not be equated with the full extent of Renaissance thought
and culture. They were, instead, a distinct group of philological experts,
trained in the reading of classical texts, first Latin and then Greek, and
devoted to deciphering and editing the scattered classical heritage they
found across Europe in medieval monasteries and princely collections.
By around 1500 they were also overseeing the dissemination of these
texts across Europe in consistent printed editions. They framed their
activities in the words of the second-century scholar Aulus Gellius: they
were engaged in the study of "*humanitas,*" that is, "learning and instruction in good or liberal arts. [For] those who earnestly desire and seek

after these are most highly humanized. . . ." Their goal and the goal of all humanists was to interpret the evidence of human lives, thoughts and actions.

By the death of Leonardo Bruni in 1444, this group of scholars, self-selected and focused on these specific philological skills, had gained immense influence in their city-states where they served as chancellors and held other high offices and elsewhere where their rhetorical and other written skills served the needs of new Renaissance states and princely courts, of the papacy and then of the universities.[7] Within the university their curriculum became known as the *studia humanitatis*, and the same Italian student slang that would label the jurists, *jurista*, for example, began to dub the proponents of the *studia humanitatis* as "*humanista*," or "humanists." The modern word *humanism* itself derives only from 1808, coined by the German philosopher Friedrich Immanuel Niethammer as "*Humanismus*." He, however, used it to distinguish between education as a practical-minded set of skills (our predominant college concentrations and earned degrees today) and education as an end in itself based on philological and literary pursuits.

Whether in public or academic life, the humanists' essential tool kits included their own skills in rhetoric, grammar and the other liberal arts, their books and then the libraries that housed these and the collections of the ancient and contemporary writings that they used. Many women also presided over or rose to prominence at court, and some even lived independent lives as poets and performing artists. Some – very few – humanists, like Desiderius Erasmus, seemed to have lived a creative life that rose above the patronage of the princes, kings and emperors that supported them.

The medieval libraries where they rediscovered their ancient Roman and Greek texts were neither as dusty nor as worm-ridden as the humanists often portrayed them, but the humanists themselves actively helped create what we would come to know as the modern library: first of all with their own collections, starting with Petrarch, and then with the collections of kings (the Angevins and Aragonese at Naples), princes (the Medici in Florence, the Montefeltro in Urbino) and ecclesiastics (the Vatican Library par excellence). These became the models for humanist libraries that, if not public in the modern sense, were certainly open to any qualified user who could read their books.

Closely tied to the library was the creation and distribution of the book: through commercial copy centers *(scriptoria)* in such university centers as Paris, Bologna and Oxford in the later Middle Ages, and then through the new print medium into the seventeenth century. Humanists set a precedent in their relationship to this new process not only in the creation of new ideas and the critical editing of old texts but in the manufacture and dissemination of the book itself: from Petrarch's and Salutati's own ideas in creating the humanist script to Desiderius Erasmus's editorial work with the pioneering Renaissance printers Aldus Manutius in Venice and Johann Froben in Basel. We thus cannot separate the work of the humanist scholar from the work of the library and the publisher: they have been integrally bound together historically from the start.

By the early 1500s "humanism" had swept the courts of Italy and then of Europe and had become such a strong cultural force that humanist educators – such as Pier Paolo Vergerio, Vittorino da Feltre and Leonardo Bruni in Italy, Erasmus in the Hapsburg lands, Juan Luis Vives in Spain or John Colet in England – had established the humanist curriculum as the only valid one for Europe's leadership classes, both secular and ecclesiastical. Grammar, rhetoric, oratory, history, poetry, all based on classical Greek and Latin models, became the classic core curriculum. It became the basis for numerous handbooks dedicated to the "education of the Christian prince," the standard for the Italian courtier, the English gentleman, the Italian and Spanish lady. Even after the Protestant Reformation it remained central for German students in secondary school (Gymnasium) as well as for the curriculum of the Jesuits in the Catholic Reformation.

The traditional university graduate specialties – philosophy, law and medicine – as well as architecture, the visual arts and the new natural sciences, all soon shared many of humanism's basic approaches and tenets: a deep respect and imitation of ancient models, the conscious efforts to rediscover and identify ancient sources, the sometimes almost slavish imitation of styles and vocabularies, to such an extent that by the end of Renaissance impulse – really the late eighteenth and nineteenth century – humanism had become almost synonymous with higher education and public culture. The architecture of humanism was the driving force of the late nineteenth and early twentieth centuries behind the grand public buildings that transformed the American urban fabric, for example, with grand public institutions (everything from libraries to train stations) and private mansions.

Humanism and its moral and intellectual concerns remained at the heart of the higher education system of the early American colonies and republic at Princeton, Harvard and Yale, for example. Even Thomas

Jefferson, a proponent of the new sciences and knowledge, based the core curriculum at the University of Virginia (UVA) on the humanist tradition: ancient and modern languages, mathematics, moral philosophy, natural philosophy, law and medicine, which matched the standard European university education of the time. In Jefferson's model we can already see the impact of the scientific revolution, the Enlightenment and American pragmatism on the humanist tradition: chemistry and more practical skills were also integrated into UVA's curriculum. This cultural legacy remained strong into the twentieth century in curricula that promoted a liberal arts education.

With the late nineteenth century, a new emphasis on "scientific" research and an empiricist methodology for humanists developed in the seminars of the great German historian Leopold von Ranke (d. 1886) – with his insistence on the scientifically derived truths apparent in the archival records. This Rankean approach began to take hold of academic life first in Germany and then in the United States. While this is a topic more appropriate to larger policy issues in higher education, these developments had a significant impact on what we identify today as the humanities. The shift in American higher education away from the liberal arts colleges of the colonial era and early republic to the research university of the late nineteenth and early twentieth centuries has had a profound impact on notions of disciplinary research specialization and the organization, publication, recognition and rewarding of work. The impulse toward "scientific" and "objective" research and writing also propelled the strict professionalization of the traditional humanist educators and their activities into the departments, schools, scholarly societies, journals and university press system that we all recognize today.

By the 1920s the goals of humanities research, teaching and publication had matched the thrust of the physical sciences and emerging social sciences: rigorously peer reviewed and professionalized within a standardized system of strict guidelines of expectations and performance. This new approach began to rapidly move the academic humanist far away from the public one: from the poet, the fiction writer, the moral essayist and dramatist, the visual artist and the architect who were the humanists of the Renaissance and early modern Europe. The new humanist – almost exclusively white and male – was to be found in departments of history, literature, classics, philosophy and the like and would be devoted to researching and teaching not only the ancient past but also his colleagues' more recent reflections on it, focusing on the evaluation of secondary scholarship that has come to mark the role of the core humanities disciplines today.

The post–World War II period inherited this system, perfected by the 1920s, and thus became the great era of the American research university. Prominent documents extolling this spirit would include Vannevar Bush's report *Science the Endless Frontier*[8] in which he laid out the basic form of today's technology-commercial–based university system, and Clark Kerr's 1960 master plan for the University of California system.[9] At the same time, the public perception of the humanities – perhaps reflecting their increasing marginalization in the national culture – evolved into something far different from what they were becoming inside the university. In 1964, sponsored in part by the American Council of Learned Societies, the famed Commission on the Humanities, which included such luminaries as Kerr, Thomas J. Watson, Kingman Brewster and Theodore Hesburgh and which led to the creation of the National Endowment for the Humanities, could define the humanities as follows:

> The humanities may be regarded as a body of knowledge and insight, as modes of expression, as a program for education, as an underlying attitude toward life. The body of knowledge is usually taken to include the study of history, literature, the arts, religion, and philosophy. The fine and the performing arts are modes of expressing thoughts and feelings visually, verbally, and aurally. The method of education is one based on the liberal tradition we inherit from classical antiquity. The attitude toward life centers on concern for the human individual: for his emotional development, for his moral, religious, and aesthetic ideas, and for his goals – including in particular his growth as a rational being and a responsible member of his community.[10]

The American university system would retain this approach into the twenty-first century and the beginnings of what we now call the "corporate university," with its emphasis on the new business-oriented forms of organization, accountability and monetization of all aspects of research and teaching – both in the sciences and in the humanities. One might say that the corporate university is promoting – in many of its most profound modes – an ironic return to the Italian system of urban education in the late Middle Ages as it existed *before* the arrival of the humanists.

The developments that we have rapidly surveyed here have direct impact on the humanities in this new digital age and present us all today with new challenges and, perhaps, new opportunities to express that basic mission of the humanities to both enlighten, according to the models of the past, and to create responsible citizens. In this regard the digital humanities might yet again be set to embrace the methods and outlooks that the very first Renaissance humanists took up: to use modern communication skills – digital iterations of rhetoric and grammar – supplemented by the creative arts of the imagination and the reflective wisdom of the historical outlook to reach contemporary audiences with interpretations of what it is to be human and what it is to be a responsible citizen.

While we have devoted a considerable amount of space to describing and analyzing the historical roots of the humanities, we have still not yet settled on a working definition of the digital humanities. That will remain the task of the following chapters as we discuss the functions, elements, materials, tools, environments and dissemination of digital work in the humanities.

2

The Organization of Humanities Research

INTRODUCTION

Humanists study the world created by humanity. Based on considerable research, and with specific questions in mind, they define a corpus of material for investigation – their evidence – whether it is the composi- tions of Mozart or the paintings of Michelangelo, the buildings of Frank Gehry or the voting records of the Venetian Senate, the cuneiform tab- lets of the ancient Near East, the land grants of the American West, the life and thought of a fourteenth-century queen or of a twentieth-century philosopher. This evidence can include text, document, object, space, performance, artifact or construct (including games, simulations and virtual worlds).

Because so many who are involved in the administration of colleges and universities may not come from a humanist background, misunderstand- ing, misconception and underappreciation of the work done by humanists can be found even within academia. Administrators are far more likely to understand how scientists and social scientists work. From biology – the study of life and living organisms (including humans) – to physics – the study of matter and its motion through space and time – researchers in the physical and life sciences attempt to understand the material world using the "scientific method," or inquiry based on empirical and measurable evidence gathered through observation and experimentation and subject to specific principles of reasoning and critique. However, from physicists to mathematicians, scientists also employ theoretical models in their work and combine theoretical with empirical approaches.

The social sciences, which include a wide range of disciplines from anthropology and economics to political science and sociology, use the empirical methods of their counterparts in the sciences when collecting

14

data on society and social groups, then process that data quantitatively to better understand how these groups function. Social science can also be interpretative and qualitative rather than quantitative, employing theories of social critique or symbolic interpretation, for example. Some distinguish social sciences from the humanities with claims that the former are quantitative (and thus more rigorous and "scientific") and the latter are qualitative. But these lines do not hold firm, and often the boundaries between the humanities and the social sciences blur, most especially in the realms of theory.

How do humanists work? A widespread misconception is that humanists read books and then write more books on their field of study: the self-evident "facts" of history or the easily read pages of literature that almost anyone with a college degree can understand. But in many ways the original research done by humanists and the high-level presentation of that research are not so different from that of scientists and social scientists. What they study may be different: humanists study human culture as created and manifested in and by individuals as opposed to the natural world or the broad patterns of human society. But all attempt to offer as close a model of the "real world" as possible: the physical sciences of the universe, the social sciences of human groupings, the humanities of the work and world created by individual humans. If they examine their capabilities honestly, none can recreate fully the worlds they study. At the very core of the humanities is this self-conscious sense of representation, and in the following chapters we shall examine the nature of such limited representation and how the humanities seek to understand and explain it.

Perhaps another of the major differences between the humanities, social sciences and physical sciences derives from the manner in which they organize the basic material of their study, how they manipulate, arrange and represent their evidence. In both the physical and social sciences data is generally arranged and analyzed in broad classes: similarities and deviations can be evaluated through sophisticated mathematical, statistical, metric and other quantitative means. This evidence is generally converted easily into digital data. But for the humanities the raw material of study has traditionally been quite different, individual and often unique: a human life, a work of art or architecture, a piece of sculpture, a work of poetry or fiction, an historical record of a deed, a property transfer, a will, a treaty, a letter or some aggregation of such individual objects that are studied in and of themselves and not reduced to statistics or patterns of data and their deviations.

Where such evidence forms unique patterns, humanists have generally turned to the study of cultures, but cultures not as represented in
broad statistical reports but again through unique examples: the Middle
Ages through Chartres Cathedral, the Renaissance through Botticelli's
Birth of Venus, the early modern era through the palace of Versailles, the
modern through the making of the atom bomb. All these are mere short-
hands (synecdoche), representations of far larger sets of evidence, but
as metaphors and symbols they also speak obliquely to the ways in which
humanists have organized their evidence for their audience. Each is put
forward to represent many more examples, each different and unique.
It is precisely difference, what humanist scholars now call "alterity," that
is the data of the humanities, and analyzing these individual objects or
events within their deep contexts and in relationship to other unique
examples over time and space are at the core of humanistic research.
In so doing they may seek to better understand similarities, differences
and cultural patterns by borrowing from the theory and findings of the
physical and social sciences. Anthropology, psychology and linguistics,
for example, have had immense impact on how humanists organize,
understand and explain the evidence they have gathered. Historically
the humanities have also organized their evidence along certain traditional lines. In the current chapter we hope to examine how humanists
are beginning to organize, manipulate and represent this evidence in
the digital environment.

It is important to remember that the evidence used by humanists is
rarely found in other books, except perhaps for the studies of printed
literature or of the book itself in theoretical work. Professional research
in the humanities required and still requires the study of original texts
and objects – ideally in their original contexts – in order to understand
who created them, why and in what settings. Thus the cuneiform tablets
collected in a museum of the ancient Middle East, the tomb objects in
a Roman gravesite, the vaulting in a medieval chapel, the paintings in
a Renaissance palace, the ledgers of a nineteenth-century industrialist
housed in a family archive, the letters of a poor farmer from Alabama
or woman immigrant from the Ukraine found in a local historical society's library all need first to be identified, dated or otherwise fit into a
context, and then deciphered using the best methods available. Only in
rare exceptions are such original and unique materials ever fully edited
or published in book form and accessible to readers by purchase or
borrowing. In addition, the materials used as evidence for humanistic

scholarship are generally limited to those directly involved in specific research agendas and disciplinary approaches.

Now with the advent of digital scholarship, however, many humanists, especially those working in collaborative environments, are exposed to vast arrays of source materials being digitized and accessible over the web as well as to materials previously considered outside the confines of their disciplines. This brings with it an opportunity for richer, deeper and different types of scholarship. In addition, the opportunities to gather materials have evolved from those labor-intensive days in an archive sifting through manuscripts and copying them by hand and those costly journeys to the far reaches of the world to view, sketch or perhaps photograph objects of study. Now that archives of texts, images, objects, virtual reconstructions, film and sound are available digitally, scholars can often do much of the basic gathering work for any project within a time frame that allows for greater flexibility, expanded scope and usually shortened schedules. This has obvious benefits – increased speed and lowered cost of research, for example. But in the digital realm it might also have some drawbacks – the temptation to analyze, interpret and publish findings too quickly.

As a positive example, a scholar of the history of science specializing in the nineteenth century might need to consult the papers of Charles Darwin. The bulk of this material, including most of his correspondence, is housed at the University of Cambridge in the library of Corpus Christi College, with some materials in the university library. His notebooks are at his home, Down House, in Kent. Referee reports can be found at the Royal Society in London and a few other items are scattered from Virginia to Buenos Aires. Previous research required extensive travel, long stays and laborious pouring through thousands of pages with no guarantee of finding the evidence sought. The digitization and online publication of this material by Darwin Online[1] now makes available on the web "over 219,804 pages of searchable text and 219,900 electronic images, at least one exemplar of all known Darwin publications, reproduced to the highest scholarly standards, both as searchable text and electronic images of the originals. The majority of these have been edited and annotated for the first time with more than 4,900 original notes."[2] Searches take only moments and results can be saved, modified and analyzed from the computer in a researcher's office or home. Secondary literature used to gain further insight or to establish theoretical frames for this source material can be assembled online from items available in thousands of libraries around the world.

REPRESENTATION

While representation remains a theme that runs throughout any discussion of scholarly communication – whether in the physical and social sciences or the humanities – in the humanities the ease with which our narratives and analyses are accessible to the broader public – and to those in other disciplines – often obscures the representative nature of the evidence we discover, manipulate and eventually publish. It is obvious to any scholar that the universe of fact, event and material that we study can never be presented in its entirety, that impossibility would make the universe a book – surely a venerable metaphor but not a model for scholarship. Every discipline, methodology and form of communication must therefore develop its own culture of representation: how the small samplings of reality that we call research findings are claimed to be truthful reflections of the world around us or of the humans who inhabit the physical and cultural world. On another level all scholars are aware of the representative nature of our extant sources. It is possible, for example, for a classics scholar to become familiar with all the written records of ancient Greece or Rome over a lifetime. But none would claim that that knowledge encompassed even a fraction of the realities of the ancient world, and all would watch as this representation was constantly modified by new findings through archeology and other scientific approaches. In other more modern fields, the research into archives, manuscript collections, printed books, newspapers and other sources both visual and aural are impossible to encompass in a lifetime, as are the increasingly vast amounts of secondary literature published on them. Thus most traditional humanistic research and writing has worked within a framework that made clear that original research and special studies were delving into mere samplings of past realities, that events and personalities chosen to illuminate the past were only highly selective representations, and that every archive or collection of manuscripts and print documents merely skimmed the surface of the deep historical realities that underlay them.

At one step further removed, the typical print monograph could offer an even smaller sense of this representation: a standard book of 250 pages might contain an additional twenty-five or thirty pages of "primary-source" documents to bolster the arguments and analysis made in the monograph. The representational nature of this sampling was so small that an unspoken understanding in scholarly communication was that such samplings were mere synecdoche, and the truth claims of such samplings became dependent upon the recognized skill of the scholar, the rigor of her methodology and the reputation of the press that published them. Thus all humanistic communication is only a representation of worlds irretrievably past and lost to full understanding. We understand that our sources cannot even remotely approach the realities we discuss. Our trust in our representations has therefore been built upon a long-standing culture of highly self-reflective reception and critique within the humanist community often neither disclosed, nor of concern, to the public at large and thus often giving a false impression of knowledge and truth claims to nonspecialists.

But in the digital realm the nature and truth claims of this representation are undergoing radical shifts. Because of vast new quantities of source material, search accessibility and aggregation and analysis tools, our representations are becoming more extensive and more accurate, offering us what might be a closer approximation to at least the complete historical, literary or visual record, if not to the underlying realities that those records reflect. At the same time, however, the digital may be diminishing our representation of reality in a paradoxical way, replacing the secondhand materiality of the sculpted, written or printed record with a virtual reality and complicating our understanding of, and ability to subject our representations to, our traditional skills of grammar and rhetorical presentation that supported the first humanists. For this digital work and its interpretations to enter into humanistic discourse, it is necessary for researchers to present their theses and their supporting documents – whether text, data, object and so forth – for the examination and consideration of the community working in any given field. Are we therefore developing a correspondingly new digital grammar and rhetoric to accommodate this new digital form of representation? How does this new digital environment affect the processes that we have come to recognize as humanities research: data gathering, classification and documentation, manipulation, analysis, interpretation, aggregation and preservation?

DATA GATHERING

Libraries, Archives and Repositories

The basic investigations that humanists undertake are now greatly facilitated by the presence of the digital and most particularly by the Internet,[3] the World Wide Web[4] and web browsers."[5] Yet these are only access tools that ultimately rely on the same aggregations of materials that characterize print culture. At the same time, however, institutions and individuals have been fulfilling the promise of the Internet by creating vast new collections of digitized material. Beginning with library catalogs, which started to be digitized in the late 1970s, the change in the way scholars have done their secondary and much of their primary research has been dramatic. Many will remember the card catalog, which was one of the primary access points to bibliographic materials. It was a great improvement over the previous shelf or manuscript lists used since antiquity and into the age of print, which were themselves volumes listing materials either by where they were located in a library, by the authors' names or by the works' titles. It is worth recalling that originally these existed only at the library itself, and a scholar would need to travel to each library to consult its holdings. Once printed catalogs became available, copies could be distributed much more widely, and major research libraries that collected the printed catalogs of other libraries could become a locus for work up to the point when the original materials needed to be consulted. Yet even here, such multivolume works as the Union Catalog, the New York Public Library, British Library and Bibliothèque nationale de France catalogs were expensive and in limited supply, narrowing access to the most important public and university libraries.

Card catalogs, a late-nineteenth-century development, facilitated the organization of bibliographic information, allowing for new materials to be easily integrated. The distribution of printed catalogs produced from card catalogs continued into the later 1970s and early 1980s, after the digitization of library catalogs had already begun using specially developed, independent systems. Linking these separate electronic catalogs became a priority of both librarians and a growing corps of information technologists. Their emerging protocols required online catalogs to use standard record data, so that computer systems could share bibliographic records. The MARC (Machine-Readable Cataloging) standards, beginning in the mid-1960s, would become internationally accepted and, with integrated library systems like the Dynix Automated Library System, would facilitate interface, communication and data sharing. The Ohio College Library Center, which began in 1967 as an attempt to create a network of Ohio libraries, soon evolved into OCLC (the Online Computer Library Center) and now comprises the collections of seventy-two thousand libraries in 113 countries. Its online catalog, now named WorldCat,[6] debuted in 1971 and itemizes all records in these collections. WorldCat is available free on the Internet, providing researchers with access to more than two billion items among the bibliographic records of participating libraries throughout the world. Searching for a title and including a postal code will identify materials by location for each user. The system also makes it possible to export bibliographic records according to several commonly used style sheets and to create bibliographies online that can be shared among users. It also provides hyperlinks to online reviews and book vendors such as Google Books, Amazon.com, Barnes & Noble and Better World Books.

As search capabilities are expanded, the representative and curated nature of the catalog is being replaced by the search engine, which often brings the researcher out beyond any one particular aggregation, institutional repository or catalog. Yet, as we will discuss in detail in Chapter 8, scholars have learned from their experience with Google Search that the accuracy of the representation of reality they get when they replace the catalog's limited samplings with the search result remains open to debate. Behind the representative sampling of research material in a card or printed-book catalog lies the expertise of subject librarians and disciplinary specialists to insure that the materials accessed are of value and have passed some basic tests of rigor and reliability whether through the reputation of the scholar, the publisher or subsequent peer and public review. Alternately broadly cast web searches, such as Google's attempt to offer the totality of reality – whether in all published books or all images – will deliver thousands or tens of thousands of references. Most of these results will remain inaccessible simply by the sheer numbers of results presented to the researcher and partly because of the indiscriminate and unmediated nature of the search engine. Paradoxically, in this the digital can approach the infinite variety and unmediated nature of "reality." One of the major challenges of the digital humanities is therefore to retain the open nature of the web and its resources while providing some degree of expert guidance in its use and in the materials accessed. Again, one of the essential roles of the humanities historically has always been to provide guidance to, and interpretation of, the world created by humanity. This remains a core mission in the digital.

Digital Libraries

Even before the invention of the World Wide Web between March 1989 and December 1990, the Internet provided the opportunity to store, retrieve and deliver materials. In 1971, Michael Hart at the University of Illinois began Project Gutenberg,[7] which may well be the oldest digital library. It now offers more than forty-seven thousand free e-books in more than fifty languages in a variety of formats. Project Gutenberg started by digitizing small, public-domain works, beginning with the Declaration of Independence, the Bill of Rights and the U.S. Constitution, and it now includes an enormous range of material, most of it previously published works in the public domain, including anything from the 1769 *Survey of Cornwall* to a 1920 volume on *China and Pottery Marks*, in addition to its vast collection of literature from Plato to Kafka and new image libraries.

As of late 2013, the Internet Archive[8] could deliver to users almost five million books and texts, 1.4 million videos and 1.7 million audio files. The Hathi Trust Digital Library,[9] begun in late 2008, is a partnership of approximately one hundred major U.S. research institutions and libraries, which to date has digitized 10,804,340 total volumes, 5,660,959 book titles and 282,038 serial titles. Thirty-two percent of the collection is in the public domain and may be freely accessed. Other material is available only to those affiliated with participating partner libraries.

Google Books[10] announced in August 2010 that by the end of the decade it would scan all known existing books (129,864,880), in total more than four billion digital pages and two trillion words.[11] By April 2013 it had reached the thirty million mark but thereafter began to plateau. Another Google product, Google Scholar, has indexed full-text scholarly literature across an array of disciplines, but this is just one of more than 120 academic databases and search engines.

Standard library materials online have been augmented by the digitization and publication of vast amounts of materials from archives containing primary source materials and institutional books, papers, theses and other works. Sometimes the online publications may be limited to collection guides or finding aids, but often the collection includes digitized versions of actual holdings. These archives may publish as national or regional collaborations like the Online Archive of California,[12] which includes more than twenty thousand online collection guides from more than two hundred libraries, museums and historical societies throughout the state with more than 220,000 images and documents. For example, the 1906 San Francisco Earthquake and Fire Digital Collection, a single digital archive, is a compilation of selected holdings from collections housed in the archives and special collections of six major institutions and includes approximately fourteen thousand images and seven thousand pages of text, which can be viewed online. Complete information on each image, including date, authorship and copyright status are published.

An outdated and incomplete online list of digital library projects[13] includes only 150, from the International Music Score Library Project[14] to the Perseus Digital Library,[15] which focuses on the Greco-Roman world. Nonacademic, cultural institutions such the New York Philharmonic Orchestra[16] and the John F. Kennedy Presidential Library and Museum,[17] and national projects in the United Kingdom, France, Switzerland, Austria and many other countries are also essential digital content creators. These form only the smallest group of samples of such digital archives, and attempts to catalog these or form meaningful taxonomies are being quickly outstripped by new materials being brought online from around the world.

CLASSIFICATION AND DOCUMENTATION

As scholars gather the information that will form the evidence for their work, the digital provides them with easy access to tools that allow them to organize and classify quickly and easily. Gone are the days of index cards and file boxes. The tools of print culture have now been replaced by databases that can store information and classify or tag it into almost infinite categories. For simple projects some scholars might prefer to use spreadsheets. While established to organize and analyze data in tabular form, and not as versatile as databases, these can serve to store and sort data, and they can be exported from and imported into databases when the need for greater computing capacity arises. Some of the best known spreadsheet applications include VisiCalc, Lotus 1-2-3, Microsoft Excel, Apple's Numbers and a variety of open-source and web-based applications, like Gnumeric[18] and Google Spreadsheets, respectively.[19] Databases are built using general purpose database management systems (DBMS) that allow users to define, create, query, update and administer them.

When classifying data, scholars can also use databases to apply multiple identifications to any object. For instance, if an investigation of Shostakovich's musical compositions is part of a research agenda, his works can be tagged within a database by date, form, instrumentation, place of composition, length, performance dates, performance personnel and so forth. The possibilities are virtually unlimited, and the researcher can decide at the outset what data is relevant to answering the research question at hand or add data fields as new possibilities emerge. Yet while the database can be quite flexible, as with many digital tools, the individual user or team must first make some important decisions about types of data, how it will be entered, sorted and reported out. Such planning often requires more rigid design and preparation than many scholars were accustomed to in the paper world.

Simply gathering the data is only one part of the research, and much time may be spent cataloguing information that is ultimately irrelevant or provides no reliable results. This cannot easily be avoided, because from the outset it is often difficult to be absolutely sure what data will be significant, based on the overall research agenda. If a scholar is looking at a trend of development within this composer's work, more detail will probably be very fruitful, but if the research question is about the impact on totalitarian regimes on artistic output, less detail might be called for. Each time a researcher sits down to classify information, these judgments must now become part of the process in ways that reflect but do not match previous analog methods.

Databases also provide scholars with a convenient place for documenting research work with details on the sources, locations, dates and bibliographic information associated with any item gathered into them. Finally databases also allow researchers to manipulate the information by sorting, performing calculations and exporting the identified and tagged material into a format that the scholar can use for the further work of analysis, interpretation and publication.[20]

MANIPULATION

One of the chief gifts of the digital is to make us far more aware of our methodologies and the various steps in our research agendas. Often the process of research requires manipulation of research findings to make them useful and amenable to analysis. In the traditional world of humanistic scholarship such manipulation was largely invisible, hidden beneath a host of methodological skills learned in undergraduate classes and in graduate school. Except in cases in which humanistic research involved the methodologies of the social sciences – statistics, for example – the data of the humanities tended to be manipulated in the sorting out of index cards by research campaigns, outlines for chapters or papers, and in the very writing process itself, where internal logic and certain rhetorical skills dictated various linear arrangements of data into narrative forms of various complexities. As any humanist scholar of the past generation can confirm, our theoretical frames have taught us that no object of research presents itself ready-made for its final dissemination in print. The very acts of selection, arrangement within chronological or thematic and theoretical frames and division into articles or chapters use skills of data manipulation to turn raw evidence into a narrative and its self-reflective analysis. In the digital realm such manipulation – carried out by a set of external and standardized tools that work within the set frameworks of their software creators – makes the process both far more conscious and objectified. The digital humanist is actively aware of the process of manipulation as something aside from the collection of evidence, its analysis and its presentation. It becomes a further step in digital research and thus itself an object of reflection that often goes beyond our usual methodological thinking.

One of the first insights presented by this new digital reality is that the process of manipulation does not mean altering the source material per se, but first converting it into digital form. This conversion presents the objects of research less as the notes or transcriptions of the print world but as files, and this basic element of digital work dramatically changes our relationship to our work. While scholars certainly created "files" in the past – and even our language carries over this metaphor into the digital – the assortments of papers brought together into a folder, a binder or a drawer were dependent upon the physical action and the mental activity of researchers to create their first transformations. The process was carried out internally and autonomously by the scholar. In the digital, however, this act too is externalized, projected from the researcher's mind to the surface of a computer screen and thus both further objectified and abstracted from the researcher. If not properly understood, this process can often be seen as alienating the scholar from her own work, taking over control at a critical period of the research project. It is therefore important that the digital humanist at the very least understand the basic elements of computer work so that even if IT staff coordinates this phase of research the humanist is neither put off by, nor aloof from, this essential task.

Such digital conversion might involve the changing of text pages into word-processing files, an image or a song from analog to digital format or a set of archival transcriptions into a useable spreadsheet or data field. That format must both maintain the original signifiers of its analog and also fit into a rigidly controlled set of coding choices that make it amenable to use and to digital manipulation: the truism that everything in the digital world becomes a set of variations on "o" and "1" thus both widely expands and narrowly levels the evidence that we collect.

A major concern is thus preserving the integrity of the original material while making it subject to digital study. As we have seen, this also raises the issue of representation in the digital realm to a degree far beyond that of print. A music score can be studied in its printed or manuscript form, but transforming it to a digital file makes it possible to subject it to a wider range of analytical techniques, although it is essential that the scholar recognize how the digitization transforms the essential and material nature of the original document.

For instance, the Marenzio Project[21] based at Columbia University – a collaboration between its Gabe M. Wiener Music & Arts Library and the Center for Digital Research and Scholarship – aims to create a complete online critical edition of the secular music of Luca Marenzio (c. 1553–99), one of the most important composers of the European Renaissance. It is using Aruspix[22] a software application designed to scan the early music prints for this edition. The scholar needs to consider what happens in the process of this conversion. What is lost or gained? How does the digital presentation of evidence alter our research, our questions and our understanding of the material?

ANALYSIS

The digital age has not changed the analytical function of the scholar, but it has created tools that can help speed the analysis by automating many time-consuming processes. The type of material under consideration often indicates what type of analysis might be required. Analysis of text, data, sound and image all require different tools, and these increase consistency and accuracy, remove subjectivity and often produce results that were not possible with manual analysis. These can generally be seen as important assets, yet objections can be raised over such issues as the necessary subjective judgment of the scholar, the suppression of exceptions, irregularities and textures in texts and art works and the loss of materiality of our sources.

Examples of the benefits of analytical tools abound. For instance, the Lazarus Project at the University of Mississippi has undertaken several remarkable projects in the arena of image analysis. Using multispectral imaging technology the project, under the direction of Gregory Heyworth, professor of English, has successfully recovered texts and images on palimpsests (a manuscript reused and overwritten with new text) and badly damaged manuscripts, including the *Codex Vercellensi*, the oldest translation of the Gospels into Latin, c. 325–50; the Vercelli Book, the oldest manuscript of Old English in existence, which was defaced by a chemical reagent in the eighteenth century; and the Vercelli Mappamundi, which suffered serious fading aggravated in a 1970s era attempt to restore it.[23] As these examples can demonstrate, such tools work best when they both speed analysis and preserve or newly uncover original sources.

INTERPRETATION

Once research materials have been gathered, organized and converted into a format amenable to digital study, the basic work of the scholar moves to the next stage: interpreting the materials. Working either from an *a priori* thesis or theory or developing a thesis from the materials at hand following empirical *praxis*, the scholar presents an interpretation regarding the material and its relationship to other interpretations within the field of study. An overwhelming amount of scholarly attention over the past generation devoted to these acts of interpretation and their theoretical turns has fundamentally altered the way in which humanists now think and work. We need not therefore expand too broadly here on the impact of theory or its relationship to empiricism or interpretation.

The digital realm has, however, had a marked influence on how theory is both implemented and validated, largely because new empirical data has begun to impact our work in ways unseen since the vast print editorial projects of the eighteenth and nineteenth centuries that created the impetus for the twentieth century's monograph culture. As Ray Siemens and Susan Schreibman have emphasized, with such vast amount of new data made both available and freely accessible to almost any researcher, even the theoretical turns of the past generation must be recalibrated.[24] While literary theory might hinge on a small circle of scholars examining minutely a relatively restricted canon of eighteenth- and nineteenth-century fiction, for example, the digitization by Google Books and others of tens of thousands of books and millions of pages of noncanonical authors opens the way to deeper and broader text mining, word searches and other analyses that can fundamentally alter the ways in which we see how this fiction was created, how it was produced and how it was consumed.

In the research of Ashley Marshall, ACLS fellow and assistant professor at the University of Nevada, Reno, for example, we can see how such methods and approaches might fundamentally alter long-held notions about eighteenth-century satire. The Book Traces[25] project under the

leadership of NINES' (Nineteenth-Century Scholarship Online) director Andrew M. Stauffer, associate professor of English at the University
of Virginia, seeks to crowdsource transcriptions of reader annotations
in the vast heritage of nineteenth-century fiction and to strike a balance between data mining and other automated processes and the
traditional concerns of humanist scholarship for the personal and particular. Readers are asked to upload bibliographic information and images
of marginal annotations or of ephemera in these volumes (from their
own or library collections) either randomly or around certain curated
authors and titles. The project thus uses advanced digital technology and
an interactive website to mitigate the effects of mass digitization and the
threat of deaccessioning the print record.

   To take another example, from American history, the groundbreaking
Valley of the Shadow[26] website created a digital archive of documents
detailing the lives of two neighboring American counties on opposite
sides of the Mason-Dixon Line during America's Civil War. Source material included a wide array of digitized newspapers, letters, diaries, census
reports, church, tax, military and veterans' records, maps and images
from the years 1859–70. From these records project principals William
G. Thomas III and Edward L. Ayers developed an interpretation of the
relationship between slaveholding and political alignment in Augusta
County, Virginia, and connections between social identity and votes for
the Republicans or Democrats in Franklin County, Pennsylvania.[27] One
of the great technological and theoretical advances of the Valley of the
Shadow project was that it was structured so that such interpretations
were neither predetermined nor unipolar. Students and other users
could enter the data and derive a multitude of evidence sets, draw dif-
fering yet still valid conclusions and view these issues from a variety of
perspectives. The digital thus opened up key historical issues and methodologies of evidence gathering, interpretation and narrative construction to far more self-reflection on the scholarly process.

   At the same time, such robust digital projects highlight the very pre-
carious and ephemeral materiality of many of our print and manuscript
sources: either by emphasizing the quotidian nature of the newspaper
or by acknowledging the risks of deaccessioning the print copies of now
digitized papers and books. Again, the digital humanities make us newly
aware of issues of materiality and preservation. They also remind us that
the small world of recent literary theory can no longer rest comfortable
when the compass of critical authority no longer points to a unique pole
and when such vast new resources explode the very notions of what such

concepts as text, textuality, intertextuality, narrative structure, author-ship and reader reception have meant in the print world.

One of the criticisms often raised against digital humanities projects is that, while they present much material in digital form – gathering and manipulating it – they do not venture into analysis or interpre-tation. The research and presentation are certainly accomplished, but many claim that without the interpretation this is not humanistic scholarship. Yet such a stance would exclude from the ranks of schol-arship the great editors and translators from the predigital era as well, from Aldus Manutius to J. P. Migne to the editors of Austen, Voltaire or Jefferson. Do the acts of editing and translation themselves incor-porate analysis and interpretation in their selectivity, their choices of methodology, their decisions about annotation, presentation and pub-lication? Do text mining, crowdsourcing and data processing incor-porate analysis and interpretation of another, decentered, sort? Or is the narrowly peer-reviewed monograph and article ultimately the only true scholarly endeavor? As we shall see further below, the praxis of the digital has in fact resurfaced this question within humanistic research.

AGGREGATION

As we have seen from the preceding examples, aggregating digital schol-arship is an important part of the process of digital humanities. Many centers have undertaken the work of bringing together related projects to facilitate discovery, cross-referencing, interoperability and compari-son. This process, however, involves far more than avoiding a series of independent "stovepipes" by matching coding systems and protocols. Institutional cultures and missions, personal research agendas, career goals and egos of principal investigators, issues of finance and sustainabil-ity, joint governance and access and sustainability loom far more impor-tantly in forging the necessary political alliances that will insure that the joined or common technologies work and remain harmonious. As we shall discuss in Chapter 10, one must conceive such larger aggregations as a social contract[28] of mutual interest among equals, recognizing their independence and agency rather than as a passive "ecosystem" amenable to top-down manipulation. In this regard, because of the larger amount of resources, money and personnel affected by aggregation, the culture of the digital humanities again highlights the ever-problematic issues of collaboration inherent in the historic humanities.

Nevertheless, good examples of such aggregation exist. The work of Thomas and Ayers discussed previously has joined an aggregation, in this case the Virginia Center for Digital History,[29] which includes not only The Valley of the Shadow, but also Virtual Jamestown; The Civil Rights Television News Archive, 1950–1970; The American Civil War Center at Historic Tredegar; The Virginia Emigrants to Liberia Project; The Countryside Transformed: The Eastern Shore of Virginia and the Railroad; Race and Place: An African American Community in the Jim Crow South; The Geography of Slavery in Virginia; and The Dolley Madison Project. At ACLS Humanities E-Book different platforms, disciplinary approaches and types of titles were brought together very early on in the project's life. While technology problems were easily solved, maintaining long-term alliances proved to be the key to building and maintaining a growing aggregation. Other aggregations and disciplinary approaches are constantly emerging and will also be discussed in the following chapters.

PRESERVATION

The preservation of digital projects is a crucial concern and will continue to become increasingly problematic as early projects disappear through lack of funding, institutional support and individual resources. And preservation is only the beginning of the problem, because as the web evolves many early projects (and their platforms) have to be updated, require continued curation and need to be linked to newly developed projects. Individual scholars can only accomplish a small part of the work involved in digital preservation. With the historical rise of libraries, scholars were no longer required to preserve their own books or the books that they used. An institutional solution was at hand. The institutional solution for the preservation of digital scholarship is currently being undertaken in isolated environments, awaiting the development of a system that might bring all of this work together. We will discuss this issue in greater depth in Chapter 8.

3

The Elements of Digital Humanities: Text and Document

With the advent of digital scholarship, humanists are increasingly using both traditional materials and those previously considered outside the parameters of their disciplines. This brings with it an opportunity for richer and more collaborative types of scholarship. By describing the variety of elements that one can incorporate into digital research, the following two chapters hope to explore the scope and boundaries of traditional disciplinary considerations. Our discussions will also link these elements with tools that incorporate this material into digital scholarship.

HUMANITIES DATA

At this point, it is important to reiterate one of our initial distinctions: while physical scientists draw their data from the natural world and social scientists from human groupings, humanists draw their information from the world created by humans: most concretely from historically created objects, but also from the record of human discourse either about that record or about human discourse itself. Thus humanities data might be about the record of events – what we commonly call facts – or about the texts created about them, whether these texts are written, oral, visual, aural or spatial. Humanists have therefore tended to talk more about texts or cultural and artistic objects; but now under the impact of the digital, a certain leveling of language tends to group all these under the rubric of "data."

The Merriam-Webster Dictionary defines *data* as "factual information (as measurements or statistics) used as a basis for reasoning, discussion, or calculation." More broadly, however, data can be the individual fact or event, statistics drawn from data points or other items of information: visual, aural or physical evidence amenable to collection, analysis and exposition. While we tend to think of "data" in terms of the physical and social sciences, humanities scholars also work with data, most often with reference to the first two functions of the above definition: reasoning and discussion. While humanities data might not always be as succinct and number friendly as the data of the sciences, often it can be just that. Asking questions about the number of hospital beds during the Civil War, for example, might lead a scholar to a better understanding of the conflict and its physical toll and cultural impact. But more often a humanist's data is not as statistically based as a scientist's or a social scientist's data. From where do most humanists gather their data?

Any scholarly project or research campaign must take the important initial steps of developing a plan by defining the data or parameters of the study. This involves identifying a body of evidence or a thesis, establishing the possible sources for the data, estimating the amount of data and setting limits – whether by type, location or date – to that evidence to clearly delineate the scope of the research agenda.

For the purpose of this discussion – and keeping to a broad common description among the sciences and humanities – we will divide data into two types: raw and processed. That is, data in its original format versus data that has been collected and organized. For example, raw data could be the English visionary painter Samuel Palmer's original sketch books, while processed data could be an edition of those notebooks with introduction and apparatus, such as notes. Raw data might be a medieval Italian notary's parchment records of property transfers, wills and testaments or dispute settlements, and the processed data a printed or online publication derived from those handwritten pages with appropriate annotations, analysis and perhaps a narrative.

While much basic scholarly material – both raw and processed – may be already collected in libraries, museums and archives, many scholars have to do basic work to compile the specific materials they need. Of the material already collected and processed, a small fraction may be digitally available. The work of processing collected material into digital format, including tagging and structuring it, is part of the work of the digital humanities, and much of this work is done by archivists and librarians.

Part of the challenge for the digital humanist is determining whether the material in question is of enough interest and significance to warrant digitization, especially considering the limited financial resources for the humanities. In other words, will other scholars – or the broader public – use this material if it is available in digital form? This is an important question not only for the digital humanists themselves, but also for the institutions and the funders, internal and external, who might support these projects. Some collections are used often and repeatedly enough that digitization has been a worthwhile undertaking. Given shrinking budgets, the costs of technologies involved and new research collaborations, asking such a question is prudent but often flies in the face of the current humanities culture where "research for its own ends" has become the hallmark of scholars at research-one universities and the granting institutions that fund their high-level work. Does the very act of assessing the impact of digitization alter this research culture in detrimental ways?

Because data collection from raw materials is basic to humanities research – digital or otherwise – here we will emphasize digitized materials already online – processed by scholars, librarians and archivists to the point where they are available for other researchers electronically. What are the sources of such data for humanists? This chapter will cover the basic materials: text and document; and the next chapter will cover object, artifact, image, video, sound and space.

TEXT

Over the past generation, our notions of "text" have changed radically under the impact of the linguistic and other critical turns. While the digital humanities have allowed us to see texts in many new ways that confirm these theoretical frames, renewed emphasis on the text itself as an object of digitization precisely in and of itself may also be returning us to more traditional approaches to the notion of text as autonomous subject and unique object just as the results of digitization – aggregation and disaggregation – robs it of this very uniqueness. Here therefore we will remain cognizant of both trends as we seek some basic postulates for studying the elements of digital humanities, keeping in mind constantly that the digital humanities have thus become more a fluid process than a stable object or subject of study.

For literary scholars, a text was traditionally a poem, play or novel, for example. Texts could be either fiction or non-fiction and were often preserved in written but sometimes in oral form. They could be the object of study by literary scholars, or they might provide data for studies by other disciplines. A data tree (see Figure 1) provides a visualization of literary texts. "Text" now also takes on a broader meaning as almost any

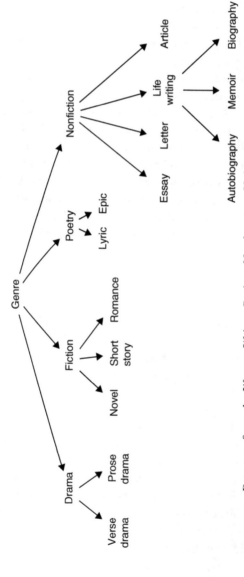

FIGURE 1. Data tree from the Women Writers Project, Northeastern University (http://www.wwp.northeastern.edu). With permission of Julia Flanders.

34

datum subject to reading. But more than this passive sense, text can also be a cultural object that speaks both to readers and to other texts; and literary theories of intertextuality are now merging with the notions of active intercommunication among computer-created objects in an era of the emerging "semantic web." Human agency traditionally conceived in terms of the active author, passive text and reader must now give way to theories that dethrone both author and reader and grant autonomy to the text as an independent agent, itself presenting and shifting meanings in a multipolar, digital environment.

Historical texts also present data using language that can be written or spoken. Although some texts were long preserved and transmitted in oral form, generally they are eventually written or captured now in electronic format: audio or video recording. Long-standing theories of textual communities, which encompass both oral and written communication independent of levels of literacy, translate well into the new digital multimedia environment, where the former primacy of the literate reader now gives way to both data gathering and publication in a variety of formats, ranging from the written word on the screen to the orally presented. Texts can be transcribed and translated; they can be copied and shared, making it possible to study them without access to the original object. This again brings us back to theories of representation and how the digital magnifies our understanding of the second-hand nature of our humanistic discourse around and about original "realities."

More broadly among humanities disciplines, meanings of "text" now also encompass cultural objects like paintings, sculpture, architecture and the like, which can now be interpreted as text if a disciplinary approach has developed consistent and rigorous methods of reading and interpreting them. Art-historical theory, for example, has long grappled with the secondary status of the visual in humanistic discourse – images being used as mere illustration of a written analysis or narration – but now, in large part because of visual theory aided by the importance of the visual nature of computing, the visual is seen as being fully the equal of the verbal both as an object of reading and interpretation and as following the same rules of intertextuality. We can now conceive of objects and data not only in formalist interpretations – tracing the influence and similarities of styles and motifs – but also in contextual terms of shared materiality, use (ritual, performance, etc.) and space. Again the digital has enabled a far broader application of such understanding of "text" through its ability to create a unified field theory of the object of study: for better or worse the digital "o" and "1" reduce all humanistic material to the same common core of data and mode of representation.

Traditionally understood texts have been the object of digitization efforts from the dawn of the digital era and, as we saw in Chapter 2, digital projects that explore the vast world of such texts are not difficult to identify. Almost anything that is now in the public domain is or will soon be available digitally – often grouping together works by an individual author or works by related authors, depending upon the disciplinary methodology or research agenda of their chief investigators. The Rossetti Archive[1] is a prime example and early model of the first type of single-author study. Conceived in 1993, it brings together not only all the verbal texts in various stages written and translated by Dante Gabriel Rossetti (1828–82), a prominent member of the Pre-Raphaelite Brotherhood, but also images of all his drawings, paintings, designs and photographic works. This collection is richly encoded so that users can apply sophisticated search and analysis tools across all these materials. Such a project has been groundbreaking in this regard, for "text" therefore includes both the verbal and visual, in both formally published and "preparatory" stages, as equally autonomous cultural data. It was no coincidence that its chief investigator, Jerome McGann,[2] is both a leading literary theorist and an early digital experimenter.

The British Women Romantic Poets Project[3] is an example of a multi-author study focusing on many original authors, most noncanonical, and "lesser" figures in terms of traditional approaches to literature. It brings together works by authors related not by critical acceptance or adherence to set standards of taste but by geographical and chronological proximity and comprises an online archive of poetry by British and Irish women written between 1789 and 1832. Such a collection by its very criteria of selection thus moves us away from traditional forms of humanistic criticism: seeking to trace the formal influences of one great author upon another in a diachronic procession of literary progress. Instead, it seeks to offer a closer representation of a time and place through a synchronic presentation of many forms, styles and levels of skill, independent of traditional critical reception but more in touch with current literary theory of authorship, textual community and intertextuality.

One of the chief criticisms of the early stages of such focused digital projects was their lack of interoperability. That is, they were often seen as creating "stovepipes" of data and interpretation that stood alone as fine exemplars of digital scholarship but that lacked the basic forms of intertextuality seen in the long-inherited habits of publication and reading acculturated through print. Over the past decade, however, such interoperability has become a major focus of both investigators and the institutions and foundations that support such research.

The Rossetti Archive, based at the University of Virginia, and the British Women Romantic Poets Project from the University of California, Davis, for example, are brought together on the web through NINES (Nineteenth-Century Scholarship Online),[4] which is a peer-reviewed collection of resources for this period aggregated in an electronic space that provides capability for cross-searching and interoperability. NINES also provides other scholarly tools for the researcher, facilitating textual interpretation. NINES is built on Collex, an open-source collection builder, that enables this type of scholarly work and is also the basis for a sister project of NINES, 18th Connect,[5] which is doing for eighteenth-century research what NINES has accomplished for the nineteenth century.

DOCUMENT

As with almost everything else in the digital age, even the most familiar objects are transformed by new techniques of observation and analysis. We are all familiar with the definition of a document as a written or printed paper furnishing information or evidence. It comes into English from French and derives ultimately from the Latin *documentum* ("example, proof, lesson"; in Medieval Latin "official written instrument," from *docere* "to show, teach"). Since the early eighteenth century, the word has meant "something written that provides proof or evidence."

With the twentieth-century development of information science, which was originally called "documentation science," the term *document* has become a basic theoretical construct that stands for anything, independent of form, that can be preserved or represented to serve as evidence.[6] Suzanne Briet, who wrote the foundational work in the modern study of information science, has provided examples: "A star in the sky is not a document, but a photograph of it would be; a stone in a river is not a document, but a stone exhibited in a museum would be; an animal in the wild is not a document, but a wild animal presented in a zoo would be."[7]

In many ways, according to both traditional and new theoretical frames, the document is therefore the next level of evidence for humanistic research, since it places the raw data or text into a more active relationship with the investigative process. The document is seen in both historical and literary terms as possessing a greater degree of authority, a text that can speak in and of itself as a guarantor of some truth claim to authenticity to represent either a past event or some human agency or intent. Thus *Merriam-Webster* defines *document* as "an official paper that gives information about something or that is used as proof of something." In other words, some form of authority has been assigned to a text in order to make it a "document," and that document is thus assigned to represent an underlying reality. Lorenzetti's *Good and Bad Government* frescos in Siena thus may be used to represent the political and social theory of the fourteenth-century Italian city-state; the Magna Carta, the aspirations of the baronial class against royal power in thirteenth-century England; Austen's *Pride and Prejudice*, the values and aspirations of the British gentry in the early nineteenth century. All can be seen and used variously as documents.

How are documents defined and created in the digital? Consider the digital collection called Probing the Past,[8] published by the Roy Rosenzweig Center for History and New Media.[9] This collection includes a searchable version of the transcriptions of 325 probate inventories from the Chesapeake region of Maryland and Virginia from 1740 to 1810. The underlying texts were used for administering the estates of deceased persons and generally provide an appraised inventory of items owned by the individual. During the period under question, the inventories would include anything of value: furniture, tableware, linens and fabrics, books, tools, animals and – given their historical context – slaves. Once the texts were transcribed, the data was entered into a database, making the entire collection searchable. In a very straightforward interface, the reader can look for people by name, for particular household items or livestock and can refine these searches by county, by male and female estates, by estates holding slaves or not and by rural versus nonrural estates.

Does the very act of choosing texts for digitization add greater weight to the representative selection chosen, making them more significant and thus more valid than the other archival materials available to the researcher? In order to avoid such subjective selection, must the research team digitize the entire run of all materials available? Who ultimately makes these decisions and based on what scholarly or pedagogical criteria? What meta-professional, personal, financial, political and cultural factors go into such choices? Historians and literary critics a generation ago discarded as naive Leopold von Ranke's claim that one could examine texts to view the world and its events "as it really is," but has the comprehensiveness of digital collections again led us into a false sense of documentary realism?

With these important distinctions and qualifications in mind, we can still postulate that the texts that we choose to regard as documents are often official and formulaic records that encapsulate significant data-bearing marks that carry authority and a greater truth claim to an authentic representation of some aspect of the past. We know that literary texts can include anything from letters and notebooks to fiction and poetry manuscripts, books, newspapers and magazines and in the modern era song, photograph, film and recording. Among more narrowly defined historical texts, various resources have also been used as documents for literary and other disciplinary studies. As these become increasingly available in digital format, their use is likely to grow accordingly. We offer the following examples.

Charters: Scholars have long used charters – documents from superior authorities to recipients granting an authority or right – for historical research. Digitization has increased their discoverability while providing easier access to researchers. Interesting examples include such widely varying materials as a collection of labor union charters hosted online by Missouri State University Libraries[10] and two sites (ASChart: Anglo-Saxon Charters[11] and Kemble: the Anglo-Saxon Charters Website[12]) that give access to a range of material on all known Anglo-Saxon charters.

Wills: Wills are legal declarations by which a person, the testator, provides instructions for the disposal of his or her property (estate) at death. The Atlantic County Library System of New Jersey provides digital images of the handwritten record of wills, searchable by name, dating from 1837 to 1921 based on a microfilm record of the original.[13] The British government has made it possible to search for and obtain (for a fee) the will of any soldier who died while serving in the British armed forces between 1850 and 1986.[14]

Deeds: Deeds are legal documents often executed under seal and delivered to effect a conveyance, usually of interest, right or property. Many states and municipalities have digitized the deeds pertaining to their regions. For example, the Archives of Maryland provide access to all verified land record instruments in that state.[15]

Leases: Leases are contractual arrangements calling for the lessee (user) to pay the lessor (owner) for use of an asset; often these are rental agreements in which the asset is tangible property. Rushden Craig has compiled indexes of leases for the western portion of New South Wales, Australia where a system of homestead leases was introduced in 1884. They are available online for private study.[16]

Receipts: Receipts are written records for the purchase of goods or services specifying items and sums of money. Examples of digitized receipt books include one that belonged to the Kansas State Central Committee and recorded various monies, provisions, clothing and so forth that were distributed throughout the territory from October to November 1856. It was digitized by the Kansas State Historical Society and includes both page images and transcriptions.[17]

Before the age of the digital, scholars needed to travel to various archives and libraries to consult such documents. Digitized collections, however, make a great deal of research possible without traveling. Just one example of such a collection is London Lives[18] – a collaboration of the University of Sheffield and the University of Hertfordshire with funding from Britain's Economic Research Council – which makes available, in a "fully digitized and searchable form, a wide range of primary sources about eighteenth-century London, with a particular focus on plebeian Londoners. This resource includes over 240,000 manuscript and printed pages from eight London archives and is supplemented by fifteen datasets created by other projects. It provides access to historical records containing over 3.35 million name instances. Facilities are provided to allow users to link together records relating to the same individual, and to compile biographies of the best documented individuals."[19] London Lives also includes criminal registers, account books, pauper examinations, apprenticeship records, workhouse admissions registers, court records, coroners' inquests, hospital admissions registers, tax payments and fire-insurance registers.

The distance between the existence of an evidentiary text and its transformation into a humanistic document has thus become far shorter in both spatial and temporal terms, as well as in the process of reflective study and analysis. New technologies have improved our access to texts in other ways, as well. For instance, the use of imaging technology makes it possible even in reproductions to see elements not formerly visible to the eye, increasing their scholarly value as documents for researchers. This technology has had wide applications in science and medicine, but its applications in digital humanities sometimes vastly increases the value of representations of original documents. An example from the Lazarus Project at Ole Miss shows how this technology reveals the damaged text hidden from the naked eye in the *Codex Vercellensi*, the oldest translation of the Gospels into Latin (see Figure 2).[20]

As our traditional sources of evidence in archives of all sizes and types now open themselves up to far more rapid study and evaluation – as

FIGURE 2. An example of the application of multispectral imagining technology to the *Codex Vercellensi*. Left is before processing and right after processing. The Lazarus Project at the University of Mississippi. Images courtesy of the Biblioteca Capitolare di Vercelli and curator Timoty Leonardi.

well as to aggregation – the nature of representation of the past begins to evolve in many ways that will still depend on traditional humanistic philological skills of interpretation but that may also quickly outpace the individual researcher's ability to make sound judgments based on vastly larger and more complete sets of evidentiary representation. Is the advent of the semantic web in which computers increasingly speak directly to computers a natural outcome of human limitations or will the humanities be able to develop methodologies that account for the sudden collapse of the wall between the remnants of the past and our representations of them?

4

The Elements of Digital Humanities:
Object, Artifact, Image, Sound, Space

INTRODUCTION

In this chapter we will continue to investigate the elements of humanities scholarship, moving on to the object and artifact and to visual, aural and spatial studies, including performance and ritual. Not coincidentally with the rapid spread of digitization of all forms of scholarly communication, a new scholarly turn focuses on "materiality," especially among premodernists influenced by anthropology, archaeology and new methodologies of textual editing of manuscript sources. As Walter Benjamin observed, in an age of technology and mass reproduction, "even the most perfect reproduction of a work of art is lacking in one element: its presence in time and space, its unique existence at the place where it happens to be."[1] His insight takes on new meaning as the digital realm ironically emphasizes the study both of the original and of its very materiality. Hence the digital humanities refocus our attention on the materials of scholarship long taken for granted in Leopold von Ranke's empiricist tradition as the passive – and transparent – media of reality. Materials now are seen to have their own agency that transforms our understandings about both their particular existence in time and space and about the larger grounding of reality that lies beyond them. In the digital era the relationship of the scholar and researcher to these materials creates a new dialog as the very notion of material existence comes into sharp focus in face of the all-leveling "o" and "1."

At the same time, space and time take on new active agency in humanities scholarship as digital tools both offer new forms for their representation and inform the researcher and audience of the autonomy of these dimensions. Digital tools can now reproduce surface and depth in 3D modeling and 3D printing, offering vast new possibilities of reproduction and representation, while the uniqueness of the objects of study becomes both problematic and contested. How should we respond to the digital in light of Benjamin's observation that "the presence of the original is the prerequisite to the concept of authenticity"? As humanists how do we grapple with his truth that "the uniqueness of a work of art is inseparable from its being imbedded in the fabric of tradition"?

OBJECT

While we can describe all the data, evidence or text that the humanities study as objects, in this section we will touch briefly on the object as that unique material entity in time and space. Google defines an object as "a material thing that can be seen and touched"; while *Merriam-Webster* defines it as "a thing that you can see and touch and that is not alive." Broadly speaking inanimate objects in the natural world are studied by the physical sciences, while animate ones – depending on one's perspectives and definitions – are examined by the biological. But both these can also become objects of humanistic scholarship due to their vibrant presence in history or literature: Anglo-Saxon poetry's emphasis on water and rock, for example.

Our understanding of the object and its copy in the modern industrial age has been the subject of intense study and speculation at least since Benjamin's famous essay. But because the digital now allows this secondhand experience on a far broader and even deeper level than our industrialized society of mass production and multiple copies, our consciousness of this loss of the original has led us to make cultural fetishes of once-ubiquitous objects that are no longer of practical use in our lives. In an age that has left behind the industrial economy, the nineteenth-century brick factory has morphed into the contemporary art museum, and the glowing neon lights of Kentile, Pepsi-Cola and CITGO have become nostalgic icons of departed neighborhoods and livelihoods; amid energy crisis, sclerotic highways and urban traffic bans, the vintage auto and the muscle car mark aspiring wealth and mythic freedom of movement; in an era of digital downloads of books and music, the unique artist's book and the vinyl LP reassume special status; against the ubiquity of the digital image, young photographers turn to vintage film cameras and darkroom techniques; with the mass adoption of the smartphone, the ink pen and cahier distinguish the new urban chic. Such fetishizations speak both to a certain nostalgia for a past slipping away but also, and as importantly, to a new ability to refocus on the uniqueness and individuality of the particular object in the face of the rapid digitization and its capacity for replication. One scholarly response has been the recent trend in the arts and humanities to study the object[2] and its materiality.

Traditionally objects did need to be studied physically, and while this may still be an important aspect of some research agendas, many unique objects can now be examined virtually through 3D imaging. Off-the-shelf software allows users to create rotating 3D images, and museums and art archives have made objects in their collections available online in 3D format. As just one example, the Smithsonian National Museum of Natural History presents a 3D collection of fossils, primates and other animals,[3] allowing users to view, rotate and examine objects in the museum's collections that were scanned to generate the 3D models. Another example is the Petrie Museum of Egyptian Archaeology.[4] It is one of the largest ancient Egyptian and Sudanese collections in the world, and in collaboration with University College London's Department of Civil, Environmental and Geomatic Engineering and a business partner, Arius 3D, it has been creating 3D images of objects in the collection, which are available in low resolution online and high resolution at the museum itself. The project focuses on creating a workflow for 3D processing and evaluating the potential of 3D imaging for cultural heritage collections.

ARTIFACTS

Because humanities scholars are charged with studying the human record, generally the objects that they study are artifacts created by other humans, from pottery to automobiles, from cathedrals to skyscrapers. Google defines an artifact as "an object made by a human being, typically an item of cultural or historical interest." *Merriam-Webster* defines it as "a simple object (such as a tool or weapon) that was made by people in the past." To work off Briet's notion quoted in Chapter 3: a star in the sky is an object, while a photograph of it is an object as well as an artifact. However, a stone in a river and a stone exhibited in a museum are both objects. A book is an artifact, although the materials that make it up, such as parchment, ink, pigments, may be studied as objects. The contents of the book may be studied as a text, as indeed may the book itself as an artifact of cultural production. An institution like the university or church may be an artifact of culture, as may a piece of music, depending on the researcher's perspective. Artifacts are traditional research materials for art historians and archaeologists, who study objects such as sculpture, paintings, buildings, jewelry, coins or pottery shards. But other humanists also incorporate artifacts into less traditionally materialistic disciplines.

The new theoretical turn of materiality is now grappling with the specific and local nature of such artifacts, focusing not on their content as text but on their material existence in time and space. This theory of material culture has newly highlighted the impact of the digital across the broad spectrum of humanistic evidence and the artifact's reducibility to computer data. Historical or cultural artifacts are usually preserved in museums. Despite the fact that in museums they are alienated from their unique location in time and space, they often need to be visited in order to be studied, although much preliminary work remains possible through photography, 3D modeling and video. Websites have facilitated access to digital representations of such artifacts as well, and scholars can look at Renaissance medals on the website of the Victoria and Albert Museum[5] or pre-Columbian earrings on the website of the Dumbarton Oaks Research Library and Collection.[6] Usually these sites include full descriptions of the artifacts and links to publications that discuss them. The Visionary Cross Project,[7] for example, is an international project that uses digital scanning technology to examine several Anglo-Saxon artifacts, including the Ruthwell and Bewcastle standing stone crosses and the Brussels Reliquary Cross. The project aims at contextualizing them within a multimedia presentation with digitized images of the Vercelli manuscript and its two pertinent Anglo-Saxon poems.

A very different project, in terms of scale and materials used, is the Cuneiform Digital Library Initiative (CDLI),[8] a project of UCLA, the University of Oxford and the Max Planck Institute for the History of Science. Of the half a million known examples of cuneiform dating from c. 3350 BCE until the end of the pre-Christian era, about 290,000 have been cataloged by the project. This collection involves digitizing data about physical artifacts and transcribing, translating and digitizing the texts and incorporating all the data into a searchable online database that provides universal access. It is possible to search the CDLI collection with criteria such as data collection, accession number, provenance, publication, date, type of artifact or material. While this is a work in progress and not all records are entire, the most complete will include an image of the artifact with a transcription and translation of the cuneiform text. For instance, a search on the term *lugal* (king) brings up this record for a stone seal in a private collection (CDLI Seals 006338, see Figure 3). The

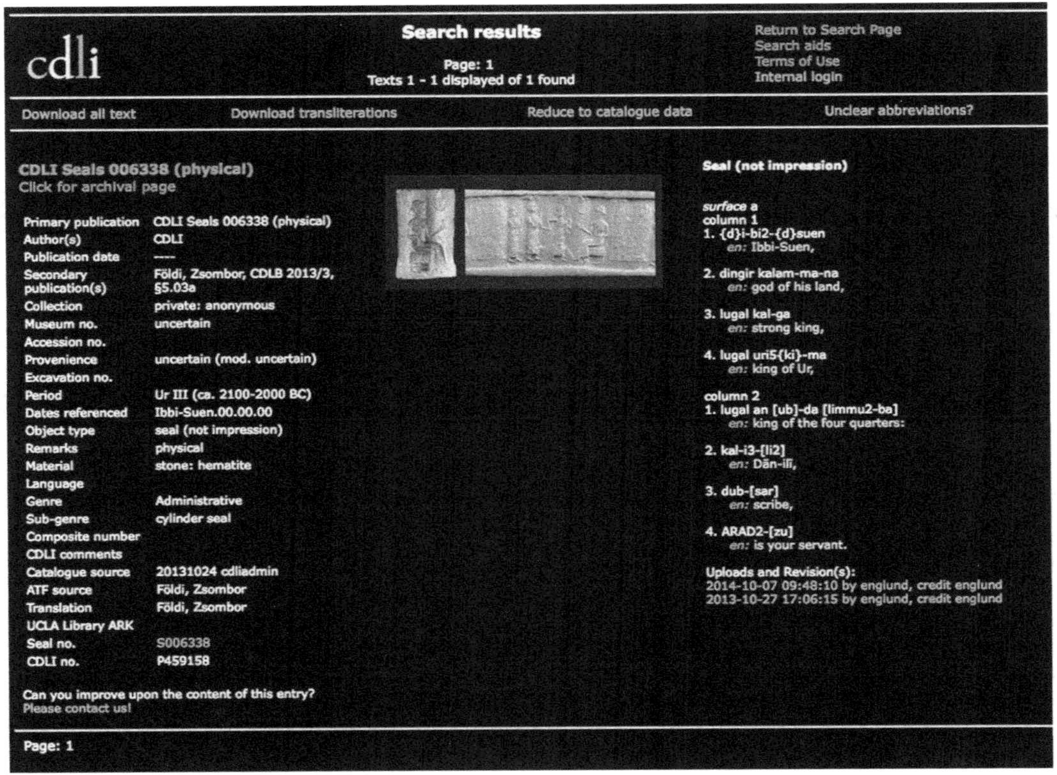

FIGURE 3. Record of a seal in the CDLI collection (http://cdli.ucla.edu). With permission of Robert K. Englund.

FIGURE 4. Image of the seal (left) and of the impression of the seal (right). CDLI collection (http://cdli.ucla.edu). With permission of Robert K. Englund.

48

record includes the translation of the seal's text[9] and an image of both the seal and of its impression (see Figure 4).

In the same way that the digital can alter the study of physical objects and artifacts, it can also transform the traditional notion of the critical edition, bound to the fixity of print, and return to a more fluid understanding of the text as it was for medieval and early modern readers. By bringing together digitally a variety of exemplars of the same work in manuscript, for example, a reader can assess the work of writing and reading as process and can better appreciate the unique materiality of each manuscript as it reflects context, copyist, resources available to that exemplar and the like. The University of Cambridge Centre for Material Texts (CMT),[10] for example, describes itself as "an initiative aimed at pushing forward critical, theoretical, editorial and bibliographical work in a field that is currently galvanizing humanities scholarship. Addressing a huge range of textual phenomena and traversing disciplinary boundaries that are rarely breached by day-to-day teaching and research, the Centre fosters the development of new perspectives, practices and technologies, transforming our understanding of the ways in which texts of many kinds have been embodied and circulated." While the actual work of centers like CMT closely resembles the traditional activity of paleographers, codicologists and textual editors, the description of texts as "primarily mental events" that can be unified and purified in a critical edition is paradoxically transformed in the digital realm. The very insubstantiality of the digital again leads us to focus on the particularity of the unique manuscript, its production and its historical and social contexts.

The advantages of online aggregations of artifacts is readily apparent: artifacts are provided with consistent metadata and cataloging information, presented under ideal visual conditions and offered to researchers with few restrictions on access or publication. While aggregators might have widely different aims for their endeavors – from practical to intellectual, financial to idealistic – underlying them is the goal of preserving a record of a group of artifacts with all the associated accumulated knowledge about those artifacts and generally of making it widely available. Trained humanists will readily recognize the nature of such online aggregations: the researcher or reader is not viewing the original artifact but a digital representation. However, such collaborative projects can eventually become so comprehensive and all-inclusive of the available artifacts in any given class of evidence that the aggregation is no longer representational in terms of available evidence but comprehensive. The digital thus allows aggregations that cut across space and time, that join together materials from a wide variety of locations and collections, curatorial and display cultures and bureaucratic access schemes. In such increasingly realizable cases the available artifacts could represent the complete reality of the evidentiary material, if not the full reality behind the evidence they offer.

IMAGE

The images that a scholar studies can be prints, drawings, photographs, paintings or computer renderings as representations of the original artifact, object, building or work of art, performance, ritual or social event; or they might be the very same images collected, aggregated and studied as objects themselves. They might be two-dimensional representations, and they might be studied for their intrinsic significance, for instance a seventeenth-century painting of Chinese court ladies and children. Or they might be studied for the information that they convey about the subject of the image, for instance, a photograph of a Parisian street by Eugène Atget. Because either of these could easily be studied for their materials, their intrinsic artistic or aesthetic value or for the cultural and historical information that they convey, art historians and social historians often approach these two types of images with very different questions.

Recent theories of visuality[11] that encompass both the nineteenth century's assumptions of the object from an imperial, male perspective and now a postmodern recasting of visual *subject* also allow new readings of visual culture from any number of points of view, paralleling the dethroning of the author-object-reader dynamic within verbal texts. With the era of the digital such questions now effect more than theoretical understandings but have had a major impact on research methodology and practice that is still being felt and assessed. The technical capacities of the digital now allow any number of perspectives and portals into the consideration of the visual artifact that go beyond the passive object and the fixed gaze of the viewer and interpreter. Such visual subjects might be the participants in a ritual or performance in a video taken from their own multiple viewpoints, rather than that of the aloof anthropological observer; or they might be the digital representations of a series of sculptural heads surrounding the reconstructed figure of Epicurus in the Capitoline Museum[12] now viewable not merely from the viewpoint of the analyst in a predetermined visual field that sets our expectations of importance and place but from any number of angles or fields of view that do not fit orthodox conceptions of object and viewer. At the same time, the very substantiality of the object or artifact that gives it agency seems to disappear in the digital's very ability to level out all such perspectives and points of view. In Benjamin's terms again, "Even the most perfect reproduction of a work of art is lacking in one element: its presence in time and space, its unique existence at the place where it happens to be." In the digital age this reproduction can achieve such a highly refined state that there is some danger of ignoring the original itself "in time and space" and thus losing the essential materiality that returns all humanistic studies to their basis in human existence and activity.

In manuscript studies, again, the microfilm copy of a medieval text was long considered to be adequate for the scholar to read and derive a text, note contents and foliation, or identify specific hands for the main body and its annotations and examine mise-en-page and other elements of design. Further study of the manuscript for issues of provenance, questions of bindings and content assembly, inks and medium, images and other codicological issues generally required a trip to the library or archive for a firsthand examination. With the digital and the rapid advance of both reproduction and analytical tools, much of this evidence is now also available to the scholar online, and often with far greater levels of magnification and detail (including spectral analysis) than could be possible with even the trained eye in the presence of the manuscript itself.

Parker Library on the Web[13] is an excellent example of such a digitization project. It is a web-based workspace for the study of the manuscripts in the Parker Library at Corpus Christi College, Cambridge and is a collaboration among Corpus Christi College, the Stanford University Libraries and Cambridge University Library. While the project is predominately image based (see Figure 5), it also accomplishes the important work of preserving a full record of the entire collection beyond the faithfulness of the best print facsimile. It provides data on each medieval manuscript in the collection, with provenance, foliation, language, dates and the title, incipit and explicit (beginning and end of each text) and notes any rubrics and illustrations in the manuscript. Most importantly, it also offers an image of each page in the collection. Parker does limit its data because it is as yet unable to digitize badly damaged manuscripts or ones with very fragile bindings. It does, however, include a record of these books and provides images of the exterior and some pages, where possible.

How does the richness of the visual data thus produced effect the reader's understanding of and response to this visual textuality? In

of record company catalogs from international labels. Music is not the only recorded sound to be archived, however, and the British Library's "Sounds"[16] includes fifty thousand recordings of music, drama and literature, oral history, wildlife and environmental sounds worldwide. Access to some of this material is restricted to affiliates of higher education institutions in the United Kingdom, but much of it is freely available.

While many institutions have sound and audio collections, countless are still awaiting digitization in order to make them available online in any way – free or paid. The cost of digitization is often beyond the budgets of the original collectors, whether individuals or institutions. As digital collections grow in size and complexity of organization and access, the resources required to both aggregate and sustain such collections and the increasingly corporatized nature of the web become real concerns both for the scholar and for the broader society that the humanities serve. Yet digitized material need not be on a grand scale to be accessible and sustainable. Smaller specialized collections with special focus can be discovered at many libraries and academic institutions. For instance, the Moffitt Library at the University of California Berkeley has an online media collection that includes the recordings collected by the Social Activism Sound Recording Project,[17] a partnership between the UC Berkeley Library, Pacifica Radio and others that preserves and makes accessible resources from the 1960s and 1970s from the Berkeley Free Speech Movement and the Black Panther Party, as well as materials from Anti-Vietnam War protests and the LGBT movement. Such archives once again question the older Rankean positivist and philological approach to the sources: if our sources are increasingly no longer restricted to written archives, their interpretation and reception becomes far more multivalent and multipolar than the old relationship between single author/interpreter and reader. In this sense the openness and multipolar nature of the digital overlaps with some of the political cultures from the examples just mentioned.

Both folklore studies and linguistics also make extensive use of recordings, as do sociologists and anthropologists generally. Making and sharing recordings are often an important part of the field work in all of these social sciences and create valuable resources for humanists. University College Dublin[18] has a collection starting from 1897 that comprises approximately ten thousand hours of recordings of both Irish and English speakers on wax cylinders, gramophone records and magnetic tape, presenting aspects of Irish custom, belief, oral history and narrative, plus music and song. While some samples are now available, the entire collection is not yet online. Other collections have also taken up the task of making text transcriptions from audio files. For instance, the Northern Utah Speaks Collection,[19] part of the FIFE Folklore Archive at the Merrill-Cazier Library at Utah State University, has transcribed several of its oral history recordings, including a collection of 124 interviews on the Teton Dam disaster of July 5, 1976. Putting them into text format makes these sound recordings amenable to digital processes like text and data mining.

But must the humanities be tied to the written text and the singular act of reading a "page"? The digital breaks down this dynamic to make the visual and aural far more pervasive and present, sensation far more immediate than that carried out only through the visual process of eye upon written text, and it therefore makes possible processes of cognition quite different from that experienced in the predigital humanities with their basis in textual and philological tools.

FILM/VIDEO

As with audio, there is now a growing number of digitized collections of film and video available online that humanist researchers can use as the basis for their work. Video has been used to capture live-action events, making them amenable to the reflective processes of humanistic study. Whether it is a play or a dance, a demonstration or a revolution, a TV drama or an inauguration, a sports competition or an opera performance, the ability to capture, preserve and share events in digital format has created a wealth of documentary material for scholars and is especially relevant for scholars working in twentieth- and twenty-first-century studies. At the same time, as with anthropological research and methodology, the application of disciplinary tools to the past disrupts traditional ways of approaching the individual, the event and the deep cultural structure. Comparative and quantitative approaches similarly replace older ways of reading individual films or videos that mediate the work of the single artist to the single viewer. While film and video have long been understood as mass media in their sociological, economic and cultural impacts, aggregated readings are now becoming established modes of reflective research and scholarship. As a corollary of this trend, new appreciations of visual and aural culture, heavily influenced by the ubiquity of these media in modern studies and society, is changing the ways we also view ancient, medieval and other premodern societies.

The cost of digitizing can be an obstacle for video as well as audio collections, but funding is sometimes available from such sources as The

Andrew W. Mellon Foundation, which is working with Indiana University and the University of Michigan to create the EVIA digital archive[20] of video from ethnographic field investigations encompassing almost fifty collections. Many of these are videos of music, but others include such subjects as "Vodou Rites in Port-au-Prince, Haiti," a collection gathered by Lois Wilcken, a ethnomusicologist who works for a center for folk arts in New York City; "Parading Traditions in Northern Ireland" from Jackie Witherow, a PhD candidate at Queen's University Belfast; and "Mundane and Spectacular Events among the Cajuns and Creoles of Louisiana" from John Laudun, assistant professor at the University of Louisiana at Lafayette. At the time of writing, many of these videos were still in production and not yet available online.

For American cultural studies, Duke University has been in the process of digitizing a collection of thousands of TV commercials from the 1950s through the 1980s from the New York ad agencies Benton & Bowles (B&B) and its successor D'Arcy Masius Benton & Bowles (DMB&B). AdViews[21] currently has a small sample of these available online. The Smithsonian Museum's National Anthropological Archives collects, preserves and makes available to researchers historical and contemporary materials in ethnology, linguistics, archaeology and physical anthropology. While it includes traditional materials such as journals, photos and maps, as well as sound recordings, its Human Studies Film Archives[22] curates about eight million feet of original ethnographic film and video.

Such aggregations can range from the narrowly thematic to the more broadly inclusive. The Center for Holocaust and Genocide Studies at the University of Minnesota,[23] for example, makes available free a collection of almost fifty video interviews conducted with survivors who were living in the Minnesota region. On the other end of the spectrum, the Steven Spielberg Film and Video Archive[24] at the United States Holocaust Memorial Museum archives has approximately one thousand hours of footage – including Nazi propaganda films from between 1930 and 1945 – on topics such as prewar Jewish and Gypsy (Roma and Sinti) life, Germany in the 1920s and 1930s, the Nazi rise to power, persecution and deportations of Jews, internment and displaced persons camps, refugees, resistance movements, postwar trials and immigration to Palestine.

SPACE/PLACE/ENVIRONMENT

Space is the three-dimensional realm in which objects and events have location and direction. A cathedral can be an object, but it can also be a space, depending on the scholar's perspective. Other spaces might include gardens, landscapes, public squares and domestic quarters. Places are spaces with an identity ascribed by human experience. But space can also be a cultural referent and locus of value. As the geographer Yi-Fu Tuan wrote: "Place is security, space is freedom: we are attached to the one and long for the other."[25]

Coming to the fore almost simultaneously, the new spatial turn and its relationship to architecture, dance, performance and ritual cannot be separated from the impact of the digital in everything from easier access to prints, drawings and architectural renderings to build-ups, GIS and virtual-reality (VR) environments. These immerse students and researchers in newly three- and now five-dimensional spaces that also include diachronicity. The digital humanities extend the core reflective function of the traditional humanities by making it possible to study space without actually occupying that space. In this regard the digital humanities combine the most advanced technologies with the most traditional humanist study of past material, visual and artistic cultures. Often the physical space might still exist, but given current human habitation, sensitive ecological concerns and deep cultural or religious associations, certain aspects of the space might be accessed better through a digital recreation. At other times the space is historical and can no longer be accessed in any case, as in ancient Rome or Revolutionary Paris, and the tools of digital humanists make it possible to offer representations of these in the form of highly accurate digital and 3D recreations.

One example of a representation of currently existing physical space is Hamilton College's Digital Mesopotamia Project,[26] which is still in its initial phase and which envisions employing digital resources such as satellite maps and global positioning systems (GPS) with the help of archaeological, anthropological and historical resources to create a diachronic picture of the geography, cultures, subsistence patterns and political organization of the last twelve thousand years of Mesopotamia up to the present. Another example that is still in development is a collaboration between the University of Redlands and the Hopi Cultural Preservation Office (HCPO) called the Hopi Archaeology Project.[27] It plans to document and preserve Hopi culture using conventional archaeological data and Hopi traditional knowledge to produce 3D reconstructions of the spaces of ancestral Hopi villages and ultimately a virtual ancestral Hopi landscape for fly-through exploration.

Representations of historical space include Rome Reborn,[28] which is creating 3D digital models of Rome from c. 1000 BCE to c. 550 CE.

This is one of the most completely realized digital humanities projects accessible today. It relies on archaeological evidence of buildings – of the Coliseum, for example (see Figure 6) – and the digitization of a scale model of ancient Rome – the Plastico di Roma Imperiale from the Museo della Civiltà Romana at EUR, Rome – as well as the extant fragments of the Forma Urbis Romae, the ancient Roman marble plan of the city.[29] The site provides both photos and video fly-through versions of the 3D model. Fly-throughs have been successfully integrated into museum exhibitions such as the Learning Sites'[30] tour of the northwest palace of Ashur-nasir-pal II, Nimrud, Assyria, in the Metropolitan Museum's *From Assyria to Iberia*.[31]

The complexity of such projects reveals one of the impediments to the success of digital humanities projects within the university. Humanities faculty may have to face even greater dislocation if untenured and the possibility of giving up tenured positions to migrate with their key digital projects for access to greater opportunities and resources. While Digital Hadrian's Villa[32] has thus far cost more than $1 million with support from a philanthropist and the National Science Foundation, Rome Reborn, which was incubated at the UCLA Center for Digital Humanities,[33] received a total of more than $2 million in support from philanthropists, foundations and industry between just 1996 and 1998. It then moved to the Institute for Advanced Technology in the Humanities (IATH)[34] at the University of Virginia with its principal investigator, Bernard Frischer, a professor of classics and art history. After his subsequent move to the University of Indiana as a professor of informatics, Rome Reborn has been independent of any particular academic institution, although collaborators have included the Virtual World Heritage Laboratory of the University of Virginia,[35] the UCLA Experiential Technologies Center,[36] the Reverse Engineering Lab at the Politecnico di Milano, the Ausonius Institute of the Centre national de la recherche scientifique and the University of Bordeaux-3 and the University of Caen. Such broadly interwoven collaborations can point the way to sustainable future projects, in which a wide variety of stakeholders participate.

In contrast to such university-incubated projects, a similar one, Paris 3D,[37] like the Assyrian palace project mentioned previously, does not appear to have any academic affiliations. This is a virtual recreation of Paris in a variety of different periods – Gallic, Gallo-Roman, medieval, Revolutionary and the 1889 Exposition Universelle – developed and hosted free online by Dassault Systèmes. These last two projects might signal that the commitment of resources to develop and maintain such

FIGURE 6. 3D rendering of the Coliseum from *Rome Reborn*.

high-end digital projects is outside the scope of even major research universities. Such corporate hosting – and the willingness or necessity of academic humanists to seek out permanent and sustainable funding from nonuniversity sources – reveals certain anxieties long felt in the academic world, most especially exposure to commercial interests and pressures that could compromise their work. By contrast, the opening up of the humanities beyond the university may hold an important key to their very survival and vibrancy within an increasingly commercial and technocratic culture.

Geographers study space and place, but so do historians, architectural historians, literature, landscape and garden scholars. Environments are the aggregate of surrounding things, conditions or influences. They may be natural, like a river valley, or built, like a green space. New York City's new linear park, the High Line, is an example of a built space: a 1.45-mile-long public park built on an historic freight rail line elevated above the streets on Manhattan's West Side. The Helford River in south-west England, which is a coastal inlet formed by a drowned river valley and fed by seven creeks, is an example of a natural environment now designated as a Special Area of Conservation, Site of Special Scientific Interest and Area of Outstanding Natural Beauty.

While spaces, places and environments often need to be experienced physically, digital technology makes it possible to represent and recreate them in ways that may partially substitute for the actual experience. More significantly, the digital can enhance those experiences by providing models that can be studied in different ways. Several medieval and Renaissance scholars have been doing just such work on Florence and Venice, providing digital palimpsests for these cities so that it is possible to experience both their present and their past.[38]

The digital and the more traditional approaches thus collaborate to form a more complete representation, whether of a foreign place or of the past itself seen as a foreign place. Yet both offer only representations and thus turn back to the core function of the humanities, which has always been to represent remote human experience in forms conveyable to our present understanding. As such virtual environments continue to improve and develop new features, they will have great impact on humanistic research in two ways: first, in eliminating that sense of distance and difference from the past that led Petrarch and the first humanists to postulate a long, dark middle age between themselves and antiquity. Without this sense of loss and alterity, however, can humanists retain their sense of the past and the perspective that allowed it to become a cultural force? Second, if such virtual worlds finally allow the researcher or reader to recreate the world of the past with an unparalleled immediacy, would this not be fulfilling Petrarch's and his colleagues' desire to relive and restore the past with both their mind's eye and their physical avatars? In this regard, the digital can pose among the greatest challenges and offer the greatest possible benefits to humanistic research.

PERFORMANCE/RITUAL

A performance is an event in which a performer or group of performers behave in a particular way for another group of people, an audience. A ritual is a performance that is repeated in a specified way, usually by a specially trained performer and often before a select audience. The former usually is an expression of art, the latter an expression of tradition, collective memory or deep mythic and religious belief. Thus a performance can include everything from dance to musical recitation to symbolic movement; while ritual might present itself in everything from a wedding celebration to a funeral to a procession or a football game.

In each some underlying perception of reality is offered in a set time and space. In performance the perception might be that of the individual artist or composer: the audience is generally considered outside the performer. In ritual the perspective is that of a more collective grouping: the audience and the performer may be one at the same time or in rotating roles dictated by special standing, age, gender and so forth. In ritual this tradition may still be vividly present and alive, or it may be a projection back into the past of our present aspirations and ideals, in which case the traditional begins to border on the mythical. In this sense too both performance and ritual express in physical form our understanding of remote experience – whether temporally or geographically. They convey through verbal, visual or spatial metaphors and symbols our understandings of these realities as processes of change and transformation. While the social sciences, especially anthropology and sociology, might document and analyze these practices, the humanities might use their traditional tools to connect present to past practice, to historical circumstance, to mythic and symbolic systems in religion. In general they seek to understand how these performative and ritualistic practices embody and enshrine the understanding and expression of our experience of the alterity of time and place, that is how people reflect back upon their past in ways that go beyond literate textuality or the objects and artifacts of their culture. They seek to understand these performative actions as another form of text capable both of rigorous study and agency. We have already noted how digital representations of such performance and ritual can free studies from their single perspective of aloof analyst and the object–subject dichotomy by multiplying points of view and voices in ways that were not possible in print.

Dance and music can be both performance and ritual: when the Alvin Ailey American Dance Theater might be read simply as dance, it is a performance; Sufi whirling, read solely as a form of physically active meditation, might be seen as pure ritual. Yet decades of study have made clear to us that either can be both, and depending upon the intent and agency of the performers and participants, either or both can contain many layers of meaning. How our contexts and social uses define them at a particular moment is largely determinative of these meanings. The humanist can therefore study them for these meanings in the same way that she might study a literary text or archival document.

Recording/playback technology, especially digital technology, has made it possible to capture these visual and audio materials for study in ways that real-life viewing does not always allow and hence to make the border between performance and ritual all the more fluid and porous, either dissolving or crystallizing meaning and understanding in new and myriad ways. Whole works can be taken apart, slowed down, stopped, sped up or reversed to allow more or less detailed examination. Platforms like YouTube allow anyone to archive performances and rituals, among many other things. But commercial and academic platforms are also growing. The Routledge Performance Archive,[39] for example, is a resource produced in partnership with Digital Theatre, which provides access to more than fifty years of documented works direct from practitioners and specialists and ranges across the entire spectrum of theater topics. The Kennedy Center, a public-private partnership in Washington, DC, provides free online access to its Millennium Stage performance archive[40] from Imani's October 1998 performance to last night's show. Andrew Apter of the African Studies Center and the Department of History at UCLA has made available online his Yoruba Ritual Archive[41] with video segments of three Orisha festivals in Ayede-Ekiti in Ondo State, Nigeria, recorded in 1990 and 1993. Again, however, scholars must weigh the unique performance against the recorded version, recalling once more Benjamin's admonition that "even the most perfect reproduction of a work of art is lacking in one element: its presence in time and space, its unique existence at the place where it happens to be."[42]

With such increasingly accessible and voluminous resources becoming available to both scholars and the public, how will the digital humanities affect our broad cultural understanding of these forms? How will access and almost limitless repetition affect an individual culture's understanding of its sacred and unique rituals? How will an artist's sense of owning a performance stand up to any number of interpreters who see ritual as performance or artistic performance as sacred ritual? These issues are not unique to the digital: at the Cloisters Museum in New York City, for example, the Langon Chapel had to be reconfigured to discourage its use by a Virgin Mother cult, just as its Bonnefont Cloister has been monitored to prevent the scattering of burial ashes. At a 2004 Byzantine exhibition[43] at the Metropolitan Museum of Art, the almost life-sized replica of an apse image of the Madonna was repeatedly kissed and blessed by Greek Orthodox parish visitors to the exhibition as if it were a sacred icon. Representations – whether textual, visual or architectural – take on a reality based less on any original intent than on their social and cultural contexts and audiences. They become powerful constructs of some other reality: of space or time, secular or sacred. Through its ubiquity and exactness, however, the digital increases such possibilities manyfold.

CONSTRUCT AND MODEL

The term *construct* is used here to denote something that has been created or devised to stand in for or simulate a real-world object, place, process, system or event over time. The linguistic and literary turns of the past generation have made all humanists aware of the constructed nature of their sources and of the narratives that they create from them. As Hayden White has observed, history itself is less discovered than constructed,[44] and our contemporary humanities practice is keenly aware of the constructed nature of its work and the necessary theoretical underpinnings to its understanding. The digital, by its rapid reassembly of the sources and discourse of the traditional humanities, has made us even more aware of the constructed nature of our subject matter, of our interpretation of that and of the complex interrelationship between the object/subject of our discourse and of our discourse itself.[45]

In order to study and understand part of our human past, scholars have often constructed models. These often started as three-dimensional representations, like a model of a ship or a building, and the architectural or sculptural models created by Michelangelo or Bernini, for example, are themselves highly prized cultural artifacts, revealing the creative processes of people in past times and places. Now these models can be created digitally and constructed so they change over time to simulate actual events or processes.[46]

VIRTUAL REALITY

The architecture of humanism is nothing if not a virtual reality. Beginning with Alberti and Brunelleschi, working all the way through Jefferson's University of Virginia campus, to the early twentieth century in the mansions, train stations and libraries of Carrère and Hastings, McKim, Meade and White, architects inspired by the ideals of humanism constructed physical environments in deep imitation of the remains of the ancient world in order for the citizens of the modern world to recapture the spirit of the ancient in their very physical lives. Living, working in or moving through these buildings, humanist architects believed, would recreate the sense of Rome's ancient past and physically impact those who did so. Raphael's painting, *The School of Athens*, for example, with its cast of the great philosophers and religious thinkers of Greece and Rome composed amid an ancient architectural setting, is actually a representation of the nave of Michelangelo's St. Peter's Basilica populated with historical personalities, "antiquity incarnate."[47] By taking the building blocks of the ancient world – pavement, stair, window, column, arch, dome – and using them as the basis for their own constructs, Renaissance architects and those influenced by them thus recreated ancient worlds and expected to produce both intellectual and physical effects on their inhabitants. By the time of the great Chicago Columbian Exposition of 1893, the architecture of the Roman Empire had become the literal setting for the new American one.

In the same way digital virtual reality worlds are computer-simulated environments through which users can interact with one another and use and create objects within an imaginary setting that recreates some specified aspect of the historical or present world. These range from online groups like Second Life,[48] "a 3D world where everyone you see is a real person and every place you visit is built by people just like you," to Bernard Frischer's Rome Reborn,[49] and UCLA's St. Gall Project,[50] which provides 2D and 3D models of the medieval St. Gall Monastery based on the famous manuscript plan housed at St. Gall[51] and other surviving contemporary visual and architectural evidence. As we have already noted, virtual reality reconstructions can also provide a platform for research by providing spaces for synchronic and diachronic comparison, interpretation and analysis.

The 2015 Sundance Film Festival's VR presentations of Oscar Raby's *Assent*, Nonny de la Peña's *Project Syria* and Chris Milk's *Evolution of Verse* reinforce the reality that non-academic content creators are also embracing new digital tools to produce serious reflections on our past.[52]

GAMES

Games are voluntary, intrinsically motivated activities normally associated with recreation, and they have also been used to help study and analyze historical events and have long been used in teaching. A good deal of debate still swirls around the classification of the game as a traditional humanistic activity. Ancient funeral games, gladiatorial and naval contests as well as medieval jousts could be viewed as performance, ritual or game depending on the context. Scholars have long been familiar with the medieval and Renaissance literature surrounding the game of chess: each figure had its own character and history, its moves and its allegorical or moral equivalents for day-to-day life and action. The tarot also offered symbolic or representational instruction of a less participatory and more curated nature. The art of the courtier depicted by Castiglione and others offered a rich array of behaviors and attitudes that might win favor, honor and prestige. The life of the courtier was a game, one brought to stark modern terms in *The Game of Thrones*, for example.

In much the same way, today's sophisticated digital games can present scholars and students with compelling recreations of past events, and within their parameters reveal deep structural forces that allow or hinder certain historical or cultural developments. Under carefully controlled circumstances they can also present counterhistorical scenarios, alternative fictional plots and reader/audience participation in artistic creation, all revealing the constructed nature of any humanistic narrative. They can also reveal much about an individual's character or a group's dynamic: choices offered in sophisticated digital games that can be ethical or expedient are visual presentations of computerized logic and are constructed to allow the player to use them on any number of symbolic levels to good or bad effect. In such cases – though often far less explicit and determinative – they replicate the moral literature and practical advice to the prince that were a mainstay of humanist discourse.

Issues ensue, however, when hiring, tenure and promotion (HTP) committees must evaluate such digital work to try to fit it into the traditional forms of publication allowable for such decisions. Can we read the game as a book?[53] And if so, who then is its author(s), who is its reader(s)? Again, the disruption of the traditional humanist dynamic of single author, medium and reader must be balanced against the increased ability of the humanist to reach wider and wider audiences with rigorous research that employs modern iterations of the age-old humanist skills of rhetoric and grammar.

There are many examples of digital gaming that take full advantage of both theoretical approaches and technical capacities, although most are teaching tools and few of them fall under the rubric of humanities research. The BBC has made available online a series of games in history,[54] covering ancient history, archaeology, British history and the World Wars. The University of Southern California's Annenberg Center for Communications has published "The Redistricting Game," which is now hosted on Games for Change[55] and allows users to explore the system that creates the districts that sent representatives to the U.S. House between 1950 and 2009. Scholars can both use these games to create scenarios for study as well for evaluating user reactions. However, funding can still be an issue for serious gaming. For instance, an online game engine that would allow students, researchers and others to explore Rome Reborn has remained unfunded for several years, leaving the project in an unfinished state.

5

Digital Tools

On the most basic level, the tools[1] of the humanist have been standard and unchanging since the fourteenth century: the liberal arts of rhetoric (we still say rhetorical "device" in referring to some of these tools) and grammar whereby the humanist constructed texts and presented them in books, speeches and letters. These have evolved and expanded into the essential philological tools that most humanist scholars continue to use. Next come material tools, including the pen, ink, sheet of paper or parchment and the codex. At the next level, these might include the nearly uniform elements of the humanist's study so often depicted in Renaissance paintings, as for example in Ghirlandaio or Van Eyck's portraits of St. Jerome in his study: a walled-off space, writing and reading table, storage structure for research materials and a private collection of books, letters and visual materials; and musical, calculation or other instruments. In the case of Antonello da Messina (see Figure 7) this expands out in a grand contextualization of the scholar within a far broader environment: St. Jerome set amid the sacred space of the Church. Finally we might also think of tools as the public aggregations that humanists use: the archive or library, the collection of objects, whether in a cabinet of curiosities or a gallery of drawings, prints, paintings or sculpture. As a physical extension of the letter and of the study, humanist scholars have also convened in classrooms, symposia, lectures, seminars and conferences for centuries. Used consciously for pedagogy or modes of scholarly communication these too might be considered tools. In short, all these provide the immaterial, performative and material bases for humanistic work.

At the same time, everything from the scholar's desk and shelves, study, studio, rehearsal and performance space, lecture halls, campuses,

FIGURE 7. *Saint Jerome in His Study* by Antonello da Messina, c. 1475.
© National Gallery, London/Art Resource, NY.

research institutes and convention halls can also legitimately be considered environments. Only most recently with the digital has this kit of
tools begun to change rapidly and fundamentally. Yet in many ways these
new digital tools carry on, in analogous ways, the same functions of the
traditional humanities. We are only now discovering and analyzing how

these new digital tools may be transforming these methods and this basic work. Is the very computer upon which humanists rely so heavily still a tool, something akin to their medieval writing tablets? Or has it become an environment, its screen no longer a blank sheet on which to write but a window or portal into the entire digital realm, which acts upon the humanist as much as or more than she acts upon it? As such tools become even more integrated with the human body – Google Glass or the new Apple Watch, for example – will the distinction between tool and environment disappear even further? Might we be approaching the time when the distinction created by the term *homo faber*, the human as maker, outside and above the world of her creations, becomes meaningless in the world of the semantic web and 3D bacterial printing? With such questions and ambiguities in mind, let us now examine where – and whether – we can still make clear-cut distinctions between tools (this chapter) and environments (Chapter 6) to begin to create a working taxonomy.

Digital tools are generally considered software applications for the analysis, manipulation and presentation of data. Over the years, and particularly over the past decade, humanities scholars have collaborated with computer scientists to build tools to facilitate these essential functions of the humanities in new ways. As we have already discussed in Chapter 1, scholars generally date the beginnings of this collaboration to 1949 when Thomas J. Watson helped Roberto Busa with tools for indexing the works of Thomas Aquinas.[2] The tools that have been developed since that time have helped scholars to collect material, encode it, study it with text mining and data analysis, map it using anything from Google Maps to geographic information systems (GIS), visualize it – sometimes using video, 3D or virtual reality recreations – create digital archives, incorporate and analyze sound – anything from speech to music to noise. All these tools help with organizing and analyzing and thus facilitate the real work of the humanist, which, as noted, is to interpret the evidence of human lives, thoughts and actions.

These changes were already in the air sixty years ago – two years before Roberto Busa approached Watson – when in July 1945, Vannevar Bush, a pioneering engineer in the development of analog computing, published an article[3] in which he introduced the Memex – a hypothetical instrument to control the ever-accumulating body of scientific literature. He envisioned an active desk that performed like a storage and retrieval system. A Memex user would consult a book by tapping a code on a keyboard and bringing up a title page. The Memex had many features that are now familiar components of e-books: pages, page turners, annotation capability, internal and external linking and the potential for storage, retrieval and transmittal. However, Bush envisioned that all this would be accomplished through microfilm.

Although tools might comprise the infrastructure for digital humanities and facilitate their work, they do not form the basis for discovery, authentication, valuation and communication of digital scholarship any more than we might reduce the rise of the original late medieval and early modern humanists to the availability of scribal offices or the printing press. Many more, and complex, cultural elements would have to be factored into any satisfactory analysis of the origins and spread of humanism in the early modern world. A clear-cut definition of what constitutes the same infrastructure for the digital age (cyberinfrastructure) is still a matter of debate.

In the quickly changing digital world, many tools come and go. Some older tools are still in use even though they are no longer supported by the institutions and organizations – either commercial or not-for-profit – that developed them. Many a tool was developed and made freely available in the hopes that it would be monetized once adopted by a large number of users and then acquired by a large developer. If that strategy proved successful, the tool was often folded into a larger, multipurpose application. Older suites of tools may be disaggregated and offered piecemeal via new apps. Previously free tools may move to a purchase or subscription model or an advertisement-supported website. Sometimes they just disappear from the web, their URL bringing up a "404: Page Not Found."

The following sections will discuss types of tools and provide an overview of various categories of digital tools and how they are used. These tools are arranged here broadly, first, according to the material being used (text, image, etc.); then according to the desired process, output or result. Most projects or research agendas in the digital humanities do not employ single tools; even the simplest projects can require text and image processing, storage, analysis and presentation, deploying multiple tools either simultaneously or in succession. Tools themselves can grow and expand to add additional features. Some tools are very simple and can be used by young children; others are fully developed, and their websites will present everything one needs to implement them; while others still appear to be in some stage of development – and the scholar might even be invited to participate in testing. Then again, some tools that are still available may no longer be functioning effectively. To learn how to use various tools there often will be tutorials on product websites, and for the most popular tools, tutorials are frequently available on YouTube,[4] Lynda.com[5] and other websites where users can find a considerable amount of basic instruction – free or fee-based.

The software tools and applications used on a designated machine might be installed locally or on a local area network (LAN). They might include word processing programs, graphics applications or video editing software, for example. Web-based applications are accessed using a browser and might include anything from linguistics programs to mapping programs like Google Maps. Tools and applications vary greatly in price, and many are available free, especially for smaller-scale academic research. Many programs that are not free are either available on a monthly or annual subscription basis, or there are often free but less sophisticated versions available. Sometimes research can be carried on up to a certain point with the free versions, after which a subscription or purchase might be warranted.

Examples of specific tools can be found in the Appendix, where they are listed in particular categories, although many perform multiple functions in addition to those highlighted there. Tools in the Appendix are listed to illustrate the possibilities available and are not necessarily recommended by the authors. Some – particularly free, web-based tools not requiring a registration – have been minimally tested by the authors, but even that is no guarantee that they are still functioning. For the most part descriptions of the tools in the Appendix are based closely on the online descriptions provided by their developers.

As discussed in Chapters 3 and 4, humanists now generally employ a range of materials broader than the texts and documents of their predecessors, including objects, artifacts, space, performance and construct. Despite the almost limitless possibilities of the digital to present all forms of data from two-dimensional page to three-dimensional reconstruction, texts and documents traditionally understood still constitute a major proportion of the material.

The caveats about the nature of text and document discussed in Chapter 3 notwithstanding, all areas of the humanities depend variously on the written records of the past and the published research of recent and contemporary scholars. Dealing with these texts and documents and integrating them into current research is a priority. Scholars need to convert texts and documents into digital form, create data from that material and then analyze it for answers to research agendas. Tools for handling these materials are therefore a major component of the digital resources available to humanists. Following are several ways of processing text into a digitally useful form. Most are by now well-known and universally used. While their importance may thus be disguised or underestimated, they remain the most ubiquitous digital tools for humanists.

TEXT-BASED TOOLS

Text Analysis: The simplest and most familiar example of text analysis is the document comparison feature in Microsoft Word, but there are other free and commercial applications. The most basic function of text analysis is taking two different versions of the same document and letting these tools highlight the differences. More sophisticated tools can perform high-end linguistic analysis, such as tagging parts of speech (POS), creating concordances, collating versions, analyzing sentiments and keyword density/prominence, visualizing patterns, exploring intertextual parallels and modeling topics. See also **Text Mining** and Appendix, Section 27.

Text Annotation: On a most basic level, digital text annotation is simply adding notes or glosses to a document, for instance, putting sticky-note comments on a PDF file for personal use. But annotation can also be done on web pages and HTML files and shared among a community of readers, thus recreating the textual communities formed by glossators and other marginal annotators in the manuscript and print worlds. Annotation usually involves a body, an anchor and a marker: that is, the text of the note, the material to which it specifically refers and the way the connection is indicated (e.g., with a circle or underline). These markers are by now common and well-known and they derive from the same notation culture first formulated in medieval manuscripts. See Appendix, Section 24.

Text Conversion and Encoding: Every text in computer format is encoded with tags, whether this is apparent to the user or not. Everything from font and point size, bold, italics and underline, line and paragraph spacing, justification and superscripts are the result of such coding tags. Common encoding formats include RTF, plain text and robustly coded text. Text converters transform all these tags from one format to another so they can be used in different applications. Originally many of these converters were stand-alone applications. Now they are add-ons, or they are embedded within a program so that a user can, for example, create a PDF, an HTML or an ASCII file from a Microsoft Word document or create an EPUB file directly from an Adobe InDesign file. Commercial and many free converters are available for formats not included within original text-processing software applications. See Appendix, Section 25.

Text Editing and Processing: These tools or applications generally allow users to perform the following operations in text documents: write, search, cut, paste, format, do and undo, check spelling and grammar, outline and generate tables of contents. They can also include capabilities for HTML processing. Among humanities scholars these are among the most commonly used digital tools. See Appendix, Section 26.

Text Mining: When text material is incorporated into scholarly research, it often first needs to be converted into information that can be analyzed for patterns. Developing software to derive this information from text has been a major undertaking of several digital humanities efforts. These programs extract data from text according to certain parameters and deliver the data in useful file formats. Often these are also referred to as Data-Mining Tools. See also **Text Analysis** and Appendix, Section 27.

Text Recognition: There are several different types of recognition tools that automatically convert input into a standard text file format.

Optical Character Recognition (OCR). These tools automatically recognize characters and create documents from digital images of text. An image that exists only on paper is first converted to a digital file through a scanning process. This is particularly effective for standard type, such as printed books and magazines, but great advances have even been made on recognizing handwritten documents and a vast array of non-Western alphabets. Often the software for this task is bundled with scanners, but stand-alone applications also exist. See Appendix, Section 5.

Handwriting Recognition (HWR). These tools allow users to transcribe handwriting and produce documents and are often used for converting personal handwritten notes. Some newer apps are also able to analyze handwriting and produce documents automatically. Their effectiveness for reading manuscript books has evolved greatly over the past decade, but they still require much direct intervention or "instruction" on the part of a researcher or other investigator. See Appendix, Section 13.

Music Recognition. These tools can process a printed score and create editable music files. See Appendix, Section 17.

Speech Recognition. Speech recognition software enables a user to automatically convert audio files, such as mp3s, to text. It is particularly useful

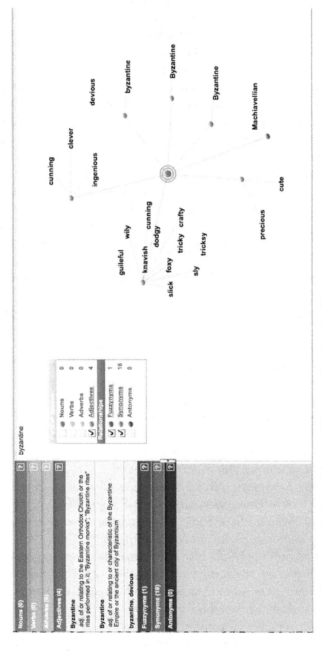

FIGURE 8. A semantic map of the word *Byzantine* from Lexipedia.
http://lexipedia.com.

for personal notes, but also for interviews, and can be applied to both user-created materials and materials downloaded from other sources. See Appendix, Section 22.

Text Transcription: There are several different types of transcription tools that assist a user in converting images or recordings of words into digital information in a standard text file format. There are also tools that facilitate crowdsourcing documents on the web for transcription. Through the New York Public Library's *What's on the Menu?*,[6] for example, participants have transcribed more than one million dishes from more than ten thousand menus.

Speech to Text Transcription. These tools allow users to transcribe audio files in various formats (e.g., .mp3 or .wav). Many of these facilitate the process by eliminating the need to alternate between an audio player and a text editor. For instance, a user can load an audio file of a speech and have tools to control the audio on the same page where there is a window for transcribing the text. See Appendix, Section 23.

Text to Text Transcription. These tools allow users to make transcriptions of the digital images of documents in the same interface, presenting the image alongside a text-editing window. For instance, a user can upload an image of a handwritten letter in one window and transcribe the letter into text format in a window alongside. These may also come with a variety of tools to help with specific types of documents. See Appendix, Section 28.

Text Visualization: These tools take text and create various visual representations of texts and words, such as semantic maps (see Figure 8) and word clouds (see Figure 9). See Appendix, Section 29.

DATA-BASED TOOLS

Database Management Systems (DBMS): Database management systems are software systems designed for defining, creating, querying, updating and administering databases – large collections of data – from XML-driven databases to dedicated databases. See Appendix, Section 9.

Data Collection: Data collection can be a large part of any scholar's work. Much of this is done manually, using **Database Management Systems** to store and manipulate collected data. However, in some disciplines data can be collected through surveys and polls administered

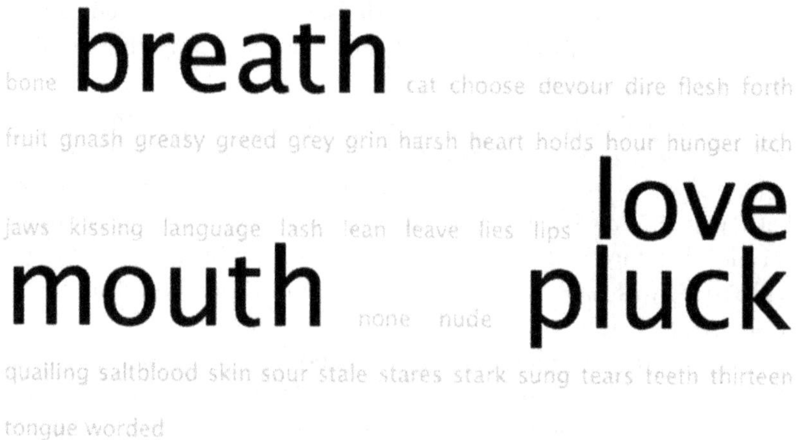

breath

bone **breath** cat choose devour dire flesh forth

fruit gnash greasy greed grey grin harsh heart holds hour hunger itch

jaws kissing language lash lean leave lies lips **love**

mouth none nude **pluck**

quailing saltblood skin sour stale stares stark sung tears teeth thirteen

tongue worded

FIGURE 9. WordCloud of James Joyce's "A Memory of the Players in a Mirror at Midnight" from TagCrowd. http://tagcrowd.com.

electronically. Methods might include a census of everything or everyone in a group or samplings that include only part of a given population. There are trade-offs in cost/time versus accuracy/reliability. Whatever the method, there are tools to make the collection of data efficient, thorough and systematic. See Appendix, Section 10.

Data Analysis: To be useful, once data is gathered, it must be inspected, cleaned, transformed and modeled to discover useful information, arrive at conclusions and support decision making. There are tools to assist with qualitative and quantitative data analysis, processing complex phenomena in text and multimedia, grammatical structure and natural language, ego (data point) network, sequential events and geographical names. Many of these maintain the traditional philological role of humanistic work: identifying, collating and contextualizing text to properly understand its full meaning. See Appendix, Section 8.

Data Management (including Data Migration and Data Storage): Once data is gathered, for it to remain useful it must be clearly defined, standardized, quality controlled, stored, monitored and secured. Both commercial and academic organizations have worked to develop tools that try to insure the preservation and integrity of data. These tools also facilitate querying, managing, enhancing, sharing and publishing data. See Appendix, Section 11.

Data Visualization: Similar to **Text Visualization** processes, data visualization applications create visual representations of structured data

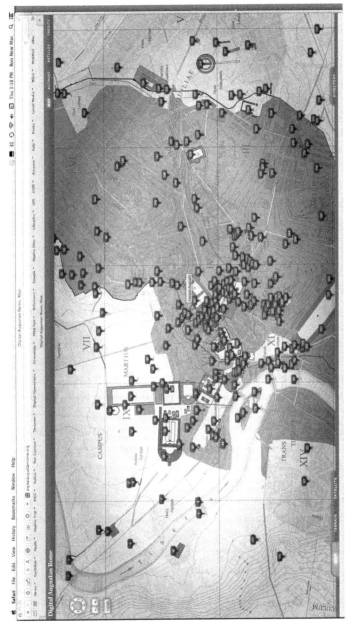

FIGURE 10. Digital mapping of Augustan Rome after *Mapping Augustan Rome* (Supplement 50, *Journal of Roman Archaeology* Series, 2002). http://digitalaugustanrome.org/map. With permission of David Gilman Romano.

based on lexical, linguistic, geographical, tonal, temporal and a wide variety of other parameters. See Appendix, Section 12.

Mapping Tools: Although mapping might generally refer to any visualization (text or data), mapping tools deal specifically with geographic data, otherwise called cartography. Figure 10 shows a mapping of Augustan Rome. These tools may use GIS, GPS or other geospatial data to create base maps, overlays, historic maps, interactive maps and maps with timelines and then to share them with users or collaborators. See Appendix, Section 16.

IMAGE AND SOUND BASED TOOLS

Image Creation: Scholars can create images in a digital environment or convert analog images to a digital format. Many software applications are available, often bundled with a computer or a device, such as a digital camera, smartphone or tablet. Some of these tools also provide a drawing environment with graphics editing and styling capabilities. See Appendix, Section 14.

Image Processing, including Editing, Annotation and Markup: Image processing involves taking a two-dimensional image that has been converted into digital format, making enhancements such as sharpening, changing color balances, saturation and exposure, cropping or straightening; annotating by adding metadata for location, date, content and so forth; and setting parameters such as color mode, compression format and size. See Appendix, Section 15.

3D Modeling: The process of 3D modeling creates a mathematical representation of a three-dimensional object that can then be processed to be displayed in two-dimensional space. This processing can include modeling, alteration and animation. See Appendix, Section 1.

3D Printing: This process creates a three-dimensional solid object based on computer-generated models. 3D printing is an additive process, that is, layers of material are added successively to achieve the exact computer-designed pattern in real space. This contrasts with traditional machining techniques, such as the lathe or chisel, which involve the removal of material by tooling processes such as drilling or cutting. Depending on the sophistication of computer programs and printers, humanists can now recreate in minute detail everything from an ancient Greek kylix to a scale model of a baroque-style ball gown, offering students and colleagues a representation far closer than anything in print

FIGURE 11. 3D Printing. Pia Hinze's gold Neobaroque dress made with a
3D printer.
http://hinzepia.wix.com/muted. Photo by Olivier Ramonteau.

or on screen and emphasizing the unique materiality of the evidence
(see Figure 11). See Appendix, Section 1.

Video and Audio Processing Tools: These control the alteration of
digital acoustic and video files and can include enhancement, cleaning, mixing and cutting, annotation and compression. For instance, a
sound file of a speech can be enhanced to remove background noise

that interferes with its clarity; or background noises might be added for dramatic effect, like the sound of aircraft behind a World War II speech. See Appendix, Section 2.

OUTCOME-BASED TOOLS

The following categories of tools are arranged by the goal of the scholar rather than by the material at hand and might be considered the digital equivalent of anything from the letter, lecture, symposium or convention. All are both instrumental and performative simultaneously and thus can be characterized as more general tools that can be employed when constructing the material for any project in the digital humanities. While clear distinctions existed in the print era between publication and pre- and postpublication modes of scholarly communication (e.g., the article, book and review versus the letter and the conference paper), in the digital various tools can now perform a wide range of such functions. Below we attempt to sort out the essential uses for each mode but recognize that multiple uses might apply to each activity.

Blogging: Informal and pre- or postpublication communication with fellow scholars to share research questions or results was traditionally carried out through letter-writing, then by phone or fax and in the digital age variably through Gophers, forums, chat rooms, RSS feeds, wikis, listservs and e-mail. Blogging is a way of discussing or sharing information on the web by uploading posts (discrete, usually brief notices). These are often displayed with the most recent item at the top. Some blogs are maintained by groups of scholars involved in similar, related or the same projects. Others can comment on the posts, although sometimes this feature is disabled or restricted to individuals approved by an editor or moderator. *PEA Soup*[7] is a good example of a multicontributor blog in the humanities. It covers topics like philosophy, ethics and academia. See Appendix, Section 3.

Brainstorming: Idea gathering is at the core of much scholarly research, and brainstorming is a group or individual technique for generating ideas with the effort focused on creating lists of as many spontaneous ideas as possible without evaluation. It is often used in engineering and business and quite amenable to digital culture, if not to the traditional model of the solitary reflective humanist. See Appendix, Section 4.

Collaboration: In the environment of digital humanities, collaboration is important and sometimes disruptive, again because humanities scholars are generally solitary workers. There are tools that facilitate collaboration on anything from text annotation to reviewing and coding to simple document sharing. Tools are also available to help conference organizers pull together their meeting by topic, date, time and other criteria. See Appendix, Section 6.

Communication: These tools provide the means for more efficient communication, particularly on projects. While many scholars still use e-mail as a basic communication method, many other specialized applications have emerged to set up meetings, virtual and video conferencing, social networking, desktop sharing and web-based discussions. See Appendix, Section 7.

Organization: Borrowed from the business and publishing worlds, in which schedules and coordination of forces are critical, such tools are available to help researchers manage their projects and organize their materials for more efficient workflow. Examples include Microsoft OneNote, Pliny and Zotero. See Appendix, Section 18.

Publication and Sharing, including Website Development: The process of publishing materials in digital environments offers many opportunities for sharing research and scholarship in various stages of development. From web publication to print, there are tools to make the process easier for scholars to create volumes, edit content, manage workflow, track manuscripts, manage journal and dissertation submissions, create page layouts, share metadata and create e-books. See Appendix, Section 19.

Peer Reviewing: The opportunity for pre- and postpublication review is one advantage of online publishing. There are a few specialized tools to help with organizing everything from comments to peer review. See Appendix, Section 20.

Searching(including Visual Searching): Most users are familiar with search engines like Goggle and Yahoo, but others are also available that have special capabilities or features and might sometimes better fit a researcher's needs. See Appendix, Section 21.

6

Digital Environments

INTRODUCTION

In our previous chapter on tools we made note of the traditional setting of humanistic work: the private study and the public library, archive,
classroom and the meeting space. In that regard our discussion of tools
overlaps with that of space and environments. For in the digital age the
desktop computer plays a highly volatile and multipolar role: it is the passive tablet or manuscript upon which we write and keep our records; but
it is also a window upon a vast world made accessible by the Internet or
recreated through the wide array of digital programs now at the humanist's disposal. In this regard it is therefore far more like a work environment. At which point did the function of the Renaissance scholar's
pen, desk, shelf, specimen jars and other accessories cease to function
as tools and at which did they become an environment? The example
that we presented in Chapter 5 (see Figure 7), illustrates this sense of
the individual scholar set within a broad social and intellectual context.
When do our other tools become such environments as well? Corbusier
had famously declared – and carried out in his architecture – the prin-
ciple that "the house is a machine for living."[1] Over the past century
the American driver has turned the automobile from a simple tool of
travel, a machine on wheels, into a built environment, an extension of
the driver's personality, social status, material success and sense of personal space and security. It is the most familiar and highly cherished
environment in which Americans still live.

The computer and its associated applications and networks, whether
local or global, can also be viewed as both tool and environment. With 3D
imaging and virtual realities our tools have also become our environments
and vice versa. As advances in cyber design accelerate, however, even this

distinction seems to be disappearing as the actual desktop device is rapidly giving way to both portable computing (tablets, smartphones and the
cloud) and to other more truly cyber-devices that extend or replicate human
forms and actions. How different will this process be from the realization
of Renaissance humanists like Desiderius Erasmus that they lived in and
through a great republic of letters?[2] That textual community used the tools
of the age of print to project their work and their personae across a newly
receptive Europe where thousands knew them almost exclusively from their
life in print. In sharp contrast to the ideal image of St. Jerome, living in
his cluttered manuscript environment, in his official portrait by Holbein,
Erasmus wished to be known solely as the lone individual with pen, ink and
paper. Nothing else was pictured or mattered. In this sense throughout the
age of print, the book has also long been the sole environment in which
author conversed with reader. What has the digital done to accentuate or
diminish an awareness of the humanist as the lone, disembodied voice of
human agency? When one reads the phrases, "digital humanities" or "digital
humanist," does one's mind's eye summon up the image of an Erasmus at
his desk or of a computer, a tablet or a software program?

   The current, and still evolving, environments for creating, publishing and working with digital scholarship therefore include everything
from personal equipment to institutes and software to cyberspace.
Despite the signals that digital humanities is a highly technical, sophisticated and rarefied endeavor, the working environment for those
engaged in digital humanities is often the same personal-computing
environment that we are all familiar with: desktop computers, laptops,
tablets, smartphones or other mobile devices. These are all frequently
used to conduct research and construct scholarship. Some digital
endeavors, however, like virtual reality, are so data-intensive that they
do require larger-scale computing, involving mainframes and UNIX
systems, and in this regard we may consider the impact of our highly
techno-industrial society in comparison to that of medieval scholars,
the first humanists of the Renaissance. During the Middle Ages, the
costs of parchment, inks and bindings, of housing for books made it
virtually impossible for any but the wealthy or those with institutional
ties (cloister, church, university, palace) to have sufficient resources
to accumulate a library. In the early age of print, likewise, the high
costs of presses (which put many of the first generation of European
publishers quickly out of business) also involved massive capital outlay
and careful allocation of collaborative effort. One of the great lessons
that social history and new materiality studies are now teaching us is

that once again ideas do not live in the ideal or abstract; social forces and contexts, including those of technology, are always at play. They are the chief ways our ideas reach others.

THE INSTITUTIONAL ENVIRONMENT

Between the larger working environment of the Internet and the personal working space so necessary for humanities scholarship, most digital humanities take place in an institutional environment. As with traditional humanistic work, major research universities have been in the forefront of providing these environments whether as separate institutes or centers or within existing structures, such as libraries. Archives and museums also provide digital environments, although these are often closely related to the holdings and mission of those institutions.

Digital humanities institutes and centers vary widely in their scope and offerings. Many simply provide networking and host talks and perhaps workshops. Some provide equipment, although the level varies widely from a handful of computers and a scanner to sophisticated digital imaging technology. Some centers host, curate and preserve projects created by scholars. Others provide support for digital pedagogy but little for digital research. A very few offer degrees and certificates. And some offer a complete array of equipment, expertise, software development, skilled collaborators and project hosting/curation.

CAMPUS-BASED CENTERS

The following list provides an overview of some model centers that offer humanists significant support for digital research.[3] Descriptions have been drawn largely from the centers' own websites and provide a good index of the current breadth of thinking about what digital humanities might mean in a variety of settings. Moreover, this environment is ever changing, with centers closing their doors, being absorbed into other institutional structures or never really getting off the ground, despite a great deal of public rhetoric.

Brigham Young University

- Digital Humanities and Technology Program (http://dight.byu.edu), in conjunction with the Office of Digital Humanities (ODH), offers courses on the use of computer technology in humanities disciplines, with an undergraduate minor program.

Brock University

- Centre for Digital Humanities (CDH, http://www.brocku.ca/ humanities/departments-and-centres/digital-humanities) is a teaching and research unit that focuses on the intersection of interactive technologies and the humanities. Facilities, including multimedia teaching labs and seminar rooms, as well as research and development labs, comprise Brock's Interactive Arts and Science (IASC) program and the GAME program, the latter in partnership with the Department of Computer Science and Niagara College.

Brown University

- Virtual Humanities Lab (http://www.brown.edu/Departments/ Italian_Studies/vhl_new) provides a portal for interdisciplinary projects in Italian Studies at Brown and a platform for the encoding and annotation of a mini-corpus of late medieval and humanist texts. Current projects include Decameron Web, the Pico Project in collaboration with the University of Bologna, Florentine Renaissance Resources and The Theatre That Was Rome.
- Center for Digital Scholarship (http://library.brown.edu/cds) is a cross-departmental group in the university library that supports digital scholarship at Brown by building infrastructure, interfaces, tools and systems and by developing new digital projects. It engages in research and experimental development work on tools and technologies that support its infrastructure and projects and that contribute to the broader understanding of digital scholarship and scholarly communication. It also serves as a locus of expertise in digital scholarship.

Columbia University

- Center for Digital Research and Scholarship (CDRS, http://cdrs .columbia.edu/cdrsmain) is a library initiative that offers faculty, students and staff access to a digital repository, data management systems, journal hosting services and conference and video services.

George Mason University

- Roy Rosenzweig Center for History and New Media (http://chnm.gmu .edu) produces historical works in new media, testing the effectiveness of these products in the classroom and reflecting critically on the promises and pitfalls of new media in historical practice. Projects include Making the History of 1989, Children and Youth in History and Popular Romance Project.

Hamilton College

- Digital Humanities Initiative (DHi, http://www.dhinitiative.org) is a collaboratory to promote humanities-based teaching, research and scholarship through the use of new media, computing technologies and interdisciplinary models and methods of collaboration between faculty and students. It sponsors faculty development workshops, media literacy programs, conferences, symposia, seminars and a fellows program.

Harvard University

- Digital Arts and Humanities (DARTH, http://www.darthcrimson.org) is an initiative to facilitate digital technology solutions for research questions in the arts and humanities making use of the Harvard Academic Technology Group's resources – including online tools for collaboration, visualization and simulation – and the Harvard Center for Geographic Analysis (CGA), which provides access to hardware, software and data, offers training programs, performs research-project consulting and develops tools and platforms for use with open-source and proprietary GIS systems.

King's College, London

- Department of Digital Humanities (formerly the Centre for Computing in the Humanities and Department for Digital Research, http://www.kcl.ac.uk/artshums/depts/ddh) and Centre for E-Research (CeRch, http://www.kcl.ac.uk/innovation/groups/cerch) studies the possibilities of computing for arts and humanities scholarship and – in collaboration with local, national and international research partners – designs and builds applications to implement these possibilities, in particular those that produce online research publications. It offers three MA programs and a PhD in digital humanities. Some current projects include Atlantic Europe in the Metal Ages, the Online Chopin Variorum Edition and the Corpus of Romanesque Sculpture in Britain and Ireland.

McMaster University

- Sherman Centre for Digital Scholarship (http://scds.ca/about -the-centre) provides research support for digital scholarship based on library/researcher resource sharing, including IT infrastructure; technical support and consulting services such as programming, data management and systems administration; meeting and work spaces; and archival and access initiatives. It offers graduate fellowships in digital scholarship and two-year postdoctoral fellowships in digital humanities.

Michigan State University

- Matrix: The Center for Digital Humanities and Social Sciences (http://www.matrix.msu.edu) creates and maintains online resources, provides training in computing and new teaching technologies and creates forums for the exchange of ideas and expertise in new teaching technologies. It offers student internships. Projects include the African Online Digital Library (AODL), the Vietnam Project Archive and the Quilt Index.

MIT

- Digital Humanities at MIT Hyperstudio (http://hyperstudio.mit .edu) collaborates with faculty in the humanities and social sciences on media-rich digital projects for teaching, learning and research. It works from project conceptualization through development to integration and evaluation. Projects include the Comédie-Française Registers Project, Arab Oral Epic and Global Shakespeare.

Occidental College

- Center for Digital Liberal Arts (https://www.oxy.edu/center -digital-liberal-arts) helps faculty and students integrate teaching, learning, research and scholarly work with emergent technologies and services. It sponsors a speakers series and an annual Mellon Digital Scholarship Institute and supports new course research and design. It advises students on scholarly resources and research strategies.

Princeton University

- The Center for Digital Humanities at Princeton (CDH, https:// digitalhumanities.princeton.edu) facilitates advanced humanistic scholarship and interdisciplinary and cross-disciplinary collaboration and provides support for digital humanities projects. It is a research center within the library.

Stanford University

- Center for Computer Assisted Research in the Humanities (http:// www.ccarh.org) is engaged in the development of large databases of musical and textual materials for applications in research, teaching and performance. Projects include Muse Data, Themefinder and Historic Calendars of Europe.
- Center for Spatial and Textual Analysis (CESTA, http://cesta.stanford .edu) pursues research that utilizes data and information visualization within a variety of methodologies, disciplines and departments. It comprises three labs and several affiliated projects and offers a graduate certificate in digital humanities. Current projects include Chinese Railroad Workers and Poetic Media.
- Literary Lab (http://litlab.stanford.edu) discusses, designs and pursues literary research of a digital and quantitative nature. Projects include the Taxonomy of Titles in the 18th Century Literary Marketplace, Loudness in the Novel and The Emotions of London.

University of Alabama

- Alabama Digital Humanities Center (ADHC, http://www.lib.ua.edu/ digitalhumanities) provides consultation with experts about project development and digital research, collaborates on innovative research and teaching projects and hosts events. Projects include "To See Justice Done": Letters from the Scottsboro Boys Trials, Southern and Western American Sacred Music and Influential Sources (1700–1870) and Shakespeare au/in Québec.

University of Birmingham, UK

- Institute for Textual Scholarship and Electronic Editing (http://www .birmingham.ac.uk/research/activity/itsee/index.aspx) uses digital tools to locate and view original materials, to transcribe them into electronic form, to compare texts, to analyze patterns of variation and to publish the texts electronically. Current and recent projects include The Greek New Testament, The Pauline Commentaries and The Codex Sinaiticus Project.

University of California, Los Angeles

- UCLA Digital Humanities (http://www.cdh.ucla.edu) provides services, instruction, resources and programs in collaboration with a variety of partners and affiliates. Current projects include ICEMorph and Sites of (re)Collection.
  - o Digital Humanities Program (http://www.cdh.ucla.edu/instruction .html) offers a minor and a graduate certificate program in digital humanities.
  - o Experimental Technologies Center (formerly the Cultural VR Lab, http://etc.ucla.edu) promotes collaborative, interdisciplinary experiential research in the use of new technologies in diverse disciplines including architecture, the performing arts, classics, archaeology, foreign-language studies and education, among others. Projects include RomanLab, Island of the Sun, Lighthouse at Alexandria, Karnak, Saqqara, Hypermedia Berlin and Qumran.
  - o Institute for Digital Research and Education (IDRE, https://idre .ucla.edu) supports research and education in computational thinking using high performance computation, data visualization and data analysis. IDRE collaborative projects include Hypercities and the UCLA Encyclopedia of Egyptology.
  - o Keck Digital and Cultural Mapping Program (http://www.cdh .ucla.edu/research/dhprojects/555.html) includes projects such as Taosi and the Sacred Landscape and Cities and Flooding: Past and Present.
  - o UCLA Digital Library Program (DLP, http://digital2.library .ucla.edu) includes the following projects: Cuneiform Digital Library Initiative, The Minasian Collection of Persian and Arabic Manuscripts, The Strachwitz Frontera Collection of Mexican and Mexican-American Recordings and The St. Gall Monastery Plan and Manuscripts.[4]

University of Glasgow, UK

- Humanities Advanced Technology and Information Institute (HATII, http://www.hatii.arts.gla.ac.uk/index.html) offers an academic program in humanities computing at introductory, honors and postgraduate levels, supports collaborative research projects and manages its own research program. Current and recent projects include A History of Working-Class Marriage, 1855–1976, Early Cinema in Scotland and Commemorations of Saints in Scottish Place-Names.

University of Illinois at Urbana-Champaign

- Institute for Computing in Humanities, Arts, and Social Sciences (I-CHASS, http://chass.illinois.edu) provides resources, both human and computational, and offers humanities, arts and social science scholars access to hardware, computer applications, graphical user interfaces and portals and educational opportunities to train in using these resources. On a basic level, it offers simple encouragement and guidance but can create new – and adapt existing – applications for more sophisticated projects.

University of Kentucky

- Collaboratory for Research in Computing for Humanities (http://www.rch.uky.edu) provides physical and computational infrastructure, technical support and grant-writing assistance to university faculty who wish to undertake humanities computing projects.

University of Maryland

- Maryland Institute for Technology in the Humanities (http://www.mith.umd.edu) specializes in text and image analytics for cultural heritage collections, data curation, digital preservation, linked data applications and data publishing, creating frameworks for developing new methods and tools for the exploration and visualization of digital materials and tools for preserving and archiving born-digital artifacts of recent and contemporary cultural heritage. Current projects include Foreign Literatures in America, The Shelley-Godwin Archive and "O Say Can You See": The Early Washington, D.C. Law and Family Project.

University of Nebraska at Lincoln

- Center for Digital Research in the Humanities (CDRH, http://cdrh.unl.edu) – a joint program with the University of Nebraska–Lincoln Libraries – advances interdisciplinary, collaborative research and provides research consultations, project coaching and support, access to resources – including hardware, software, staff and materials – work space, project and professional development funding and professionalizing opportunities. It hosts a summer digital scholarship incubator for student-led digital research and scholarship. Projects include Cuban Battlefields of the Spanish-Cuban-American War, The Journal of the Lewis & Clark Expedition and The Willa Cather Archive.

University of Oregon

* Digital Scholarship Center (http://library.uoregon.edu/digitalscholar ship) provides support for faculty and student projects using digital tools and technologies and access to, and preservation of, materials from faculty and student collections, special collections and university archives and local organizations. Projects include Oregon Petrarch Open Book Project and We Are the Face of Oaxaca.

University of Sheffield, UK

* HRI (Humanities Research Institute) Digital (http://hridigital.shef .ac.uk) provides research and development services for arts, humanities and heritage research. Current projects include Cistercians in Yorkshire, London Lives and Online Froissart.

University of Victoria, British Columbia

* Humanities Computing and Media Centre (HCMC, http://hcmc .uvic.ca) assists or collaborates with grant applications, with project planning and management (consulting, workstations and other resources), software development and data preparation and development. Projects include Maclure Architectural Drawings, The Diary of Robert Graves and Seventeenth-Century French Marriages.

University of Virginia

* Institute for Advanced Technology in the Humanities (IATH, http:// www.iath.virginia.edu) provides its research fellows with consulting, technical support, applications development and networked publishing facilities. Recent projects include Leonardo Da Vinci and

His Treatise on Painting, Silk Road: The Path of Transmission of Avalokitesvara and Virtual Williamsburg.

- Scholars' Lab (http://www.scholarslab.org) offers advanced students and researchers across the disciplines partnership on digital projects, expert consultation and teaching focused on the digital humanities and geospatial information.
- Virginia Center for Digital History (VCDH, http://www.vcdh.virginia.edu) provides experience and expertise in digital publication, design and development of innovative technology for digital history. Projects include The Valley of the Shadow, Virtual Jamestown and The Dolley Madison Project.

West Virginia University

- Center for Literary Computing (CLC, http://literarycomputing.wvu.edu) offers consulting, outreach and support for innovations in humanities scholarship. It provides practical experiences for graduate students and undergraduates. Projects include Computing Literature, Creative Reading Podcasts and Electronic Book Review.

Yale University

- StatLab (http://statlab.stat.yale.edu) offers support for research and quantitative analysis and consulting on data management, statistical software, quantitative methods, data and geospatial resources and emerging technologies to support interdisciplinary scholarship. In partnership with the library it provides technology, classrooms and computing facilities.

COLLABORATIVE CENTERS

The following list includes umbrella organizations for the digital humanities that may provide networking support for smaller centers.

Alliance of Digital Humanities Organizations (ADHO, http://www.digitalhumanities.org) represents constituent organizations in digital humanities. The effort to establish ADHO began at the 2002 ALLC/ACH conference. Activities include a publishing program, oversight of an annual conference and model presentations for humanities computing. It is focused internationally and includes six organizations:

- European Association for Digital Humanities (http://eadh.org)
- Association for Computers and the Humanities (http://ach.org)
- Canadian Society for Digital Humanities / Société canadienne des humanités numériques (http://csdh-schn.org)
- centerNet (http://digitalhumanities.org/centernet)
- Australasian Association for Digital Humanities (http://aa-dh.org)
- Japanese Association for Digital Humanities (http://www.jadh.org).

American Association for History and Computing (http://www.theaahc .org) is dedicated to exploring the intersection of history and technology across teaching, researching and representing history. The *Journal of the Association for History and Computing* was published from 1998–2010 and is archived at http://quod.lib.umich.edu/j/jahc.

Association for Computers and the Humanities (ACH, http://www .ach.org) is an international professional organization for people working in computer-aided research in literature and language studies, history, philosophy and other humanities disciplines. It engages the relationship between digital technologies and humanities methods.

Association of Internet Researchers (AOIR, http://aoir.org) is an academic association dedicated to the advancement of the cross-disciplinary field of Internet studies.

Canadian Society for Digital Humanities (CSDH-SCHN, formerly the Consortium for Computers in the Humanities COCH/COSH, http:// csdh-schn.org) is an association of representatives from Canadian colleges and universities aimed at drawing together humanists who are engaged in digital and computer-assisted research, teaching and creation. It provides opportunities for publication, presentation and collaboration.

Coalition for Networked Information (CNI, http://www.cni.org) is an alliance of some 220 organizations dedicated to supporting the transformative promise of digital information technology for the advancement of scholarly communication and the enrichment of intellectual productivity.

European Association for Digital Humanities (EADH, http://eadh .org), formerly the Association for Literary and Linguistic Computing (ALLC), brings together and represents the digital humanities in Europe across the entire spectrum of disciplines that research, develop and apply digital humanities methods and technology.

HASTAC (http://www.hastac.org) is an alliance of individuals for sharing information and materials focused on technological innovation and its impact on pedagogy and research.

Text Encoding Initiative Consortium (TEI, http://www.tei-c.org) is an international organization whose mission is to develop and maintain a standard for representing texts in digital form.

THE FUNDING ENVIRONMENT

The history of the first two decades of the digital humanities was one of bright expectations, robust experimentation and collaborative institutional participation. Yet at the end of these two decades few of the original projects or groupings that began the digital turn have survived. As the 1990s and 2000s went on, it became clear that sustainability was rising to the top of the list of priorities for any digital project to consider, most especially in an environment where the humanities themselves were under pressure from a variety of directions.

Various models and definitions of sustainability were proposed, tested and proven workable or not, ranging from purchase and subscription models, to open-access schemes that included every model from author pays to institution pays to foundation pays to end-reader pays.[5] Whatever the combination of funding models, two factors have become clear. First, that no digital project can now be launched without a clear sustainability model that takes into account recurring expenses for hardware, software and personnel. And second, that once that model is locked into place, it must be maintained. This has become especially true in the case of institutional and foundation support – the most robust and high-profile type – which frequently promises enough to launch and maintain a project for a few years. Once funds are exhausted or the funding agency shifts priorities, however, irreparable damage is often inflicted on these projects, their principals, staff and users.

On another institutional level – the university – this issue becomes even more urgent, as it is the very pressures of the host institution – hiring, tenure and promotion (HTP), research grants and prestige – that might launch a project on its course but also sets performance expectations and then finally renews or denies further funding. At the same time, the competing agencies within the university – faculty, library, university press and administration – have variously been charged with responsibility for devising and insuring long-term sustainability plans;[6] yet little coordination among these parties has resulted over the years, leading to the failure of a good many university-supported projects as well.

While several learned societies in the humanities have lent important prestige and financial resources to furthering digital research and publication – including major professional bodies such as the American

Anthropological Association (AAA), the American Historical Association (AHA), the College Art Association (CAA) and the Modern Language Association (MLA)[7] – many smaller societies in the humanities have neither the resources nor the internal expertise to launch more than token digital projects, generally including an e-version of their journal, an improved website, member services modules and perhaps a few digital monographs. University presses and other scholarly publishers have been experimenting – with mixed results – with various forms of digital publishing for the past fifteen years. We discuss their role in greater detail in Chapter 10.

In effect, funding specifically digital research and scholarship still takes place at the institutional/university level, and there are few funding opportunities specifically designated for digital humanities that are available outside that framework. However, as digital research becomes more the norm – unless research is aimed at creating new tools – general humanities funding can usually be used for most projects in the digital humanities. A few funding opportunities specifically focused on digital grants to individuals and collaborative teams include:

Alfred P. Sloan Foundation, Digital Information Technology Grants (http://www.sloan.org/major-program-areas/digital-information-technology) provide support for data and computational research, scholarly communication and universal access to knowledge.

American Council of Learned Societies, ACLS Digital Innovation Fellowships (https://www.acls.org/programs/digital) support digitally based research projects in all disciplines of the humanities and related social sciences.

Andrew W. Mellon Foundation, Scholarly Communications and Information Technology Grants (http://www.mellon.org/grant_programs/programs/scit) focus on the development of sustainable tools, organizations and networks of scholars and other professionals supporting the creation, use and preservation of original sources, interpretative scholarship and other scholarly and artistic materials. Grant applications are generally solicited by the foundation, but letters of inquiry are welcome.

National Endowment for the Humanities (NEH) has two programs in digital humanities, but as of June 2014, only 3.7 percent of the NEH's budget was devoted specifically to the digital humanities.[8]

- Digital Humanities Start-Up Grants (http://www.neh.gov/grants/odh/digital-humanities-start-grants) are small grants to support the planning stages of innovative projects that promise to benefit the humanities.

• Institutes for Advanced Topics in the Digital Humanities (http://www.neh.gov/grants/odh/institutes-advanced-topics-in-the-digital-humanities) makes grants that support national or regional (multistate) training programs for scholars and advanced graduate students to broaden and extend their knowledge of digital humanities.

THE GLOBAL ENVIRONMENT

Outside the university and the university library, the world of the digital humanities not only survives but thrives. Most of the tools that digital humanists employ in their work are created outside the university (see Chapter 5 and Appendix 1). Although humanists may have their own social media sites, like Academia.edu, humanists still generally rely on popular social networking sites like Facebook, content communities like YouTube, Vimeo and Google Groups and blogs and microblogs like Twitter and Tumblr. Humanists also participate in online collaborative projects hosted by libraries and museums and in independent projects like Wikipedia and Wikimedia.

The web is the ground on which all of this participation takes place, and participation is not limited to those with academic affiliations. Online publishing opens the work of humanists to readers and reviewers. As the line between content creators and audience, producers and users converge on the Internet, the constraints of academic considerations, like hiring, tenure and promotion (HTP), become less important than the communication of ideas and information.

Given this new environment, the digital may be freeing much of the humanities from the university and its strict disciplinary bounds, its HTP requirements and its narrow specializations. Would a return of the humanities to their disruptive role as exercised in the century of Petrarch and Boccaccio be a good thing? Would the equation of the humanist with the public intellectual be a natural one once again? And are the humanities ready to break away from the nineteenth-century German university model to become less a series of disciplines and once again a methodology and attitude for approaching the issues of the present with a deep knowledge of the past? Has the digital presented the new humanist with the necessary access, tools and publication possibilities so that the university setting is no longer necessary? Or will the digital humanities simply take their place as one more walled-in academic specialty, speaking only to its members?

7

Publication: Prerelease, Release and Beyond

Once a digital publication is ready for release, what issues surround it and how do they affect reception and use? What are the mechanisms in place for prepublication and postpublication peer review of digital projects? How are digital projects used by other scholars? What are the various and possible criteria for evaluating digital scholarship? Do digital projects count? For what and to whom? Must digital projects be scalable and replicable? Should they be interoperable with other scholarship? How is a project connected to the humanities community through the digital tools that the community uses: forums, blogs, wikis, listservs and so forth?

The meaning of publication and its forms have changed considerably over the past five hundred years and continue to do so. In the two hundred years that separate Petrarch and his first conscious attempts to define a new humanist movement and Desiderius Erasmus, who took full advantage of the new technology of the printing press, most humanists chose to publish in a few set forms. These ranged from the letter, closely modeled on classical examples most especially those of Cicero, where the communication sent from one scholar to another was both a private and a very public matter; to the edition of classical texts (secular and religious) culled from manuscripts in monastic and princely libraries; to the treatise – whether on education and manners, arms or architecture. Great works of history based on classical forms raised Renaissance historiography from the chronicle and its sequential recording of events to new thematic and interpretative formulations. By that time, Erasmus, Thomas More and other Renaissance humanists were writing for a print audience, and they had amplified these forms to include more popular alternatives, including the dialog, satire and essay. In the hands of writers like Erasmus and Montaigne, the essay became one of the chief media of political, religious and philosophical thought. Poetry, whether love or epic, and drama were also well-known types that adhered as closely as possible to ancient models or that used the approach of classical authors to forge new types of writing.

As Renaissance gave way to the early modern and the scientific revolution, works of science of all kinds also became a large part of humanist output, most especially in an age where much of natural science was indebted to classical texts for their basic models and content. The scientific treatise and the reference work formed a substantial part of humanist output into the nineteenth century. With the nineteenth century and its impulses to search for national origins and narratives came the new emphasis on a more "scientific" form of writing: the treatise and essay started to be supplanted by the work of scientific history, with evidence drawn from vast national archives, as well as major critical editions of narrative and literary primary sources, often published in grand series. Scholars henceforth began to communicate with one another not using the classically inspired letter but through "scientific" papers, whether in physics or philosophy or history. Theses presented might first be tested before other scholars, not in the symposia and academies of the fifteenth and sixteenth centuries inspired by Plato, but in more formal conferences where exposition might be met with heated debate. The resulting dialectic of fact and interpretation well matched the new sense of struggle found in so much nineteenth-century thought. As we shall discuss in more detail, the traditional forms of letter, essay and narrative were no longer considered scientific – or masculine – enough for the new world of science, competition and global empire. The conference paper, the article in the scholarly journal and the monograph forged over years of research now held sway and were to become the models for scholarly communication enshrined in the research university of the twentieth century. Scholars and researchers continued to keep notebooks and to write letters – voluminously in some cases – but these were meant to open up an area of discourse informally, to seek advice or consensus, to criticize or respond privately and to prepare for some formal publication.

ARCHIVES

Most humanist scholars would probably still agree that most new and valuable research begins with the archive, whether of a poet's letters and other unpublished material or with the government records of a city-state, for example. In digital form there are now true archives, that is, nearly complete digitized versions of the slowly accumulated documents placed in a depository for record keeping, and libraries have taken the lead in creating the infrastructure to house and access that data. Archaeologists have already begun archiving digital data. For example, Open Context[1] reviews, edits and publishes archaeological research data, and it archives that data with university-backed repositories. Another example is the ALIM project,[2] which is the digitization of several archival sources for the history of medieval Naples and Campania. Here an almost complete digital version of this archive is possible only because so much of the original archival material was destroyed in World War II, and the digitization process could reasonably quickly encompass all previously printed collections of these now lost sources. Digitization of the surviving copies of these documents, or alternative archives based in Marseilles or Barcelona because of historical reasons, remains ongoing.

Far more common are representational archives, digital collections of documents chosen by their researchers to offer the reader a far more robust sense of the materials available from the past than the ten or twenty documents usually appended to a print monograph. An excellent example of this is The Valley of the Shadow.[3] This digital archive offers a robust number of letters, diaries, newspapers, speeches, census and church records from the Civil War period for two neighboring – but opposing – counties in Virginia and Pennsylvania. This was the work of a team of people under the direction of Edward Ayers, its founder. But few digital archives can even approximate the completeness of original document archives. The task of digitizing complete runs of U.S. Civil War archives, for example, remains daunting and requires major institutional collaborations and sustainability plans. In the meanwhile, the representation of the archive provided by The Valley of the Shadow – though collected somewhat subjectively – still gives the reader some sense of the vastness of historical records and the multidimensional nature of research agendas and conclusions that can be drawn from a multitude of archival materials.

Digital archive projects are generally collaborations, and they offer new ways to share knowledge and create connections between scholars and the public. They have the potential to reinvigorate the traditional humanistic formula of scholars delivering neatly bound "reports from the archives" in print monographs. The University of Oxford, for instance, has brought together The Great War Archive,[4] which contains more than sixty-five hundred items contributed by the general public – with every item originating from, or relating to, someone's experience of World War I, either abroad or in Britain.

One of the more impressive endeavors in terms of collaboration and ambitious scope is The Medici Archive Project (MAP),[5] which brings together scholars who work on a single archive, the Medici Granducal Archival Collection (Mediceo del Principato). This archive comprises more than four million letters distributed in 6,429 volumes and occupying a mile of shelf space and covering the years from 1537 to 1743. It documents the political, diplomatic, gastronomic, economic, artistic, scientific, military and medical culture of early modern Tuscany and Europe. As of August 2011, the Documentary Sources database contained more than twenty-one thousand letters, fifteen thousand biographical entries and eighty thousand geographical and topographical tags; the online version of the database was recording an average of twenty thousand monthly hits.

Building upon this base, the project realigned its priorities to produce original, individual research in the form of books and papers, while creating an accessible archive where scholars from all over the world could view digitized images of archival documents, enter transcriptions, provide feedback and exchange comments. At first the path toward a workable model of collaboration was not always clear. Initially the project allowed individual scholars to focus on their own research agendas and to transcribe related documents. The result was a spotty and inconsistent digital archive. But as the project, its management and its technology matured, the Medici Archive has evolved into a model of rigorous collaborative effort with a clear mission and workable interim goals. In the decade following its founding, graduate students, university professors, museum curators and independent researchers paid regular visits to MAP's workspace at the State Archive in Florence in order to access unpublished documentary material or to seek help with archival research strategies related to their scholarly endeavors. At the same time, thanks to the NEH Fellowship Program and other similar funding, generations of researchers, experienced in archival and paleographic studies, have worked continuously to populate MAP's database with new material gleaned from the Medici sources. Initially accessible only in situ, this vast repository of transcribed and contextualized documents was published online in April 2006, free of charge. With funding from The Andrew W. Mellon Foundation, MAP has been able to update its (BIA) platform and make it accessible online to researchers all over the world.

In the hands of seasoned researchers both familiar with the archives under consideration and with proven ability to construct meaningful interpretation from these digital materials, the results can be startling. We will discuss here one example in some detail. The Rulers of Venice, 1332–1524: Interpretations, Methods, Database[6] took up a long-standing and vexing question in Venetian historiography: What accounts for the rapid rise of the Venetian colonial administrative class beginning in the fourteenth century and carrying on into the sixteenth? The traditional consensus interpretation, derived from long hours, days, months and years of individual researchers pouring through the Venetian archives, one fondo, one folio, one line at a time, using a standard historical method of representation, was to select a few salient details, choose a single individual and follow that person's career, his "prosopography" of family and connections, office holdings, geographical moves, honors, appointments and elective offices, then publish the findings and join in the scholarly conversation with other very specialized studies published in other journals and monographs to come up with a working hypothesis. That consensus has long been that the sudden increase of the Venetian administrative class was a fourteenth-century stimulus program created by a stagnant government bureaucracy in response to economic depression, plague, political and military crisis.

This question was one of the many addressed by a collaborative international research team that included American and European, senior and junior scholars, archivists, the American Council of Learned Societies and its Humanities E-Book, the Delmas Foundation, the Mellon Foundation, the University of Michigan Libraries, the Renaissance Society of America and the Archivio di Stato of Venice. The team first identified all available archival sources for this question – whether print or manuscript – then masterfully transcribed the documents into a database and arranged for digitization of the original documents, creating links from their transcribed texts to the digital reproductions of the original archival materials for other scholars to verify readings and replicate their research and conclusions. At the core of the database is a powerful search engine to identify individuals, families, offices and posts within the Venetian Mediterranean empire.

The first version of the work was completed in 2009. The result was more than sixty thousand archival records online in a single cross-searchable database. Within weeks of the completion of the database, this team had the evidence to overturn a generation of established archival research. With dozens, hundreds and thousands of examples now available to trace the careers of every known Venetian nobleman who held office, lead investigator Benjamin G. Kohl and his colleagues Monique O'Connell, Andrea Mozzato and Claudia Salmini were able to verify a simple, yet important preliminary conclusion: the huge increase in the Venetian administrative class was not the result of a public-works stimulus project, the sign of a decaying welfare state, but quite the contrary: it was the direct response to the very real and urgent needs to staff the expanding, enriching – if often endangered – Venetian colonial empire. Government grew not to feed welfare programs but to serve the Venetian people in a time of vast change, challenge and opportunity. Venice was thus documented to perform up to its contemporary reputation: the best example of a state governed by reason, law and justice.

It is an easy temptation to become overenthusiastic about the digital, to overclaim its impact on current methods and scholarly consensus, to see "paradigms" shifting, being disrupted and reformed, newly emerging everywhere one looks. Nevertheless, The Rulers of Venice has demonstrated clearly the effectiveness of the digital to answer traditional research questions. Beyond this it demonstrates the clear advantages of collaboration in humanistic research – a benefit yet to be widely embraced within the academy. In addition, this digital work, like so many others, now lives independently of any one scholar, team, research agenda or IT department and is open access and available to all, hosted and sustained institutionally. It comprises interpretive essays, interactive maps, images of archival materials and transcriptions. Despite the groundbreaking nature of the work and its findings, however, this project has never been reviewed. And this is one of the major issues that remains for digital humanities scholarship.

Yet even with tens of thousands of items in these new electronic archives, their digital nature only emphasizes their representative quality: first as a digitization of existing hard-copy records and, secondly, as subjective selections of such records, chosen by an individual scholar or a team for what they consider to be supportive of their research, pedagogy or analytical work. They do, however, point to a day when – with proper resources and funding – all hard-copy archives can be digitized. At that point they would change from being representational to true archives. But considerations other than technology may in the end determine what archives are completely digitized: funding, sustainability, the skill sets of researchers and public response to the materials digitized will remain far more important. In this regard humanists may again need to play the role they took in the fourteenth and fifteenth centuries: launching campaigns to identify and transform ignored or unknown manuscripts for new editions.

Again, we must still face the question about how closely any text or document can mirror its underlying historical reality. As this happens, the traditional approach of the humanist to the text begins to alter. The single scholar no longer converses with the historical author – Petrarch with Cicero, for example – and the resulting discourse is no longer dependent upon an individual's analysis and judgment: the Renaissance metaphor of the past as a single perspective point in space no longer holds. A multitude of polarities both in the text sources and in the audience are refracted through the prism of the digital.

REFERENCE WORKS

Dictionaries and encyclopedias have been part of the Western tradition since antiquity. Pliny the Elder, Isidore of Seville, Vincent of Beauvais and Denis Diderot all attempted to encompass some representation of all useful knowledge within the pages of the bound book. Today there are enormous digital reference works that adhere more closely to specific disciplinary boundaries and rarely make an attempt to be all comprehensive. Often these encyclopedic projects are collaborative and undertaken to cover an entire field. For instance, there are two major works in philosophy: The Stanford Encyclopedia of Philosophy (SEP)[7] and The Internet Encyclopedia of Philosophy[8] hosted by the University of Tennessee at Martin. These are collaborative, peer-reviewed collections of signed articles by recognized experts; each collection has an editorial board and presents the most current research available in completely searchable archives.

There are also many digital reference works produced outside academia, for example, The Digital Encyclopedia of George Washington,[9] which is published online by the Mount Vernon Ladies Association. This is a thorough reference work on Washington with approximately four hundred entries prepared by a team of more than sixty contributors, a third of them with PhDs and just less than one-third with higher education teaching positions. Perhaps the best known and most used digital encyclopedia is Wikipedia,[10] which because of its open access and collaborative, wiki structure, has the best ability to be all-inclusive. Yet for all its virtues,[11] Wikipedia still suffers from the doubts among many professionals over its accuracy and objectivity. Most of this criticism is based upon the old humanist formal preferences and presumptions of a single author working on clearly delineated field, the necessity of professional peer review and expectations about the immutability of the text until a new authorized edition.

Nonetheless, this type of digital reference reaches a broad audience. It is usually researched, assembled and written in a digital environment and is certainly published digitally. Internal review by the editors is also often done digitally. For example, SEP has password-protected web interfaces for authors and subject editors, which facilitate posting encyclopedia topics, commissioning, submitting, referring and reviewing, editing and updating, accepting and rejecting articles, comparing revisions, publishing and cross-referencing articles, providing citation information and tracking readership.

However, because these works are not considered original research – even though original research might in fact be included – they will seldom receive academic peer review and therefore will not count for the purposes of hiring, tenure and promotion (HTP). Conversely, because it is not considered work that is pertinent to HTP, it will not receive peer review. Some maintain that because no new knowledge is generated, these works do not count as scholarship, despite the fact that trained scholars produce them.

ONLINE BIBLIOGRAPHIES

Another form of reference publication is the online bibliography, and there are bibliographies for just about every subject imaginable, as well as bibliographies of bibliographies. However, constructing bibliographies – even annotated bibliographies, which were an important scholarly undertaking of the 1970s and 1980s – is no longer considered of scholarly (i.e., academic workplace) merit. It is not surprising, however, that online bibliographies are very valuable resources, and publishers like Oxford University Press[12] have made enormous investments in this area. These bibliographies are subscription based and are produced collaboratively by scholars and librarians. Marketed as a cross between annotated bibliography and a high-level encyclopedia, these reference works are kept current with entries constantly being added and updated. The Getty Research Institute[13] provides access to material published between 1975 and 2007 in the Bibliography of the History of Art (BHA) and the Répertoire international de la littérature de l'art(RILA) at no charge, while the International Bibliography of Art (IBA)[14] charges for materials after 2007.

Individual bibliographies can also be found on the web, and these were often launched in the earlier days of website building and at some time were brought together into collections of bibliographies, but unfortunately many have not been updated in the last five to ten years. In medieval studies both the Internet History Sourcebook[15] and the Orb: Online Reference Book for Medieval Studies[16] remain useful resources but only up to a certain point in time. It is not surprising, considering the work involved in keeping a bibliography current, that most online bibliographies have faced the prospect of either charging for access or discontinuing updates.

Again, scholars who dedicated their efforts to building online bibliographies – even projects that required years of work and constant research – failed to receive academic credit toward HTP. But the work of publishing bibliographies online continues, perhaps not only from academic corners, but now also from other organizations. The Historic New Orleans Collection and the Historical Text Archive, for example, both publish online bibliographies on topics ranging from culinary history to voodoo.[17] There are also monumental online aggregations, such as OCLC's WorldCat[18] that allow users to search and browse through any topic, find titles from all the member libraries and compile open-access, online bibliographies around specific fields or research agendas.

EDITIONS AND TRANSLATIONS

The edition of the Greek and Latin texts and the translation of Greek works into Latin and then into the vernacular were fundamental activities of the first humanists. This work was once highly valued in the academic community. The editions of great collections of sources stretching from the seventeenth into the twentieth century became legendary. The *Acta Sanctorum, Monumenta Germaniae Historica*, the Roll Series, the Papers of Benjamin Franklin have all had fundamental impact on humanistic scholarship. So too the work of translation in such series as the Loeb Classical Library, Harper Torchbooks, the Penguin Classics or the Columbia Records of Civilization. In the late twentieth century, however, under the impact of both new theory and the pressures of the job market, the critical edition and the translation became forms to be avoided, as only the interpretive monograph could open access to HTP at most institutions.

By the early twenty-first century scholars were therefore often forced to rely on old editions and translations while awaiting newer ones promised in accordance with current practice. By then, however, digital tools for preparing editions, online dictionaries and other resources had given rise to a significant increase in the number of new online editions and translations in many fields, from musicology and literary studies to art history and religion. Online publication of editions and translations broadens the audience for these works, which previously were often available only in small print runs and in specialized libraries.

For example, A New English Translation of the Septuagint and the Other Greek Translations Traditionally Included under that Title[19] is a translation of the Greek Jewish Scriptures. The International Organization for Septuagint and Cognate Studies sponsored this translation by specialists in Septuagint studies. A translation manual is provided online with guidance for the translators, and each submission is thoroughly reviewed before publication. Originally published in print by Oxford University Press, even a work like this, with a print component, appears to have had only one review (*Journal of the Evangelical Theology Society*). Meanwhile, the University of Maryland has published a series of scholarly editions on a website called Romantic Circles.[20] The website emphasizes that "each edition is based on the highest scholarly standards and is peer-reviewed." Reviews of these online editions are very rare, with only one appearing in *Review 19*,[21] an online review journal.

One of the more promising projects that weds the traditional philological outlook of the humanist with the digital attempts to kick-start the online editing and dissemination of classical and later Latin texts is the Digital Latin Library (DLL).[22] The DLL is a partnership among the Society for Classical Studies, formerly the American Philological Association, the Medieval Academy of America and the Renaissance Society of America. Similar in intent to a traditional public research library, the DLL will have a catalog, a variety of collections of texts and reference materials and working space for both individuals and groups. Unlike a traditional research library, it will also provide tools to facilitate the creation and publication of open-access, born-digital critical editions and other scholarly and pedagogical resources that take full advantage of powerful technologies. Rather than relying upon the digitization of previously edited texts, whatever their source or quality, however, the DLL seeks to publish works that will follow their newly created textual editing standards. It anticipates that this process will result both in new editions and in a new community of textual editors familiar with the latest editorial and digital practices.

Despite such innovations, old problems remain: depending on the field and the extent of introductions, annotations and other apparatus, editions may or may not be reviewed. Translations – no matter how scholarly – are seldom reviewed in academic journals. As with the case of encyclopedias, work on editions and translations is rarely given credit toward HTP within the academy, particularly if the publication is not reviewed in the important scholarly journals.

COMPENDIA/COLLECTED WORKS

Digital compendia are generally websites that include all of the items in the preceding discussion. We are familiar with published series like the complete works of Mark Twain or Charles Dickens, but in the digital realm these collections break out of the bindings of books. While these may not include new research, they are often the place to find out about it through introductory surveys, notes and bibliographies; and while they may not all be essential for other scholars, they do provide important resources for teaching and learning. They are seldom reviewed in specialized journals and rarely cited in scholarly literature.

The University of Virginia's Rossetti Archive,[23] curated by Jerome McGann, on the Pre-Raphaelite painter and poet, Dante Gabriel Rossetti, for instance, includes access to all of his visual and textual works. It also includes what publishers would call a companion volume, a large contextual corpus of materials, mainly from Rossetti's own lifetime, but some stretching back to the fourteenth-century sources of Rosetti's Italian translations. The Princeton Dante Project[24] includes the full text of all of Dante's works, the texts of lectures, maps, audio files of readings and links to full-text secondary works. It also links out to approximately ten other Dante websites. Often when these sites derive from the long career of an individual scholar, they suffer from stagnation and neglect: the bibliographies do not keep up with current research, links are broken and in the worst cases the hosting institution fails to maintain the site. The best of these compendia are collaborative projects, which helps to guarantee continuous updating.

The Perseus Digital Library,[25] while focused on the Greco-Roman world, is a model for exploring how collections of materials in a field move from being discreet units – books and articles – to being a part of digital libraries as the components are aggregated into a single interconnected platform. Perseus is one of the greater success stories in digital humanities. Everyone in the field knows it, and almost everyone uses it. Whether or not the pioneers behind this massive, thirty-year-old undertaking achieved academic recognition commensurate with the achievement, the site continues to be used long after most monographs published thirty years ago have since been deaccessioned and forgotten.

ARTICLES

The scholarly article is the most contested form in the digital realm today. Originally growing out of the early modern humanist essay, under the influence of Leopold von Ranke's scientific history, the article took on a rigidity that it has retained into the present. A single scholar takes up a research agenda that might take years or decades to accomplish – conscientiously plowing through vast written archives, the work of a painter or sculptor, collections of papyrus or cuneiform, reports of archaeological digs, the works of a single composer – and carefully crafts a "report from the archive" about current research findings, with theoretical frames to examine evidence and substantial citation of secondary work to enter into a dialog with the current consensus of scholarly opinion. Before publication the author might first present a basic thesis and its evidence to an academic conference to receive comment and scholarly approval. She then would submit a proposal to a scholarly journal, whose editor would first read the piece for its original contribution, scholarly standards and appropriateness to the journal's scope. Then, if the journal editor found the article worth consideration, she would send it on to a specialized area editor who would be familiar with the current state of the submission's very specialized field. If that editor found the article of value, the journal would contact peer reviewers within the tight field of that specialization.

Peer review would be carried out in several ways: "double-blind" in which the author did not know the identity of the peer reviewers nor the reviewers the identity of the author; single-blind or reviewer-blind, in which the author would not know the names of the reviewers but they would know the author of the submission, or double-open or open review, in which all identities were clear. The more blind the review, the higher the prestige of the process and the journal. The article might run from twenty to forty pages in print, most often in a scholarly journal supported by a specialist learned society in any number of humanistic fields. In this the humanist article differed little from that in the physical or social sciences: intended for a professional audience, using a technical vocabulary common to the field, designed to push forward the boundaries of current specialized knowledge.

Upon publication – most often in random order of submission or editorial completion in a journal issue containing some four to six articles of unrelated subject and period within the disciplinary specialty – the author would then await the "impact" factor. This could come quite quickly – through a best-article reward – or far more slowly through private communication from other scholars and finally through the cumulative process of citation in other articles, monographs and then in surveys and more popular work. Such a model follows not historical humanist practice but that of the scientific scholarly society or academy of the nineteenth century, where the humanities were held to the same standards of evidence collection, evaluation and dissemination as the sciences for and by highly trained specialists. It became the perfect vehicle for the twentieth-century university, and most humanist scholarly societies were built around the publication of the specialized article. While the educated public and nonspecialists greeted the highly technical scientific article with respect and tolerance for its often opaque language, the same audience might often receive the advanced humanities article with derision for its narrow focus and specialized language and citations: again a function of the assumed ease and transparency of humanist research.

Yet another venue for the article – one increasingly embraced by humanist scholars at the turn of the twenty-first century – was to publish it in collected works, first in *Festschriften* – volumes presented in honor of a distinguished teacher by her students – and increasingly more prevalent, in collections built around certain set themes within a discipline, very often intended to present the state of the field or introduce new theoretical models. Many scholars, sometimes frustrated by long delays, apparently arbitrary peer-review reports and escalating rejection rates at increasingly overworked journals, saw such volumes as the best way to present their work. Yet this alternative held certain disadvantages: they were not strictly peer reviewed (most often reviewed solely by the same volume editors who had invited the article), they were dependent for their dissemination and prestige upon the reputation of the book publisher, and they faced a hierarchy of impact metrics that placed such venues lower down than the most prestigious journals.

The digital began to change the nature of article publication and its dissemination almost immediately. In 1995, one of the very first digital aggregations, JSTOR,[26] initially funded as a preservation project and then directly administered by the Mellon Foundation, began to retro-spectively digitize the complete runs of print journals. It now hosts more than two thousand journals and serves up more than fifty million pages reaching more than 9,200 institutions worldwide through a subscription model now also available to individuals. Standard contracts with schol-arly societies or other journal publishers call for a "moving wall" that allows the original publisher to retain both rights and distribution to the most recent issues. The project became an almost instantaneous success in terms of access and distribution and in changing scholarly culture. It did so both in its technical innovation but also – and more importantly – through the net effect of its day-to-day adoption as an academic stan-dard. It was transformative not because of platform (later replaced) but in changing academic *habitus* of research. JSTOR's interface and access model made it possible for far more users to access the articles than was previously possible with bound volumes on library shelves; secondly, users quickly became aware that JSTOR's sophisticated search mechanism – developed at the University of Michigan Libraries – would cross-search thousands of journals and millions of pages and that search results were soon being brought up from sources never before considered.

JSTOR was soon joined by several imitators. ACLS's Humanities E-Book,[27] discussed below, applied the very same technology to mono-graphs, while Project MUSE[28] of The Johns Hopkins University Press launched a similar journal plan in 1995. The History Cooperative was launched in 2000 by the American Historical Association (AHA), Organization of American Historians (OAH), the University of Illinois Press and the National Academies Press. Meanwhile large university and commercial publishers, including Elsevier, Oxford, Cambridge, Chicago and Routledge, pushed forward rapidly with their own proprietary aggre-gations, vastly expanding the access to and reach of individual articles and deepening the impact of search-engine findings.

At the same time, JSTOR made it possible for both researchers and theorists to realize that the digital had begun to actively disaggregate both the article and its texts from the context of the narrowly defined journal and sponsoring society. With the advent of text-mining tools this disaggregation became even more pronounced. Scholars and publish-ers also began to both theorize and actively implement the publishing possibilities that the digital offered to change the basic structure of the article in the digital era: no longer restricted by the publishing costs and schedules of journals to a set number of pages published periodi-cally, the digital article freed itself from page counts and fixed release dates. While its purpose – to announce initial findings or very targeted research – remained intact, the digital article now could take on almost any format, adding images and other features, expanding the amount of primary source material or linkages to more closely resemble what had long been the preserve of the print monograph. Access was also now completely changed: whereas once the article was first received by the subscribers to the journal – generally the members of the scholarly society that sponsored it – in the digital the audience could be as wide as access schemes, open or paid, would allow. Impact could now be measured quickly and easily, either with the statistical tools imbedded in commercial or not-for-profit hosting software or through third-party aggregations like Academia.edu, where authors can see the changing numbers of views and downloads of their work daily at the click of a mouse. Prepublication versions of the work could circulate freely online, outside the normal limitations and confidentiality schemes of traditional peer review. Articles could both resemble monographs in their structure and conference papers in their initial form, as authors could now post preliminary work online in article form, receive comment and criticism and incorporate such community review into a "final" version.

Another side to the issue quickly developed, however. Because of the relative – or perceived – ease of publishing online, many authors, especially after viewing online readership statistics, began to reconsider the importance of the entire editorial process: who needs editors, printing presses or distribution networks when one can write and post online immediately and freely? Such attitudes also contributed to calls for open-access publishing (which we will discuss below). The JSTOR model – one of mass digitization and standardization based on scans of printed pages – began to come under critique, and calls for new born-digital articles were sounded across several scholarly societies. One of the early experimenters with these possibilities was the *American Historical Review*, which posted two born-digital articles over the years. The first was intended as an introduction to the theoretical construct of Robert Darnton's grand pyramid of digital publishing.[29] It presented an electronic version of his AHA presidential address, "An Early Information Society: News and the Media in Eighteenth-Century Paris," featuring layers of graphics, documents, maps and sound files. The original version, which appeared on the site of the University of Indiana Press, is no longer available, although the text with hyperlinked footnotes and low-resolution image files is still online.[30] The second was the William G. Thomas III and Edward L. Ayers article, "The Differences Slavery Made,"[31] which drew on the resources and collected evidence in their Valley of the Shadow project. An over-view appeared in the print version of the *American Historical Review*, while the electronic article was originally published on the site of the former *History Cooperative*. The article is now hosted on the site of the Virginia Center for Digital History.[32]

The digital article continues to confront authors, publishers and readers with some essential questions about the digital humanities. In a digital realm of radical aggregation and disaggregation how unique are the research findings and impact of the individual article? Does tra-ditional peer review still work, and if so what weight is given to rigor-ously peer-reviewed digital work?[33] Must the digital humanist continue to write for a small, restricted audience of specialists? Can one maintain a rigorous standard depending on community input using social media and other means rather than on a few nameless peer reviewers? What role remains to the library when its rows on rows of shelves lined with print journals no longer attract readers and when the researcher and student can now sit at home and call up a vast array of the most rigorous and recent scholarship on any given topic? What is happening among the learned societies when one of the chief mainstays of their survival – income from print journals – quickly disappears? Will society members retain their loyalty to the club once its most highly prized resource, its journal, can now be accessed remotely through libraries' digital collec-tions? Are the old strict forms of publication that clearly distinguished article, book, survey, textbook still valid? What is the difference, for example, between an online article of forty "pages" of analytical text and 160 pages of documents, visual sources, hyperlinks and other features and a two hundred-page print monograph in which analysis is spread out over several chapters and the same documentation cited and analyzed but not presented to the reader? How must we now assess their content and impact?

DIGITAL MONOGRAPHS

Because "the monograph is the coin of the realm" in academic human-ities, what author would chose to publish a *digital* monograph if a print publisher were willing to publish it and if one's academic career depended on this publication? Not only would few scholars choose a digital-only monograph, but there are few places where one could pub-lish one. Rice University Press, which was reestablished in 2006 to pub-lish digital monographs, ceased operations in September 2010.[34] The

University of Michigan Press[35] has published several titles, but while one of these resembles a scholarly paper, the others are even less like monographs. JSTOR has taken on monograph publishing,[36] but to date the works are digital reprints of recent monographs (primarily post-2000) from a variety of publishers, mostly university presses.[37] These books are based entirely on the print versions with only the limited digital capabilities of a simple PDF book rather than a truly enhanced, interactive publication.

ACLS Humanities E-Book (HEB),[38] originally the History E-Book Project, was established to publish new digital monographs as one part of its mission, and it was originally mandated to work with university presses to develop these titles. The university presses, however, could not envision a revenue stream from digital publications, so despite the fact that these publications were significantly subsidized by HEB, the only new titles to emerge – in addition to its very significant backlist – were titles appearing both in print and digitally. Only when HEB decided to act as a publisher itself was it able to publish a select number of digital-only monographs. To date HEB has published about two hundred original digital monographs either under its own imprint or in collaboration with its publishing partners. These titles range from minimally enhanced digital versions of print – widely critiqued for their lack of innovation – to robust born-digital scholarship. This achievement has largely been eclipsed by HEB's backlist, which currently numbers more than forty-three hundred digitized monographs and over one million pages from more than one hundred publishers.

Again, are scholarly works published digitally considered scholarship? If so, why are they not reviewed? Even if the digital works fall into several areas already closely bound with traditional humanities publishing, they are still considered different. There have been exceptions. *Florence Ducal Capital, 1530–1630*[39] by R. Burr Litchfield, for example, was published in 2008. It is based on a digital edition of the Buonsignori map of Florence and makes intense use of Brown's Florentine Renaissance Resources: Online Gazetteer of Sixteenth Century Florence[40] and the Online Catasto of 1427[41] edited by David Herlihy, Christiane Klapisch-Zuber, R. Burr Litchfield and Anthony Molho. The e-book analyzes how sixteenth-century Florence changed from a merchant city and communal republic that was the center of a city-state into the seat of a princely court and bureaucracy and capital of a regional grand duchy, a shift that affected its architecture, urban morphology and social structure.

Litchfield was not concerned with HTP issues but with the preservation and promotion of the digital work that had gone into the Florentine database project. He could therefore bypass traditional print publication and pursue an enhanced, born-digital book that linked back and forth from the text to the database. Unlike so many other digital publications, his monograph was well received and reviewed in the *American Historical Review*, the *Journal of Interdisciplinary History*, *Seventeenth-Century News* and *H-Net*. This may indicate that journals would be willing to review digital monographs if publishers – or someone else – were willing to publish them. It is also worth noting that the review problem is not entirely unique for digital publications: many print publications also remain unreviewed. As more and more monographs are published, fewer and fewer receive attention from the scholarly community.

Another important experiment in digital monograph publishing provides a few worthwhile lessons. Between 1999 and 2011, another Mellon-funded project, Gutenberg-e,[42] produced thirty-five monographs in HTML. These were young scholars' first books based on dissertations chosen by a committee of the American Historical Association. These thirty-five award-winning books garnered a total of thirteen reviews, eight in the *American Historical Review*, the journal of the American Historical Association, and only five in other journals. For all its original plans and expectations, one of the initial disadvantages of Gutenberg-e was its publication model: each award-winning scholar was matched with a team of technologists at Columbia University and Columbia University Press and given carte blanche to experiment with format, function, features and any other number of variables on the HTML website that would constitute their e-book. While adopting current theory of authorship and collaboration, this model led to two further drawbacks: these custom-made websites became overcomplicated and costs rose; while the finished books could not "talk" to one another – that is they could not be cross-searched – and the lack of standardized format made the experience cumbersome for readers. These problems of format and publishing strategy were addressed later in the project, while the questions of sustainability and access were resolved by incorporating the Gutenberg-e titles into ACLS Humanities E-Book. HEB had by then determined that consistency and interoperability were far more important in the digital environment of increased aggregation than creating a series of distinct websites, however innovative some of their features.

Such stress on consistency of format and elements should not disconcert humanists. Humanism was, after all, based on the consistent

application of the rules of grammar and rhetoric: the goal of the humanist endeavor was to perfect both structure and form according to classical models. This impulse manifested itself not only in the elegance
of the humanists' Latin but also in the purity of their page designs.
While the medieval manuscript with its numerous glosses and illuminations revealed a wealth of information and fascinating interconnection
between text and commentary, most humanist books were by comparison quite stripped down, all the better to convey the purity of language
and thought. Will the academic community ultimately opt for consistency and predictability of format – what had made print ultimately successful over both manuscript and block-books? Or will it continue to seek
an ideal of complexity in each digital publication? The test of time has
thus far borne out the HEB model. It seems clear that going forward
aggregation, common standards and interoperability will remain key to
any publishing and sustainability strategies. All humanists know how to
read a 250-page print monograph: the challenge now is to create that
same cultural *habitus* for the digital.

VIRTUAL REALITY

There are also digital projects that go beyond our traditional notions
of the publication and dissemination of scholarship: collaborations of
scholars using 3D modeling to create virtual-reality (VR) worlds that
can become teaching and research spaces in themselves: projects like
Bernard Frischer's Rome Reborn,[43] Paris 3D,[44] Digital Karnak[45] and similar projects on Babylonia and London. VR projects like Rome Reborn
allow users to drill down from visual representations to the archive of
images and texts that provided the basis for the model. Linked elements
to photos, catalogs and manuscripts function like a book index or a finding tool. These projects thus become editions of cities as grand texts: a
reconstruction and representation of the original in a curated and accessible format that uses a grammar of visual and verbal metaphor to evoke
an underlying reality. UCLA has probably done more than any other
institution in this particular area of virtual reality, but several other projects are commercially hosted.

In comparison to these other new formats, virtual-reality projects most
dramatically remind us that humanistic publishing is more of a dynamic
process than the creation of a series of distinct objects. As one becomes
familiar with the current state of reconstruction and representation of
the Roman Forum, for example, one understands the cumulative nature

of humanist scholarship: building upon and correcting what has been presented before as the most accurate representation of another time and place.

CONCLUSIONS

Each of these publication formats is based on the work of earlier humanists. In many respects they are working in much the same way that the Renaissance humanists did: gathering information, organizing, analyzing and interpreting it and disseminating findings. Yet in other respects the digital has had a profound impact on the relationship of scholars to libraries, publishers and their audiences. The old equation – the scholar researches and writes, the editor reviews, the publisher disseminates and the library archives – has been altered. Old collaborations, between the scholar and the printer for example, are being replaced in the digital era with collaborations between scholars and IT departments. Libraries, once considered passive repositories of the accumulated knowledge of the past, have now taken a far more active lead in both creating and disseminating scholarly work. Interpretative works born of the scientific approach of the nineteenth century still remain more valued than the translations and editorial work of the first humanists, but the digital has begun to readjust that balance.

Publishing models born of the scholarly academies of the nineteenth century – the scholarly article distributed to a small group of specialists and the monograph sold primarily to research libraries – are being replaced by web publication of many kinds of research material in many different formats. These new forms can draw thousands of viewers a month to resources now available in seconds that previously would have been difficult, expensive, slow or impossible to access. In this environment scholars remain concerned about standards: what guarantees the continued quality and reliability of this digital material when all the structures of scholarly communication are in flux? Scholars remain reluctant to review digital materials, and without that peer review such projects become worthless in the eyes of academic credentialing bodies. This discourages scholars from undertaking work that has the potential of reaching out to the vast audience of web users, scholars, students, teachers and the general public. At the same time new organizations, partnerships and alliances have begun addressing these issues and experimenting with different solutions. At this point, however, publication remains a constantly evolving aspect of the digital humanities.

8

The Meta-Issues of Digital Humanities 1

There are many issues surrounding the digital humanities that are beyond the question of the scholarship itself and its contribution to either the individual disciplines or to useful knowledge generally. While humanists outside academia need to be less concerned with many of these issues, academics must be acutely aware of them for their own success and the success of their work. In this chapter we will discuss the education of the digital humanist; stratification; collaboration; publication, distribution, discoverability; preservation; reader and author; funding strategies; sustainability; HTP (hiring, tenure and promotion) issues; gender, global and other divides; and digital theory. In Chapter 9 we will examine copyright and other rights, DRM (digital rights management) and open access.

EDUCATION

One of the chief hallmarks of the first Renaissance humanists was their insistence upon a new style of education that would reform the methods of the medieval schoolmen in the universities and transform individuals through a knowledge of past models and of the skills needed to communicate this knowledge for the present.[1] While humanists eventually found their place within the university and derived their name, *humanista*, from the *studia humanitatis* that they taught – largely the disciplines of grammar, rhetoric, moral philosophy and poetry (including history writing): what today would cover most humanities faculties – the impact of Renaissance humanism went well beyond academic disciplines. Pier Paolo Vergerio, Leonardo Bruni, Aeneas Silvius Piccolomini, Battista Guarino, Baldassare Castiglione, Desiderius Erasmus and Juan Luis Vives all produced treatises on education for Europe's lay elites.[2] These works covered education both in formal terms and in subject matter – history and ethical education, for example – and for day-to-day life, in practical matters of courtesy and behavior – everything from life at court to table manners to the martial arts. The education of a Christian prince and of young men and women became hallmarks of a humanist approach intended to be comprehensive and thorough, translating the virtues of the past for the present. It consisted both in skills (languages, grammar, rhetoric, history, philosophy) and in a broader approach to life infused with the wisdom of the past as a model for present virtue, both private and public. As such it moved into the university by dominating a set of disciplines. In this way it became the model for the Anglo-American higher-educational system from the sixteenth into the nineteenth century. Its public role as a model for individual behavior and citizenship fared less well when it became tied to the notion of the early modern "gentleman," a model that faded with the end of the *ancien régime*.

How then does this original humanist mission translate into the digital? Are there skills and modes of behavior for the digital era that correspond to such historical models? Are there digital equivalents of grammar, rhetoric and poetic formalism that translate into today's environment? Or are such questions no longer relevant after the impact of the nineteenth and twentieth centuries' professionalization of humanism into academic disciplines? If the latter is the case, how then does the digital fit into the modern disciplinary scheme of things? Are both the humanities and the digital a set of technical skills that bear no relevance to larger audiences or purposes and that focus narrowly on professional concerns and developments? What then distinguishes the technically proficient humanist curriculum from any other business- or technology-oriented college or professional school course offering? Do humanists need to be "trained" in the digital within the context of their graduate school education in the same way that many consider accounting or lab technology training?

There is a movement to introduce courses for doctoral and masters candidates on the "digital humanities," but if we accept one possible definition of the digital humanities as the application of digital tools to standard humanities questions, does the subject matter of this "discipline" become training in the use of digital tools? Henry M. Gladney has recently contended that the digital humanities cannot be a discipline precisely because they lack such a disciplinary core of content and that " 'digital humanities' (DH) is the name chosen by an interest group that is promoting their activities for funding and for inclusion in university faculties."[3] Can they therefore become an essential part of the graduate humanist education when Information Science, a recognized academic discipline, has already addressed most of the issues raised in far more rigorous ways?[4] Is a PhD required to be a "digital humanist"? And if so, in what field(s)?[5]

It would seem that the generation now in charge of graduate school education might feel the need for such courses, because this is the generation that still might not even know how to crop a digital photo or scan a document. At this point, however, most graduate students – and even more undergraduates – are much more familiar with the fundamentals of digital production and might not need to spend precious and very expensive time learning skills that are second nature to people who grew up after the birth of the World Wide Web. The basic skills once learned are easily extended to new tools and new methods. Quick online tutorials are available free or for small fees through anything from YouTube to Lynda.com. Most tools even come with online tutorials or support from developers. In most cases students who understand the research at hand will automatically apply digital tools to the task.

If, however, digital humanities are defined as some new way of thinking, some new paradigm for the work of humanists, it would seem that there has not yet been made a clear enough case of exactly what this is, or how it might be taught, or by whom. This is a conversation that needs to continue in more rigorous settings: at special seminars and conferences that leave behind advocacy and rigid answers and definitions and that focus instead on reaching a broad consensus on intellectual problems. At best, "what is DH education?" remains an open question at this point.

STRATIFICATION

Yet another aspect of humanist education is revealed in a story told by Vespasiano da Bisticci (1421–98) about Federigo da Montefeltro, the duke of Urbino. Vespasiano was among the most famous of Renaissance manuscript designers and copyists and also one of the period's best memoirists. His stories about some of the leading figures of his time are among the best narrative sources we possess. He was one of the most respected of book collectors and was commissioned by Cosimo de Medici to form the basis of what would become the Laurentian Library in Florence, and he also helped establish the humanist library of King Matthias Corvinus of Hungary. Vespasiano was commissioned to copy many manuscripts for the duke of Urbino, a powerful papal vassal who was both a renowned *condottiere*, or mercenary captain in papal employ,

and a well-known patron of the arts and letters. His manuscript collection of Greek and Latin classical texts, as well as of contemporary humanist authors, laid out in large elegant pages in a fine humanist script and
luxuriously illuminated in high Renaissance style, still forms the core of
one of the Vatican's most beautiful collections: the Codices Urbinates.

Vespasiano relates that Federigo refused to allow into his collection
a single book produced by the new printing press, no matter who the
author or the printer. Vespasiano closed up his copyist shop in 1478
rather than compete with the new printers. Scholars have challenged
the accuracy of Vespasiano's story about Duke Federigo, but it has the
ring of a certain truth: in an age where the reverence for the past and the
appreciation of fine art set the prince apart from and above his fellows,
a reverence for fine manuscript work and a disdain for print harkened
back to the wisdom of the ancients long transmitted in manuscript culture. It also invoked another cultural inheritance from antiquity, when
the noble disdained manual labor and the use of any mechanical device.
This sort of thing was left to the slaves and the merchant classes who
worked with their hands. One needs to be reminded that humanist culture derives from such ancient foundations: the life of the singular mind
built upon the labor of the many and on the service of a literate but sub-
ordinate class of readers and amanuenses.

Most especially in the early days of the computer revolution one heard
similar stories from and about senior faculty and their imitators: scholars who had never used a typewriter, who could not insert a floppy disk,
who could not send or receive e-mail, who could not use a word processor, let alone a spreadsheet or a database. For whatever reason the same
humanities faculty members who on a personal level drove back and
forth to work in their autos, boarded jet airliners to attend conferences
and do their summer research, used the television and radio, the home
entertainment unit and (if enlightened) the dishwasher, for some reason
could not accommodate the new digital technology and relied upon "IT
staff" or students for even the most basic routines of digital reading and
writing. Not so the hard or social scientist, for whom computer-aided
analysis and number crunching had long been essential tools and processes of their disciplines. One suspects that a certain *imitatio* of their
ancient and Renaissance models among humanities faculty – as well as
a certain class hauteur – may have accounted for much of the disdain,
some of which lingers twenty years into the digital era.

Such attitudes were often humorous personal peculiarities of
well-known and eccentric colleagues and teachers; but on an

institutional level they took on another dynamic altogether, which is reflected in everyday academic stratifications and in the institutional DNA of humanities and digital humanities curricula and institutes. While full tenured faculty are usually either the sole researcher or research team director, the day-to-day, hands-on work that involves the use of the computer, the entry, manipulation and reporting of data remains that of the IT staff or technologist; and the majority of projects, even in the digital humanities, continue to adopt this formation. In addition, the long-held divide in many humanities disciplines between theoretical and empirical work – in some sense reflecting that of the hard sciences – continues to favor the theoretician over the scholar who sifts and weighs firsthand evidence, the author of the monograph over the textual editor or translator, the project head who sets goals (often without any digital experience) and the technologists or editors assigned to carry out project objectives. In the real world of academia, this also most often translates into the great divide between the tenured and the nontenured, the full-time and the contingent, part-time or grant-funded fellow, usually with a disciplinary PhD and the (mis)fortune to be skillfully attuned to her digital times. From whichever perspective one approaches the issue – historical, technical, theoretical or professional – it appears that the digital humanities tend to exacerbate rather than ameliorate such class distinctions in a rapidly bifurcating academic society.

COLLABORATION

Collaboration and team publication are part of the scenario in many disciplines, including the social sciences, but despite two decades of focus on this issue, by far most humanities research and publication remains firmly single author. While the rise of collaborative volumes has been a step forward, most essays prepared for such a volume are usually not done in a collaborative manner. Scholars approach a specific topic from an individual viewpoint, and the essays are brought together without any reference to each other, unless an editor manages the selection process rigidly or offers thematic unities within an introduction. Except in fields like archaeology, panels at general conferences and specialized conferences rarely present more than the same amalgamation of individually created and isolated parts.

When humanists collaborate with other humanists, the process often becomes a hierarchical arrangement with a chief investigator and a team of graduate students, and publication is often only in the name of the chief investigator with assistance from others unacknowledged or acknowledged only in passing. When humanists collaborate with others – social and physical scientists or information science, information technology and other professionals – stratification remains: collaboration is seldom among equal partners, each bringing their own interests and questions to a problem. More often the others help the humanist to answer his or her own questions by solving problems or providing guidance on questions outside the humanist's own area of expertise.

Even with many digital projects that have been hailed as collaborative, the research question and agenda is often posed by a chief investigator, and others become the working hands. This is true not only for the technologists but even for the other humanists involved in the project. The Rulers of Venice, 1332–1524[6] – a collaboration of Benjamin Kohl, Monique O'Connell, Andrea Mozzato and Claudia Salmini and six organizations – was answering a question posed by Kohl. The Valley of the Shadow[7] lists four coeditors, three project managers, more than fifty other staff contributors and two institutions, but the initial question was posed by Edward Ayers.

One of the more impressive projects in terms of collaboration is the Medici Archive Project,[8] already discussed in Chapter 7. This brings together scholars who work on a single archive and produce original individual research in the form of books and papers, while creating an accessible resource where scholars from all over the world can view digitized images of archival documents, enter transcriptions, provide feedback and exchange comments. Yet here the path toward a workable model of collaboration was not always clear. At first the model allowed individual scholars to focus on their own research agendas and to transcribe related documents. The net result was a spotty and inconsistent digital archive. But as the project, its management and its technology matured, the Medici Archive has evolved into a model of rigorous collaborative effort with a clear mission and workable interim goals.

The issue for humanists in academia remains how to receive sufficient credit for purposes of HTP when the final product has so many names on it. While the academy has expressed rhetorical support for collaborative projects, it is still difficult to achieve the necessary recognition for this type of work. In the end HTP committees in the humanities still want to see single-authored monographs. At a recent scholarly meeting one junior faculty member from a major research university, when asked about collaborating with senior scholars in a related digital project at another major research university, frankly admitted, "I'm not interested now in collaborating, I need tenure."

PUBLICATION, DISTRIBUTION AND DISCOVERABILITY

The current academic culture is defined by an economy of scarcity: a very few positions sought by a very large number of highly qualified applicants.[9] If HTP committees continue to apply the methods first devised in the late 1960s to winnow out the competition – chief among them the single-author monograph[10] – what strategies and relationships should a digital humanist cultivate? One solution would be to see all publication as a continuum and to plan accordingly. The same way that a scholar once viewed a monograph as an extension of a dissertation or of a series of articles, one now should view research and writing through multiple points of distribution. Because the "monograph is the coin of the realm," one outcome will need to be either a monograph or a strong series of articles, depending upon disciplinary practice. For the foreseeable future, books from university presses will probably remain print-first with distribution of an exact version in digital format as a PDF either issued by the press or in another format from iBooks or Amazon (Kindle). Journal articles will continue to appear in print – or print and digital – but most distribution will be digital, either through the press that publishes the journal – often for a society – or through an aggregator like JSTOR[11] or Project MUSE.[12]

But there are also ways to make materials available on the web, from posting bibliographies – including annotations – on WorldCat[13] to creating a custom interactive map on Google Maps.[14] One can also upload photos and videos to sites ready-made for that purpose, from YouTube[15] to Flickr[16] to Tumblr[17] and Vimeo.[18] Blogging software like WordPress[19] makes it easy to share research agendas and findings throughout the life of a project. Colleagues with similar research interests might have a website or be willing to collaborate on one where researchers post archives, transcriptions and translations in particular fields. And although Wikipedia was once suspect, the editorial review and careful contributions of humanists, both academic and nonacademic, has made this into a resource that is judged to be comparable to the *Encyclopedia Britannica* in terms of accuracy, reliability and timeliness.[20] Open-access resource sites such as Academia.edu[21] now also facilitate the creation of online pages where one's CV, research interests and specialties, books, articles, papers, digital projects and other research and writing are listed for specific disciplinary colleagues and where – depending on a work's copyright situation – they can also be made available for free download. As of January 2015, more than 16.3 million academics had signed up to Academia.edu, adding 4.8 million papers and more than 1.4 million research interests. Academia.edu attracts more than 15.7 million unique visitors a month. Such sites multiply impact factors by many times, deliberately bypassing prepublication peer review and thus allowing the intellectual public forum to decide the value and prominence of work, independent of print gatekeepers. These and other open-access resources pose a significant challenge to the system established to maintain HTP culture.

One cannot ignore the strained environment for scholarly and academic publishing today. University presses currently work under the pressures of shrinking sales, increased submissions, peer-review requirements, electronic competition (see Chapter 7) and mandates from their universities to be self-sustaining while maintaining their mission to reflect the university's core values. Most university presses have developed coping strategies that have allowed them to survive and in some cases to thrive. These strategies sometimes, however, work against the digital humanist.[22] It is also important, nonetheless, for faculty committees to understand the publication landscape and work with revised ground rules for crediting digital work. Administrators also need to create environments at their universities where publication options – print and digital – are available to faculty, along with the editorial and production personnel to facilitate these processes. We shall discuss this landscape in detail in Chapter 10.

Related issues of access and distribution have been part of the conversation about the digital realm since card catalogs started to be converted into digital format in the 1970s. Some of these issues have been addressed by the development of the World Wide Web, where distribution and access can be almost guaranteed, particularly in any open-access and net-neutral environment. While some scholarly materials on the web are behind a pay or subscription wall, this is still an improved environment for access and distribution.

Given the immense scale of the Internet and its almost infinite number of distribution points, the original premise of its inventors – that access would be a relatively simple matter of connecting writers and readers – has been immensely complicated by a variety of factors, some caused by the very democratic and egalitarian nature of the web's fundamental architecture. Every author can now create a website and thus become a publisher, and the net-neutral mechanisms of the Internet will allow her work to be distributed worldwide almost instantaneously. This was never an issue of access, however, but of discoverability. One must first be able to identify, isolate out and group objects on the web by certain standards and research agendas, and the notion of the web as itself such an efficient engine was soon outpaced by realities.

In late 2005 and early 2006 ACLS Humanities E-Book (HEB) conducted a limited experiment to test the benefits of unlimited access to information in the humanities.[23] Because HEB was and remains relatively small, applying strict quality criteria for inclusion into its aggregation, the contrast with vast commercial search engines like Google was instructive: it quickly emerged as an issue of "too much information" and not enough mediation.[24] The experiment involved the search for a common term in fourteenth- and fifteenth-century studies: the "Black Death." It was assumed that the term "Black Death" would bring up materials narrowly focused on the great fourteenth-century plague. The first recorded results from Google Search (November 19, 2005) returned 84 million results (discreet URLs). As of March 29, 2006 (four months later, at 2:00 PM EST) Goggle had returned 204 million results. On March 29, 2006 at 6:00 PM (four *hours* later) the result was 219 million URLs.

Where does one's search through 219 million URLs begin? Where can it end? Scattered among the 219 million results was a stew of more and less reliable sites, including ones offering giant plush dolls of viruses, classroom syllabi, television docudramas, Wikipedia entries, IATH resources, distance-education and other pages, serving up overviews, selected documents and brief case studies. But such an array only begs the question: Which of these sites are reliable, and which are permanent, or at least stable, sources of information and analysis? Access began to appear meaningless for serious scholarship.

Between November 19, 2005 and March 28, 2006 the total number of sites on Google responding to this simple search term increased from 84 million to 204 million, or 243 percent. It grew by 15 million in just four hours. How many of these sites survived the four *months*, how many joined the web in the meanwhile, how many permanently disappeared? How can the scholar access result number 10,000, let alone result 10 million, even with the most advanced "search within results"? To be fair, Google has long offered an advanced search. Using this, the search was narrowed down to .edu sites focusing on "Black Death," excluding "America," and updated within three months of the initial search. From 219 million the search then served up "about 11" results, including one book, five course syllabi, two Power Point presentations (course work) and one undergrad term paper. Google has spared the researchers from viewing two "very similar" results.

Over a decade of experience with Google Search indicates that the relative stability of the most-hit sites reflects only that: what the "market" for information has decided, and more to the point, how many of these websites have paid Google for prominent placement. Without the preparation of the advanced search – still a haphazard approach – little of quality emerged. With Google's advanced search little of either quality or quantity was left. By comparison, a similar search performed on the HEB site delivered up 1,900 matches across 140 titles (out of the then 1,300 on the site), or .0000093 of Google's unfiltered results: a tiny fraction. But the result brought up a selection of the most important works in the field, which constituted 12.72 times Google's advanced search results by title and 172.72 times by "hit."

Though these results narrowly focused on some of the most important works in the field, several important conclusions emerged: first that the collection of titles accessed was of the highest quality and depth, second that search results would remain stable and as permanent as possible and third that the researcher would be able to use and then cite these online findings with complete confidence in sources and the ability of other scholars to verify findings.

A second set of results from the HEB search, however, may leave the reader somewhat disconcerted; and that is the (relatively) wide variety of studies and fields delivered up from a broad search even in this limited scholarly context. In addition to medieval Europe, the test search brought up titles from the Middle East, from Africa, from South Asia, from the U.S. Southwest, the U.S. rural South and from the impoverished life of many historical and contemporary cities. In short, "Black Death" delivered something akin to Google's unfiltered results: not just the European fourteenth century but an in-ruption of the Global South, of the historical and contemporary margins, into previously neat scholarly categories and disciplinary boundaries.

One might legitimately wonder whether it is appropriate for specialists to have such a diversity and whether the HEB collection's value might be diminished without some clear-cut methods of carefully delineating a search topic and territory. What if a student, unfamiliar with strict disciplinary boundaries or with powerful Boolean, Proximity, Bibliographic or Subject search engines, did such a search and found such results? Over the years humanists have come to realize that this type of result, this "history without borders" across a broad range of regional studies, disciplinary specialties and time frames fulfills much of the expectations of the digital realm and is exactly and precisely where the scholarly disciplines seem headed both online and in the plans of provosts, deans and many scholars.[25]

Such methodologies – whether in consciously constructed policies or in search results – by necessity break down barriers. They bring before the focused specialist and the new student familiar issues as diverse as trade and population. But they also raise issues of health, poverty and wealth, slavery and economic difference, the political structures and cultures of disease and illness, new global perspectives on marginalization and wholeness. By its very nature then, online scholarship is an instrument of such change, whether on the massive and unregulated scale that Google serves up or in even the most carefully mediated collections that ACLS and others have assembled. By its very nature the digital – far more than the old print culture and its capabilities – breaks down boundaries, permits regional and global perspectives and enables comparative approaches that are both diachronic and synchronic.

But all this is not simply or mechanically achieved. Rather, the insights gained from resources like HEB pointed to the newly emerging use of the book in the digital realm: as an essential building block of knowledge and scholarly communication, no longer isolated in its production, distribution or use. Content rapidly escaped print bindings, while the old referents of print culture – the footnote that allowed the print publication to talk to its peers – began to give way to aggregated searches. Such aggregation quickly became both a sustainability and an intellectual goal as the chief funder of such projects, The Andrew W. Mellon Foundation, began to focus on larger and larger projects that moved to avoid the creation of isolated "stovepipes." At the same time, not-for-profit aggregations like HEB, the Hathi Trust,[26] the Internet Archive[27] and Project Gutenberg[28] began to feel the pressures of commercial ventures just as Google Books[29] tried to foster a greater access and distribution model for printed materials with an aggressive approach toward orphan works.[30] The intellectual and legal battles that ensued exposed the issues of open access, intellectual property rights, copyright and fair use in important ways that are still resonating within the humanities community. We will discuss these in Chapter 9.

PRESERVATION

One of the major impulses behind the great manuscript hunters of the Renaissance – from Petrarch to Coluccio Salutati, Poggio Bracciolini and Niccolò Niccoli – in seeking out ancient manuscripts in monastic libraries throughout Europe was to identify, save and then preserve what they considered to be the crumbling records of the ancient past. They, as we, knew that left unattended, parchment manuscripts have a life of about one thousand years. Little remained for the first humanists to save and copy that had not already been copied in the centuries between the fall of Rome and the years 800 to 1000. Over and above the media of such works – the parchments and vellums of the ancient codices – the humanists were deeply concerned to preserve, edit and then transmit the texts of the ancients to both recall and recreate what they considered the purity of ancient knowledge and its virtue.[31] They therefore developed methods for the efficient and elegant copying and dissemination of manuscript books, including the humanist script that would form the basis of all modern typefaces. With the age of print, this process became even more rapid, and techniques for the editing of various manuscripts to form unified texts in "critical editions" were developed by humanists in collaboration with Renaissance printers/ publishers, like Aldus Manutius of Venice, and perfected in Erasmus's New Testament of 1516.[32]

The legacy of the past remains a paramount concern of all humanists and humanities disciplines in the digital realm. For individual humanists the problem of preservation of digital work is complicated by limited resources, both of time and money. Many digital projects have faded from the web because there was no institutional structure to sustain them. A scholar or a small team might work on a website with the most rigorous of methodologies and criteria for selection to provide texts, bibliographies, interpretation and ancillary related materials, but unless they can identify an institutional setting, their sites might either stagnate at the point when the chief author retires or moves on to other projects, or the site might disappear completely from the web. Software applications that were once easy to purchase, learn and deploy might disappear in both the not-for-profit or for-profit spheres; the hardware for that software might become obsolete; and newer versions might become prohibitively expensive or difficult for many humanists to learn.

Such concerns were among the first that information technologists and librarians began to tackle in the earliest days of computing;[33] and to address such issues the library community developed strict guidelines for everything from coding systems to versioning protocols and equipment warehousing. But there remains a great disconnect between this community of expert preservationists and information specialists and the generally less-informed digital humanist who, even with the help of department technologists, might set off to create yet another unsustainable website. This is as much a problem of the age-old culture of individualist humanist creation as of resource deployment and acculturation into a digital *habitus*. As we have noted, many of the best exemplary digital projects are those that have found permanent homes within institutional settings and whose authors have been aware of the necessity of providing for such settings from the start. Yet the larger issue of preservation is one that goes far beyond the capacities or expertise of the individual author or team and must be addressed on far larger institutional and transinstitutional levels of the foundation, the university and the consortium.

Among the earliest preservation consortia were the UK Digital Preservation Coalition[34] and the National Digital Information Infrastructure and Preservation Program at the U.S. Library of Congress.[35] As already noted, JSTOR began as a preservation project. More recently, Hathi Trust was created both as an aggregation of titles in a cross-institutional setting and as a model for preservation. The Digital Public Library of America has included strategies for preservation into its basic infrastructure from the start.[36] The Mellon Foundation's Portico[37] is a digital archive for e-journals, e-books and other electronic scholarly content, but only publishers and libraries now contribute content. Scholars are charged with getting their digital material into archivable format, and their institutions should have the resources for distributing and preserving that content either within their own systems or through collaboration with larger digital content management projects. Much progress has been made in both thinking through and establishing best practices for preservation of digital resources, but unless such issues are brought to the fore in humanities culture, a residual skepticism about the enduring value of digital scholarship and its media may continue to stymie the progress of digital humanities endeavors.

RELATIONSHIP OF READER TO AUTHOR

In the early days of the digital, there was a considerable amount of utopian thinking about the goals and transformative effects of the digital. Vincent Mosco characterized these grandiose expectations in his book, *The Digital Sublime*. The digital was going to transform our understanding of information and our access to knowledge, it would democratize the publishing paradigm and loosen the grip on dissemination then held by publishers. Through the Internet, communication of all kinds would spread around the globe freely and equally, helping the world toward mutual understanding and peace. More locally and particularly it would break down and reconfigure the relationship between author and reader so that the reader would be in part a cocreator with the author.

Such reconfigurations in the digital would coincide with the long-standing theoretical turns around textuality, in which authorial intent and reader response had been dramatically altered from traditional understandings of the writing and reading processes. Text took its place within an intertextual reality – one text speaking to or through another either by direct quotation or other referent. This was at root a humanist philological model that became a theoretical turn embraced by literary and some historical critics and that prefigured the semantic web in which computers themselves created content and talked to one another independent of human agency: an electronic equivalent of intertextuality.

On the concrete level of digital authors and readers, this reconfiguration would be accomplished through the widespread application of social media and such digital tools as annotation, comment, blog, e-mail and other software where multipolarity and simultaneity dethrone the singular voice. Crowdsourcing would almost automatically replace the need for a single scholar's long and specialized research in archives or on verbal or visual texts. Critical analysis would come about not through the insights or prejudices of one individual or subsequent peer review but through the consensus of opinion expressed in online comment or through the algorithms of text mining. Some authors did not care for this idea, retaining the humanist preference for solitary research and writing and the traditional process of peer review, publication and public review. Others embraced it as the promise of the future and a redress to the decades-long stranglehold of the few gatekeepers upon the efforts of the many in scholarly communication.

In order to test the possibilities of these new technologies, in February 2005, the *American Historical Review* sponsored an online discussion around the online publication of "Imaging the French Revolution: Depictions of the French Revolutionary Crowd" edited by Jack Censer and Lynn Hunt.[38] The work comprised six essays. The online conversation was set at one month. The project limited discussion to the authors of the six essays. Even in this carefully controlled exchange, however, there was not a great deal of communication. There were comments, and these were presented in edited format; yet the essays were not revised based on the comments. It was an experiment that was not repeated at the *American Historical Review*.

There are more robust examples, however. PEA Soup[39] hosts discussions around articles in the scholarly journal *Ethics*, published by the University of Chicago Press. The articles under discussion are available open-access through JSTOR, and each discussion begins with the publication of a critical commentary. For example, Agnieszka Jaworska and Julie Tannenbaum coauthored an article published in January 2014 entitled "Person-Rearing Relationships as a Key to Higher Moral Status." On February 20, 2014, Margaret Olivia Little and Jake Earl posted a 2,300-word commentary about the article to open a discussion. Over two days approximately twenty-five comments were posted, including some by the original authors.

Best practice lays somewhere among these results. Most scholars are too busy with their own research and writing to spend much time working on, or thinking about, someone else's, but occasionally, with a carefully orchestrated experiment, scholars do forge a conversation around a particular topic or piece. Authors sometimes post short essays on blogs and ask for comment from those who subscribe to that blog. Academia. edu, for example, now allows users to post preconference or prepublication papers, to invite a select group of scholars and to post their comments during a set time frame. The original author can then reply to comments and post a revised version. Because Academia.edu exists outside traditional academic walls, scholars can feel free to participate. Sometimes discussions are fruitful, sometimes they wander off into irrelevancy, at other times they are of the same mixed variety as the reviews posted to Amazon.com.

In any case, this new conversation between author and reader does not yet seem to have significantly impacted the way humanists write or read in the digital environment. Fears that one's work would be savaged by readers or hopes that it would be improved seem to have both been largely without basis. The digital has not automatically changed the dynamic of this relationship, and any digital humanist who wants to engage in this type of interaction needs to carefully plan how to incorporate these capabilities into the project beforehand and have a clear sense of what the feedback and conversation is to accomplish. Merely adding a digital capacity to an online resource or publication is like adding ornament to a medieval manuscript with no clear sense of how the reader is to consider it: Is it gloss, visual commentary on the text or merely a deluxe feature to please a patron?

FUNDING STRATEGIES

Funding digital projects was once considered problematic, and special programs were established to help, like the NEH Digital Humanities Start-Up Grants,[40] Alfred P. Sloan Foundation Digital Information Technology Grants,[41] the ACLS Digital Innovation Fellowships[42] and the ACLS HEB subsidies to publishers to directly fund e-book production. In truth, while individual digital humanists might still have difficulties funding digital publication, digital research has become almost indistinguishable from any other research in the humanities, and unless scholars are interested in developing specialized tools or purchasing expensive equipment, most research grants will cover most digital research. Digital tools are just the ones that scholars now happen to use, and for the most part as far as digital humanities models have developed, there seems to be nothing essentially different in the nature of the individual research.

Problems arise when scholars are at institutions that do not provide a great deal of research support in the first place, and then they must turn to outside funders. In such cases the appeal to digital humanities – for projects or new centers – may be motivated less by innovative approaches to traditional humanities research questions than by the possibility of tapping new sources of funding for ongoing work. In other situations, such as in archaeological, architectural or visual history, many projects may be conceived that are in fact innovative either in their data gathering or their publication methods, involving high-end technologies for recording, searching, analyzing and representing data. A range of solutions has been adopted, and we have noted various funding sources in our discussions in Chapter 6.

The key may lie in assembling a consortium of stakeholders to both minimize the risk of exposure for any one funder and to help spread support for digital humanities projects. The NEH continues to fund individual and collaborative projects, as does ACLS; but these are not institutional solutions. While The Andrew W. Mellon Foundation continues to fund institutional start-up and experimental projects, continuously seeking to broaden horizons and break down boundaries, it has not been as successful in long-term sustainability of such projects once launched and ongoing.[43] By involving a variety of university, museum, library, foundation and private support, humanists can scale the impact of their own research and transform what had once been the solitary efforts of single scholars into broader collaborations with some chance of long-term survival. Key to such strategies is setting clear-cut goals for institutional mission and sustainability, including both financial support for the ongoing research and development and – equally important – institutional support for the survival of such projects. The latter involves both the mechanics of hosting complex projects once completed and the proper curatorial and technical staffing for the long term. Such planning does involve a major change in humanists' thinking, a transformation that sees digital work less as the solitary achievement of a Petrarch or Boccaccio and more like the foundational work of Vespasiano da Bisticci or Poggio Bracciolini in establishing libraries. Can humanities culture change to reward such collaborative work? Is the status of the humanist diminished by such efforts? The reputations of Robert Darnton, Jerome McGann, Holly Cowan Shulman, Bernard Frischer or Diane Favro would argue not. But how exceptional are such scholars and how exceptional will they remain?

SUSTAINABILITY IN THE DIGITAL ENVIRONMENT

As indicated, sustainability in the digital environment remains one of the most vexing problems for the humanities. It involves technology, individual research and institutional missions and agendas. Many projects completed years and even a decade ago remain available, but many others, even when hosted at institutions, seem to disappear, move or be abandoned at an alarming rate.

When print books are also being rapidly deaccessioned, and scholars admit they are unable to keep up any longer with the research in their own narrowly defined specialties, perhaps the problem that we discern in the digital realm is only one more symptom of the general problem in the academic humanities where work is valued for the role that it plays in the HTP processes, but otherwise is of increasingly small impact. Rapidly diminishing print runs and escalating fees for print (and e-book) monographs would indicate that. Yet – like the Neapolitan *piastra* in the nineteenth century – the "currency of the realm" remains the undisputed medium of such exchange within academia, while it is recognized less and less in the outside world and is becoming rapidly devaluated at home.

Again, if scholars want to publish any findings digitally, they must first insure that they have a clear-cut mission goal and a strategy for preservation and sustainability that would ideally include keeping the projects vital with continued contributions and curation by new generations. This necessarily involves collaboration within institutional frameworks: everything from the library to the department to the university's or learned society's cyberinfrastructure. But in general, humanists have not practiced collaborative methods and tend to still think that their scholarship is their own, and once it is in published format, it stands finished and preserved on the library shelves. This has not been a bad model, but when it combines digital research and conventional print publication it often results in the relegation of the research data to inaccessible paper or computer files. Other alternatives can run head on into the increasingly problematic nature of the corporate university: mandatory repositories, letters of agreement that provide the corporation with first claim to an individual's research, aggressive aggregators that seek control over a scholar's work and the method of its recombination and publication, especially when published under open-access models.

As we have already discussed, another aspect of digital sustainability is the ability to have continued access to digital files created in the past, again a task often best left to institutional solutions. Continued migration to new formats and versions is often the key here and is less costly than later finding conversion houses that can decipher and translate old files to new formats. Libraries and publishers, who are charged with protecting digital materials for their patrons or authors, have found solutions to the sustainability and migration questions, but this often requires the leverage of large institutions with deep resources.

HIRING, TENURE AND PROMOTION (HTP)

For better or worse, HTP considerations are intrinsic to the work that academic scholars chose to produce and the way they create and distribute it. Many universities and colleges have expressed their belief that the age of appropriate credit for digital work is just around the corner. Learned societies like the Modern Language Association (MLA)[44] and the American Historical Association (AHA)[45] have published guidelines for effective evaluation of digital humanities and digital media, yet many HTP committees remain unable (or unwilling) to adequately assess digital work.[46] Much groundbreaking digital scholarship, however, continues to be published by scholars no longer under HTP pressures. Examples include Edward Ayers,[47] Benjamin Kohl,[48] Burr Litchfield,[49] Holly Shulman,[50] Lynn Hunt[51] and Jerome McGann.[52] Many other scholars who were not free of those pressures have produced notable digital projects but have not received recognition commensurate with their work.

It is important for humanists to weigh these matters carefully. While the digital humanities might seem like the next big turn and a path to academic success, there is no predicting how departmental colleagues will array themselves when the question is finally on the table. If a scholar is open to a career outside academia, a digital project might open many doors, especially in alternative academic careers.[53]

GENDER

The humanities began and remained male from the fourteenth century through most of their history into the mid-twentieth century. This is nothing unusual in itself: most of the work carried out in the public sphere was predominantly male, with few exceptions. While many of the most prominent poets and letter writers of the later Renaissance – including Vittoria Colonna, Gaspara Stampa and Veronica Franca – were women, the *studia humanitatis* both inside and outside the university remained almost strictly male, and the model of humanistic research and writing remained that set out by Petrarch. Today the situation within the academy has changed dramatically, and most humanities fields are seeing a female majority in both numbers of students and of faculty – even if not tenured. Lauded in most cases, this situation is also seen as problematic as the humanities as a whole are devalued in society at large, and this "feminization" is sometimes seen as just one more sign of this decline in value and prestige.

While many content editors in publishing continue to be women in the digital realm – as had long been traditional in print publishing – most designers and implementers of code and authors of digital projects themselves have tended to be male. From the leaders of cutting-edge history web sites to many of the leaders in TEI (Text Encoding Initiative), males tend to set both the tone and the agenda for digital work. Scholars of the digital humanities, such as Tara McPherson and Bethany Nowviskie, have pointedly called out this gender imbalance.[54] Will the digital humanities remain a bastion of white male techies? Or will the digital humanities, like so many new fields, open themselves, or be opened, to the emerging world at large in terms of race, gender and class? We will examine some of these issues below.

The second aspect of this question is the gendering of the *form* of digital work.[55] This may best be approached by using two recent theoretical frames: first, the gendering of history and humanities scholarship in general, and second of liberation theory. Bonnie Smith's *The Gender of*

History[56] has provided some useful insights into what she (among others) sees as the gendered male, monographic nature of current historical research: narrowly focused, scientific ("empirical" and "positivistic" are better words) and professionalized, the product of nineteenth-century structures of politics, class, race and gender.

Along the way to modern scientific history, Smith argues, the insights and methods of an entire class of historians – the feminized amateur (in fact, mostly women) – and of types of history were swept aside in favor of the research engendered by the seminar and the archive. Thus the edition, the bibliography, biography, memoir, the collection of letters and texts, popular ephemera, poetry and the novel, the play, music and dance, the translation and almost all of visual and physical culture, were rejected as improper material for the professional historian. The monograph and its little brother, the scholarly article, were the ironclad products of this process: almost exclusively textual (the visual could appear as illustration), unidirectional, mono-vocal and, even when collaboration was a clear necessity, single-authored. Student-sons were relegated to the role of "research assistants." The wives and daughters of the great nineteenth-century historians often did all the translating, editing and transcribing but were – and often still are – rarely acknowledged as collaborators. Throughout this development the visual, the aural, the tactile, the multinarrative, the immanence of the past, history as a process of recreating a spatial and temporal "other" was gendered out of the scholar's study and relegated to the drawing room as feminine, soft and unfocused, nonprofessional.

The monograph as it emerged as the paradigm of scholarship pioneered by Leopold von Ranke (d. 1886) has remained the currency of the realm in historical research ever since. But it replaces all other historical writing, even the synthetic work, as the only valid form of scholarly communication that can meet the professional requirements for HTP. Even in today's theory-driven monograph – which displaces and casts doubt on empirical history – the assertive point of view that marshals data to support itself continues to reflect a certain gendered approach. This was and remains, according to Smith, the product of two nineteenth-century developments. First of Ranke's seminar room: a male, combative, sometimes humiliating "knowledge work." The second was the dismissal of the ephemeral, the day-to-day, the family and emotion as subjects in favor of what could be salvaged from the archive. These developments resulted in what Smith calls "professional historical work":

a focus on politics in scholarship, a methodology stressing a disembodied, well-trained observer, and a set of practices based on scrutinizing state documents and displaying the resulting historical writing for the adjudication of a community of experts.[57]

As a counterexample Smith offers the work of Vernon Lee, the pseudonym of Violet Paget, a friend of Bernard Berenson and of the architectural historian Geoffrey Scott. As early as the 1880s, Lee set out to consciously criticize the methods and narrow horizons of Rankean history. Smith offers this synopsis of a chapter from Lee's *Euphorion: Being Studies of the Antique and Medieval in the Renaissance*:[58]

> Her chapter on the music scene in eighteenth-century Italy begins by taking readers on a walk through the streets of Bologna, ushering them into its Philharmonic Academy, and showing them the portraits of great musicians guarding the door of the Academy's archives. Amid the letters and musical scores in the archives, the narrator finds Charles Burney's account of Italian music, and it is through his travels that cultural history proceeds. As they travel with Burney, readers are interrupted by other accounts, gleaned from letters, music reportage of the day, and additional travelers' records. The tour comes to an end with the narrator's departure from the archives.[59]

A century before the Internet and World Wide Web, Lee set out to offer a conscious alternative to the Rankean monograph: in the process she provided the basic structure, navigation methods and multimedia approach of digital history. As Smith observes, it was the very "amateurism" – the marginalized and the disruptive – that allowed such history to break out of the narrow bounds of "professional" standards and to provide a path to innovation.[60]

With digital publishing we can now see emerging this multivoiced, multicentered type of scholarship that allows primary sources to speak for themselves and privileges the source rather than the examiner. Allowing the sources to speak for themselves necessarily displaces the gendered male overvoice of the monograph. And because digital publications can be multilayered and address a multitude of users, readers and interpreters, its sources, arguments and narratives become multipolar and multidimensional in ways that the print monograph could never be.

In a second sense, the digital can be seen as a form of "liberation" from the male monograph. Since World War II we have witnessed not so much a turning away from formal European academic theologies (the modern equivalent of Scholastic thought) as the reemergence of humanist theologies based on a multiplicity of experiences and voices: Asian, African, liberation, gay, women's, black, theologies of creation and of the earth or of the goddess. This is a not a displacement but a broadening out to other voices and centers. The digital is seen by some as opening humanistic discourse in similar ways. John Unsworth, for example, dubbed the then-emerging Open-Source movement as a "Liberation *Technology*."[61] Most important for Unsworth, this new digital work is collaborative: the author is encouraged to work with a variety of equal partners, taking into consideration sources and voices easily muted in the monograph. According to Unsworth, the organization of work is also different. The collaborative nature of digital publishing displaces a top-down hierarchy of the great scholar and his circle of assistants – whether of nineteenth-century woman copyists, twenty-first-century information technologists or those perennially "patient and helpful" spouses, editors and publishers.

Digital scholarship would also be a form of reticulative rather than linear activity that displaces former centers and opens the world of study to the margins and the peripheries, very much as liberation studies have done in theology. As Bonnie Smith has written in relation to the work of Germaine (Madame) de Staël, the great historian-novelist of the French Revolutionary world, "Reticulative thinking . . . makes history – and in this case the historian – spring from a *web* [emphasis ours] of associations and analogies rather than from a knowledge of dates, details, and facts."[62]

In the print monograph the visual, the aural – even the nonprivileged textual sources – are reduced to a series of almost inconsequential illustrations. In the digital environment, however, all of these materials are texts in their own right, open to the interpretation of the entire audience, not filtered through one point of view. They become interconnected in a web. As liberation theologies witness, passive "object" becomes "subject" and agent. This process opens the world to a new level and form of discourse. The visual and aural necessarily work on a level of symbol, metaphor and free association, they make multivalent and nonlinear connections that are rejected by Rankean history. But these nonlinear experiences are, after all, the essence of the spiritual and religious modes that have deeply shaped the humanities since their inception. The digital may hold the ability to give back to these representations their multivalent and multifocal powers.

Is the Internet inherently masculine? Is the digital inherently male? Such examples would have us conclude not: perhaps the digital will free us from the male model of the monograph and from certain forms of linear thinking. Yet, if women outnumber men in the humanistic disciplines, why are so few digital humanists women? Does it reflect a hierarchy in academia that belies the face value of the overall numbers and the nature of the new media? If this contradiction persists, will the digital find its natural home outside the academy? The success of commercial products, services and schemes, including Google, iTunes, Wikipedia and Amazon.com might suggest so. Is then the academy – with its rigid disciplinary bounds, narrow professional perspectives and strict hierarchies – ultimately inhospitable to the modern humanities?

Can only private institutions with significant endowments and public institutions with healthy state funding provide the resources to support the digital humanities? When fewer than 10 percent of the higher education institutions in the United States, and significantly less than that worldwide, provide an environment to foster faculty engagement in digital humanities, should humanists be concerned about the type of work that these divides are likely to produce? Will such digital work foster even greater divides between the few faculty who get the resources to produce it and the new majority of have-nots?

GLOBAL AND OTHER DIVIDES

From the time of Petrarch onward, humanists were bound together over distance and time through the art of letter writing. Petrarch's own correspondence contains numerous letters written to his ancient teachers, especially Cicero, while his missives to contemporaries formed one of the earliest collections of modern letter writing. By the sixteenth century Erasmus and his contemporaries had formed a "republic of letters," both in the sense of their textual and philological studies and in their continuous correspondence. Latin, the international language of learning throughout the Middle Ages and into the eighteenth century, was the perfect vehicle for the new humanist letter form, as it leveled both distance and ethnic and new national differences into a shared humanist agenda and a corps of scholars.

From very early on as well, humanists physically traveled to royal and princely courts and to the republican centers of Italy and Northern Europe. Petrarch, Boccaccio, Poggio and many other Italians helped spread the new humanist studies by meeting with friends and followers and attracting new adherents. Once Italy became widely admired as the center of the new learning and arts, Italian scholars themselves traveled north, often at the invitation of universities and courts to serve as lecturers, tutors, advisors and historians and in other official capacities and in so doing helped spread personally the learning that the new print revolution was spreading through book distribution. From Poggio Bracciolini's years in England (1418–23) right to the end of the *ancien regime*, when Giacomo Casanova (1725–98) served as librarian for Count Waldstein of Bavaria, well-known Italians were also active in remote German, Scandinavian, Polish and Russian courts as tutors and cultural advisors. Italian models of architecture, painting, poetry and music accompanied them in spreading Renaissance style.

This distinct impact of the humanities long held sway in Western culture, inspiring the French of the Revolution and the young American republic with models of ancient Rome and Greece. Reciprocally, travel to the Mediterranean became a necessity for all cultured Westerners into the beginning of the twentieth century, when the Grand Tour was replaced by mass tourism. Reproductions of paintings and sculpture in prints and book illustrations flooded the Western market increasingly throughout the age of print. The virtual was thus something that was deeply embedded in humanist culture into the twentieth century. It therefore came as no surprise that many humanists would embrace the new digital media to spread their work and to communicate with one another; and such communication quickly became the norm, far exceeding the personal contacts at conferences and other physical meetings throughout the Northern world.

Yet very early on as well, the global divide was seen as one of the major issues in the computer age: lack of capital for the purchase of computers and software, of educational resources, of basic infrastructure – most especially reliable and cheap electrification – came to the fore as the major issues of the new "digital divide." While such problems were being aggressively addressed through both governmental and private foundation efforts, the pressing needs of the Global South also surfaced in ways that effected the digital humanities. If the humanities were born and grew as the province of a small elite of Western males, and Western culture and its values were intimately bound to the humanities for centuries – most especially in the colonial and imperial eras – what concern were they to the Global South, where cultural, religious and political-economic traditions far older than Western humanist culture survived intact and with vigor? Were not even these Westernized scholars educated at major universities part of a neocolonial class of oppressors, and did not the digital merely magnify the impact and reach of such hegemonies?

When the pressing needs for economic and social development – including the most basic requirements of food, clothing, shelter and medicine – dictated forms of cultural and educational growth, how could the Western humanities have any impact? Were not the humanities, even delivered over the Internet, both an extravagance and an insult to such cultures? Why should anyone in the Global South care about the values inherited from ancient Greece and Rome? Such questions were not, of course, confined to the Global South: most urban settings in the North were also beset by many of the same basic human problems, where solutions seem to lie in social, economic and technological models, not in philology or history. To maintain otherwise was seen by many as an elitist cultural form of the neocolonialism that plagues development in the rest of the globe.

As strong as such divides remain, the new digital media also seemed to find their place easily within a new globalized culture that broke down boundaries and barriers; and the irreconcilable differences between West and East, North and South have been demonstrated to lie as much in rhetorical and political postures as in physical and geographical differences. Third-century CE Roman coins from Germany deposited in the Mekong Delta in Vietnam sometime before 800 CE attest to the porousness of boundaries and cultural exchange even in the earliest days of the Common Era. The Internet and all of its content – unless deliberately blocked by repressive regimes or command societies – make all the world's information and knowledge available at the click of a mouse; and cheap, durable laptop computers, tablets and smartphones are quickly making access a reality across the globe. The humanities are, therefore, one of many forms of expression easily and often eagerly embraced outside the West. Satellite campuses of great Western universities – NYU, Cambridge, Carnegie Mellon, Paris-Sorbonne, Northwestern and Middlesex (UK) – now afford students and faculty of every discipline open and physical access to key Western ideas and techniques. And despite the very real human rights issues in host countries, students are already receptive to such exchange because of the electronic media's deep penetration. Again, such interventions could easily be characterized as neocolonial maneuvers intended to spread elite Western domination.

In response to these technical possibilities and pressures, even before the digital era, humanists embraced the new media for the purposes of teaching and broad outreach: recordings of poetry, ancient epics, medieval drama were followed by audiotapes and videocassettes of lectures and then online and downloadable lecture series, many of which still attract large new audiences accustomed to the soundscape of the automobile environment: "books on tape" of many standard classics and educational resources are staples of this economy. Distance learning and correspondence courses have long been a part of the American university, with mixed results. In 1994, James J. O'Donnell at the University of Pennsylvania taught an Internet seminar with gopher and e-mail, on the life and works of St. Augustine. More than five hundred participants worldwide joined the seminar. More recently major universities and private corporations have begun experimenting with Massive Open Online Courses (MOOCS)[63] as a way of disseminating both introductory and higher-level teaching to unlimited numbers of students and auditors in an open and often free environment, delivered by some of the best-known and accomplished faculty. Results have been mixed, and initial, nearly millennial, expectations have been dampened, but experimentation continues and adjusts to a variety of pedagogical, economic and cultural realities.

DIGITAL HUMANITIES THEORY

Textual, historiographical, material, gender, liberation, neocolonial and other theoretical frames have informed discussions throughout this book. While we have already discussed digital iterations of many of these turns, we should also take a brief look at specifically digital theory to determine what role it might play in the digital humanities. For the most part digital theory focuses on the direct impact of computer technology upon traditional humanistic studies and can thus be characterized broadly as "humanities computing." Chief among its theorists have been Franco Moretti and his "distant reading," Stephen Ramsay and his "algorithmic criticism," Lev Manovich and his "cultural analytics" and N. Katherine Hayles's "writing machines."

Moretti is renowned as a critic and analyst of the modern novel who trained in Italy and taught at Columbia and Stanford. Among his more controversial approaches, in such works as *Distant Reading*[64] and *Graphs, Maps, Trees*,[65] has been to attempt to apply quantitative methodologies to the field of literary studies, an approach already encountered in the work of John (J. F.) Burrows, for example.[66] With the vast amounts of literary output now available through Google Books, Project Gutenberg, the Internet Archive, Hathi Trust and other digital aggregations, Moretti's approach is to decentralize the individual work and author and reject the narrow insights and discourse based upon a restricted canon in favor of statistical analyses and conclusions drawn from thousands of texts. His work also coincides with the impact of the semantic web, in which computers now displace humans as the key investigators and interpreters.

Stephen Ramsay is associate professor of English and a Fellow at the Center for Digital Research in the Humanities at the University of Nebraska-Lincoln. He is probably best known for his "algorithmic criticism."[67] Ramsay, highly influenced by the past generation of new literary criticism and theory, sees the digital humanities as a distinct "field" and its achievements as "revolutionary," a potential as yet untapped but likely to radically decenter traditional reading. This will be accomplished, he proposes, through the rigorous application of computer power to text not as distinct created work open to faulty human, subjective interpretation but as impartial data embodied in the algorithm. In the face of questions and lines of inquiry – deep comparative method for example – that the computer cannot achieve (as yet), Ramsay seems to suggest discarding such hermeneutical restraints in favor of allowing computers to do what they do best: count. Word and frequency lists are seen as "provocative" critical insights, mathematical formulae as authoritative. As Ramsay puts it:

> If algorithmic criticism is to have a central hermeneutical tenet, it is this: that the narrowing constraints of computational logic – the irreducible tendency of the computer toward enumeration, measurement, and verification – are fully compatible with the goals of criticism set forth above. . . . This is possible, because critical reading practices already contain elements of the algorithmic.

Lev Manovich is a new media theorist, professor in computer science at the CUNY Graduate Center and visiting professor at the European Graduate School in Saas-Fee, Switzerland. He is chiefly known for his theory of cultural analytics.[68] His 1998 "Database as a Symbolic Form" posited the digital's preference for a multipolar web of connections over the traditional narrative form. His term "cultural analytics," coined in 2007, refers to the use of computational methods for the analysis of massive cultural data sets and flows. Like Moretti's and Ramsay's, his interest lies more in humanities computing, the application of computer technologies to humanities data than in any historical humanist agenda. As such, Manovich sees the rich possibilities of data mining and other computer-enabled analytical procedures as key to the future of the humanities. His "Software Takes Command"[69] points both to this displacement of traditional humanistic work and to the possibilities inherent in the semantic web; and in his "Trending" of 2011[70] he speculated on the qualitative differences in humanistic research brought about by big and deep data.

N. Katherine Hayles, professor and director of Graduate Studies in the Program in Literature at Duke University, began her career as a chemist at Xerox Corporation before switching fields to English literature. She has since focused on the relationship between science, literature and technology, most specifically on what she considers the "posthuman" brought about by the computer and the eventual semantic web. While insisting that materiality and embodiment remain central to an Enlightenment view of humanity, she holds that "there are no essential differences or absolute demarcations between bodily existence and computer simulation" and seeks to study literature within that boundary between the human material and the cyber. In such books as *How We Became Posthuman: Virtual Bodies in Cybernetics, Literature and Informatics*[71] and *Writing Machines*[72] she focuses on "similarities between current literary theory and texts and the contemporary scientific models" as exemplified in computational studies.[73]

It is not possible here to survey the entire breath or depth of such digital humanities theory, but this small sampling does give us an idea of several consistent theoretical strains. First, digital theory applies almost exclusively to only one of all the humanities disciplines: literary studies. Few such theorists ever take into account history, classical and modern languages, art, architectural and urban studies, music, performance and ritual, religion, folklore, myth and philosophy, most area studies or any other aspect of humanistic research not fundamentally affected by literary theory and its digital successors. Practitioners all appear to come from either literary or computer studies. Second is the contention that "digital humanities" is a discipline in and by itself, best practiced by a relatively small number of well-theorized computer and literary advocates who have moved on from the revolutionary victories of new literary theory of the 1980s and 1990s. Third, the chief impulse comes not from traditional humanist concerns (though humanistic history and rhetorical vocabulary are often on thick, pyrotechnic display) but on the power and promise of the machine. Finally, while human ingenuity certainly lies behind the advocacy of humanities computing, the actual work of humanistic inquiry and communication seems best left to computers and their technicians.

If, as we have argued, the humanities are now inextricably wed to the digital, is this the future that the digital humanities have in store? Or is this only one possible future? If indeed such a theoretical future is inevitable, who will be its prophets and priestesses and what does such a future hold for the other thousands of current and newly made humanists? As Cathy N. Davidson has argued,[74] "in a time of paradigm shifts, moral and political treachery, historical amnesia, and psychic and spiritual turmoil, humanistic issues are central." She argues that only such self-reflection and open debate can continue to guarantee the humanities a place both within the academy and in the larger culture.

9

Meta-Issues 2: Copyright and Other Rights, Digital Rights Management, Open Access

COPYRIGHT AND OTHER RIGHTS

The practice of a writer or artist laying claim to his or her own work is an ancient one in the West and goes beyond the limitations of literacy into textual communities that included both oral and written transmission.[1] By 500 BCE, for example, chefs in the Greek city of Sybaris in Calabria were granted year-long monopolies on their culinary creations. The authorship of the *Iliad* and the *Odyssey* was long attributed to Homer even before they were transcribed into writing. In ancient Rome writers like Cicero would have their own literate slaves, or would rely on those of friends, to produce multiple copies of their works to be distributed among their textual community. The accuracy and authenticity of their texts would be guaranteed by their authors' direct supervision of this process. Writers like Virgil and Horace became celebrated writers in their own lifetimes,[2] and the Roman poet Martial complained of piracy of his works when they were recited without attribution. By the late eleventh century in the medieval West, the oral traditions of the *chansons de geste* were slowly taking on ascribed authorship as various versions became recognized. Under the late medieval patronage system, the dedication of an author's book to a wealthy patron not only guaranteed some form of income or social promotion but also acted as a means of informal princely protection for authorship.

During the Renaissance the first Florentine law that can be characterized as patent or copyright was granted to the architect Filippo Brunelleschi in June 1421. It is probably no coincidence that the first satire of this concept was Antonio Manetti's fictional tale, *The Fat Woodworker* (c. 1450).[3] Manetti relates how – in revenge for a social slight – the craftsman in question is duped in a practical joke by Brunelleschi and his friends into believing that he longer existed, but that he was actually someone else, a copy of himself. While not the first context to emphasize the notion of the original and the copy, the social situation of Florentine artists and writers most certainly combined with the humanist glorification of the individual author and artist to lend social currency to the idea. It was also during this period that sculptors such as Donatello and Ghiberti began signing their works, a practice that reached its apogee with Michelangelo.[4]

By 1474, a Venetian statute had protected a patent right, and in 1486 Venice issued the first known copyright protection to a printer/publisher. The system of French royal privileges to protect printers dates from 1498. In 1501 Pope Alexander VI issued a bull prohibiting unlicensed printing of books, and the system of copyright and privileges spread through Europe in the first half of the sixteenth century. With the progress of classical learning and new critical editions there also arose the humanists' need to protect their work as sole authors – a status jealously guarded in humanist culture.

In England, copyright was tied to several things: the manifold replication of texts, government and church interest in censoring or controlling content, early capitalist industrial culture and guild systems. In 1518 the first copyright privilege was issued to Richard Pynson, the successor to William Caxton as royal printer. In 1557 Queen Mary Tudor established the Stationers' Company with the sole right to register legal entitlements to publish. This was followed by the Printing (Licensing) Act of 1662 and the Statute of Queen Anne (An Act for the Encouragement of Learning or Copyright Act) in 1709/10. The act contained two ideas of paramount importance: the protection of the rights of authors and publishers to solely control the dissemination of their work and the "encouragement of learned men to compose and write useful books."

The U.S. Constitution carries over this twofold intent, with an even greater emphasis on the need "to promote the progress of science and useful arts, by securing for limited times to authors and inventors the exclusive right to their respective writings and discoveries" (Art. 1.8.8). This represented a change in the thinking behind the first licensing restrictions of the Renaissance, but this also enshrined the humanists' desire to disseminate their revived learning as broadly as possible. This twofold purpose has therefore often been the cause of great conflict, which arises ultimately from the inherent conflict within humanist culture since Petrarch to both spread knowledge and yet to be the individual credited with these advances.

We need not survey the history of U.S. or international copyright law here. With the Berne Convention of 1988 and the Digital Millennium Copyright Act of 1998, the landscape for authors and publishers had taken dramatic new turns, tightening and lengthening copyright restrictions in response to the prevalence of the mass media, the power of entertainment corporations and the rise of the digital. In other places throughout this book, we have noted some of the many issues involved in copyright. Recent challenges to notions of copyright, especially in the digital era, have involved several principles. These include the "nonrivalrous" nature of intellectual and cultural work: that is, such work can be distributed without limit without diminishing the original content; second, the arguments around free speech and freedom of thought and expression; and finally the theoretical models of textual community or social argument for the creation of texts: that is, not only authors and publishers but also audiences and commentators and their predecessors create "texts." Thus, the theory goes, authorship itself is a contested notion, and individual rights often take second place to larger textual communities: essentially a return to traditional modes of medieval creation before the humanist creation of the individual author. This strain of thinking was reinforced by postwar political theory – of Jürgen Habermas, for example – of the literate classes and communities and the role of "publication" in creating the public sphere and the "commons" as an alternative to royal and other overweening power. One recent response has been the founding of Creative Commons[5] in 2001 by Lawrence Lessig, Hal Abelson and Eric Eldred. It is devoted to expanding creativity and knowledge by providing legal tools and sharing digital resources. By 2011, more than one hundred Creative Commons affiliates were pressing some combination of these principles.[6]

Many recent trends have come together and been most clearly highlighted in the litigation surrounding the Google Books project. In the fall of 2004, Google introduced both its Google Books and Google Library (Google Book Search) initiatives. Originally working with a consortium of several major research libraries in the United States and United Kingdom, including the University of Michigan, Harvard, Stanford, Oxford's Bodleian Library and the New York Public Library, the project called for the digitization of up to fifteen million volumes in the holdings of these libraries and the display of short selections as search results. The idea was to open access to millions of volumes of the world's humanistic works in ways that took full advantage of digital search and access. Many of the titles were either out of copyright (largely nineteenth-century titles and series) or orphan works – books whose copyright holder could not be either identified or located. The model was an "opt-out," where books would be incorporated into the collection unless authors or publishers took advantage of a window of opportunity to opt out of the program.[7] Plans met with immediate legal challenges from both the Authors' Guild and the Association of American Publishers, both representing large-scale commercial interests and authors. But little unified resistance – or support – emerged from the academic community, despite drawn out debate and consideration. By the end of 2008, more library systems worldwide were joining the consortium, and the legal challenges were being negotiated. By the end of 2010, Google had transformed the project into a commercial e-book venture, with more than twelve million books scanned and an apparatus established to determine hits and pay royalties to copyright holders. By the end of 2013, more than thirty million books had been scanned, a tentative agreement with commercial publishers rejected by the Federal court and the entire scheme judged in Google's favor under fair-use doctrine.

Notwithstanding the many twists and turns of the legal process, the initial poor quality of many of the scans – especially of nineteenth-century texts – the theoretical arguments against the representational nature of the collection[8] and the threats to authors' control of their own work, Google Books marked a turning point in the acceptance of the digital as a robust resource for humanistic research. Not only was the great and minor literature of the nineteenth century now available freely to consult title-by-title or to data mine – changing approaches to literary studies dramatically – but the great achievements of eighteenth- and nineteenth-century scholarly editing – archival and narrative sources, diaries, letters and the like – were also becoming freely available to scholars who could access the great collections in the world's best libraries from their desktops. Google Books, in both its aggressive stance toward copyright and orphan works and in the attempt to be all comprehensive, both raised the bar for the digital aggregations of printed books and gave impetus to national and private libraries and museums to make freely available digitally their vast collections of manuscript books, images, objects and other visual resources. Google succeeded in one of its largest strategic goals: to change the *habitus* of both scholarly and popular reading and to make the digital fully capable of becoming a true representation of the historic past, itself one of the major goals of all humanities research and writing. Of equally great import, however, is the fact that throughout the process of creation and litigation of the Google projects, the academic community had little effective input, preferring instead to reflect upon developments (in true humanistic mode) or to "ride the tiger" of corporate developments, a less than positive commentary both on the humanities' public outreach and on the resources of the academic community as a whole.

Perhaps the aggressive stance of Google and the resulting commercial push-back set the stage for a more conscious and creative approach to copyright in the digital era. One of the results is that now companies like Amazon.com, its print-on-demand program, CreateSpace, and its e-book arm, Kindle, are careful monitors of the copyright status of works put into their programs, with publishers often having to provide documentation, such as contracts, to support copyright claims. At the same time, not-for-profit aggregations like the Hathi Trust (the result of Google's original content agreements with the University of Michigan), JSTOR and ACLS Humanities E-Book (HEB) have been careful to clear copyrights for their online repositories, and other projects are careful to digitize only out-of-copyright materials. What this means for most humanist scholars is that the situation for print materials is now far more clear than it was a decade ago, and much of scholars' initial resistance, based on a recitation of copyright restrictions and problems, has now been overcome, at least in print.

With the new theoretical turns of materiality and visual culture, however, the image has taken on a primacy and importance both in traditional print work but most especially in the digital. The availability of digital copies of almost every known work of art, from the greatest fresco cycles to the smallest pieces of jewelry and other examples of material culture, has coincided with these theoretical turns to push forward the use of visual materials as never before. At the same time publishing models – which previously had limited the inclusion of only about two dozen images in the standard monograph as mere "illustrations" to any text that was not specifically art historical – now saw the digital altering the old equations to permit any number of images, in color or black and white. Digital photocopying, digitizing equipment and high-quality digital photography have now also made it possible for researchers, authors and their associates to create and publish images of everything from architecture and sculpture to coinage and textiles to plans and graphs at the highest resolution for any number of media and platforms.

Simultaneously, however, many conservative forces continued to work against the possibilities that the digital offered. The early days of digital scholarly publishing saw the continuation of many traditional practices. Authors – most especially art historians and other visual scholars – continued to insist that they must not only clear permissions to use images of historic architecture, sculpture, manuscript pages and the like, but also continue to pay hefty permission fees to libraries and museums. Libraries and museums for their part saw both a threat to the integrity of their collections and the possibility of vast new financial revenues from the licensing of these very same materials. Publishers, unsure of the new rights terrain that the digital opened, often erred on the side of caution. In one famous case, a major university press, publishing a work on U.S. history, agreed to a library's request to both sublicense and pay a prohibitive reproduction fee for a digital image of the Declaration of Independence. Many long-serving editors at university presses, sideswiped by and suspicious of the digital, reinforced this caution by erecting ever new barricades against the use of digital reproduction, requesting copies of all permissions, even though authors had already agreed in contracts to warrant all permissions obligations, and in some cases going so far as to eliminate images from new monographs or to block them out in digital versions of existing print monographs.

Numerous scholars, long familiar with image rights and fees, related horror stories of the ever-escalating prices for reproductions of well-known pieces of art, long in the public domain and long part of the world's cultural inheritance. This was matched by the rising role of corporations in restoration projects, such as the Japanese Nippon Television Network Corporation in the restoration of Vatican's Sistine Chapel and its subsequent control over reproductions of the world heritage frescoes the chapel contained. As many art historians scoffed at and protested these developments, many others – powerful and experienced figures – still refrained from exercising fair-use rights out of hesitancy to offend hosting museums or libraries and thus upset long-established, personal relationships with curators and collection heads. As requests for ever-larger payments for digital rights increased, moreover, art historians and other humanists began to call upon foundations, such as ACLS and Mellon, to foot the bill for such rights, in effect moving large sums of money from one not-for-profit to another, with the humanist scholar effectively the courier for the transaction. Self-appointed digital experts began to spring up at many museum and art-historical conferences, confidentially spreading the gospel that money – and more and more of it – was the solution to what they deemed the impossible task of publishing the visual in the digital era.

Slowly several large not-for-profits began to push back against this new wisdom. JSTOR developed a fair-use regime for the materials in its collections that preempted the need to ascertain new rights permissions. ACLS Humanities E-Book adopted this model from the start, and ArtStor aggressively aggregated visual content from creators. Their actions prompted many university and departmental libraries to do the same. Tens of thousands of slides from private collections were aggregated, and software was developed to deliver them efficiently for classroom and scholarly presentation. In February 2015 the College Art Association summarized this experience in their "Code of Best Practices in Fair Use for the Visual Arts."

As pressure mounted from the robust application of fair use by such aggregators, by publishers and by other collections, libraries and museums began to reconsider their original policies. Rather than seeing the digital as either a threat to their collections or a lucrative new revenue stream – and as the cost of administering these complex permissions schemes was often not covered by the revenues they generated – libraries and museums also began to realize that the digital versions actually acted first as markers for the originals and second as pedagogical and research resources that widened the breadth of their impact. They discovered that both uses actually drew existing and new audiences into their brick and mortar buildings to view the artworks and artifacts in their original. The representative nature of the digital was fully realized on both professional and popular levels, and the main beneficiaries – after the public – of digital dissemination became the museums and libraries themselves. By the early years of the twenty-first century, museums and libraries were making available online free of charge hundreds of thousands of images from their collections – everything from paintings and sculpture to maps, papyri, manuscripts and coins – all accompanied by the highest-quality metadata.

As we will discuss in greater detail below, rights in the digital realm do remain an issue when authors and their institutions claim rights for items in open-access repositories after the same authors have already transferred their rights to a publisher. Rights to dissertations, which are being appropriated for institutional repositories, and rights to works supported by government funding remain unresolved issues in the digital environment. The Authors' Alliance[9] is one attempt to help resolve this issue. Its mission is to further the public interest in facilitating widespread access to works by helping authors navigate the opportunities and challenges of the digital age. It seeks to provide information and tools designed to help authors better understand and manage key legal, technological and institutional issues essential to what has become a knowledge economy of abundance.

The quality of illustrations themselves has long been key to humanistic research and publication. When Giorgio Vasari singled out the painter Giotto for his ability to "counterfeit and imitate nature,"[10] he summed up Renaissance humanism's approach to the world. Its accurate representation became a key to the value of the new textual studies as well as to the visual arts of painting and sculpture. The best architecture was the one that reflected the practices and values of antiquity. From the fifteenth century on, various forms of printing technologies gradually improved the ability of the machine to reproduce the original image; and the issue of the original and its copies took on more and more importance in the twentieth century as technology made imitation ever more accurate and the autonomy of the image ever more important.[11] Walter Benjamin's 1936 essay[12] succinctly summarized these cultural anxieties over representation and a mass consumer culture of manifold copies.

In the earliest days of the digital, the gross effects of low-resolution pixilated images, reproduced on low-resolution screens and low-output dot-matrix and laser printers, caused a considerable backlash over the digital among visual scholars. Publishers who began to rely upon digital technologies for textual works were often met with derision for the limited resolutions and design capabilities of first-generation computer typesetting. Gradually technology and resolutions improved to the point where in the publishing world all processes and production steps were being handled by computers, even if most scholars and even some editors were not aware of it. By the late 1990s and the early twenty-first century, all such issues had been resolved for scholarly publishing, and even the highest quality printing houses were almost universally using digital technologies to reproduce works of art in a variety of media. High-resolution scanners and cameras were also capturing the majority of scholars' own visual documentation. These were easily transferred into production quality.

One of the few remaining areas of contention remained the presentation quality of visual materials in the digital: art historians, archaeologists, historians of design and architecture continued to press for higher and higher resolution images and more and more true reproduction of color balance, tone and other formal qualities. Yet digital technology was quickly outpacing perceptions. A demonstration of NASA-funded imaging at a conference sponsored by the Getty Research Institute in

June 2006, for example, startled an audience of art historians, curators and digerati for its visual accuracy and the possibilities inherent in
mega-pixel imaging. As museums and libraries began to perfect digitization and online publication methods, the content delivered up over
the web also improved dramatically until today the researcher can find
online digital representations of hundreds of thousands of visual objects
at the highest resolution, available both for study online and for download at a variety of resolutions.[13] Throughout the process the very excellence of the reproduction technologies has brought into even more
stark relief the very materiality of the original, and scholars of the visual
have accordingly begun to include in their methodological tool kits an
ever-present awareness of the sharp distinction between the material
original and the digital copy. This has become possible only because the
digital now offers a fully viable alternative beyond derision and dismissal.

   The same developments have affected the aural and oral sources
of humanist research. Since the pioneering work of Walter Ong and
others, our theory of textual communities has developed around the
interplay of oral and written textualities, and the validity of both oral
traditions and aural sources has become well established in both theory
and practice. This trend, however, speaks more to ancient and medieval studies than to the philological, textual methodologies inherited
from Renaissance humanism and borrows much of its strength from the
demonstrated contributions of anthropology, sociology and other social
sciences. Yet humanities disciplines have now fully accepted the study of
performance, ritual, sound, song, as well as dance and other performative arts as core to humanist disciplines. As analog sound recording and
playback equipment have given way to the digital, a vast expansion of
source material has become available online in everything from sound
archives to YouTube videos documenting every conceivable social and
cultural practice.

   Simultaneously battles over sound recording and its distribution have
slowed the growth of new aurality studies and threatened to frustrate
much of the new form of digital publication around such aural and oral
disciplinary approaches. Early attempts to share music online, using
Napster (1999) for example, were met with rapid legal challenges and
severe penalties. Restrictive limitations upon scholars' ability to use such
materials under fair-use doctrine clashed increasingly with large corporate forces intent upon maintaining close control over recordings of all
types. Online projects, including e-books that contained sound files,
became increasingly difficult to publish both as authors self-censored

their use of materials and as publishers once again erred on the side of overcaution. Lawyers rather than scholars began to determine what the content of digital publication might be. In response several groups, most especially the Creative Commons, sought to reclaim both fair use of existing copyrighted work and clear definitions of work that was in the public domain. As important, the Commons offers legal guidelines and best practice, as well as links to active aggregators of music and other aural sources. Meanwhile digital oral-history platforms and archives, including collections of folklore, are becoming available freely from sources as diverse as the Oral History in the Digital Age (OHDA) Project,[14] Digital Omnium,[15] the Dédalo Platform for Intangible Heritage Management,[16] the National Archives of Singapore Oral History Centre[17] and many others across the globe.

DIGITAL RIGHTS MANAGEMENT

Digital rights management (DRM) is generally considered a combination of software, technology and legal measures that parallel the first licensing models in the print world: it is intended to limit the copying of digital materials, including software, the number of machines that might use these materials or the replication of content in either digital or print formats. First-generation DRM generally controlled copying of media, while second-generation DRM limited dissemination, copying or altering of content. While there is often considerable overlap in intent and practice, DRM must be clearly distinguished from copyright: the first is intended to protect distribution, the second to protect ownership. One can give away one's books or music without further issue but would strongly object if someone else presented that work as their own. DRM restricts the former, while copyright protects the latter. DRM regimes can be applied to most of the digital products of humanistic research: books, images and video, TV and film, music and other aural presentations and the accompanying metadata for all of the above. After some initial experimentation with controls and consumer and advocacy-group push-back, the Digital Millennium Copyright Act of 1998 made it illegal to employ software or other means to work around DRM schemes. This was followed by the 2001 European Copyright Directive, thus engaging the issue on a higher legal level. The Foundation for a Free Information Infrastructure[18] and the Creative Commons[19] have been among the major organizations fighting DRM schemes as anticompetitive, restrictive of individual and consumer rights and destructive of fair use.

DRM was once considered an enormous problem for digital publication. How could publishers protect their products in the digital environment when pirates or consumers could seemingly break into anything to either copy software or to make unwarranted copies using electronic or print methods? This problem has for the most part been less vexing than the problem of unwarranted replication of printed books using photocopy machines and course packs. Generally the pricing of digital materials, the ease of finding and accessing them and the convenience of the formats has made it less attractive for pirates to spend much energy breaking into books. Companies like Adobe and Amazon.com have also created DRM schemes within their distribution mechanism that protect against unlawful sharing and distribution of digital materials. Many scholars will choose to make their work freely available on websites such as Academia.edu, and others have a variety of protected solutions that they can choose from, even password-protecting PDFs. Clearly with the vulnerability of everything from financial institutions to the National Security Agency, it will be impossible to securely protect digital content, but is unwarranted copying worth the time, money and possible prosecution?

Reliable studies[20] have started to demonstrate that the digital versions in themselves are not cannibalizing the sales of hard-copy books and recordings, and that in many cases such digital distribution was boosting sales of hard copy. Other studies have pointed out that with the large majority of digital versus print sales,[21] profit margins remain firmly with print. This is primarily a function of average pricing formulas that publishers use when calculating profit and loss factors on titles. Unauthorized distribution of music through Napster and other file-sharing methods was, however, found to have a substantial impact on music sales, but this was an entirely different issue from the disruptive effect of legal digital downloads on analog sales. By the late 2010s, important members of the digital community, including Bill Gates and Steve Jobs, were questioning the value and validity of DRM, and Apple had removed DRM controls from its iTunes store. Private copying proved to be far less prevalent than feared, and unauthorized distribution was kept low as long as the purchase or rental price threshold was kept down. Although not all publishers have embraced the iTunes model, it is clear that sensible pricing for e-books makes it more likely that people will actually buy them instead of spending time trying to copy and distribute them privately.

This dynamic, however, feeds into another, larger concern among humanists: the commercial value of their scholarly work. As already discussed, most scholars see their work's value in hiring, tenure and pro-motion (HTP) terms, not in terms of the commercial marketplace, and they are quite willing to distribute their work as freely as possible, with-out any form of DRM. This, of course, runs head on into the realities of commercial and university press publishing, most especially the lat-ter, where individual-copy pricing is a carefully honed result of formulae that take into account everything from office overhead to warehousing costs and royalties. Margins are slim, and the fear of lowering the average retail price and profit margin through Kindle and other pricing schemes is very real. While offering PDFs or Kindle versions of humanities mono-graphs for $95 does not seem like a model for sensible pricing, the mar-ket and its analysts have not yet found an effective or convincing price point for digital versions. While experiments with DRM and non-DRM distribution are being planned,[22] no consensus has been reached, and until then DRM schemes are likely to endure.

OPEN ACCESS

Free and open access (OA) to the books and ideas of the humanities has been part of our cultural inheritance since the ancient Greeks and Romans. Pisistratus of Athens (c. 600–527 BCE) was said to have founded a public library, and the library of Alexandria contained more than four hundred thousand books by the third century CE. Public libraries appeared in Rome in the first century CE, and by 350 CE there were twenty-nine public libraries in that city.[23] The public library was an idea revived among the humanists and their supporters with the great manu-script collections of the Renaissance. The humanists made stark contrast between their own learning and that of the Scholastics – the philosophers and theologians of the medieval universities – and the learning of the monks, among whose supposedly crumbling, dusty collections of ancient manuscripts the humanists claimed to have rediscovered the learning of the ancients and brought them back into the public light. The Medici of Florence, the dukes of Urbino, King Matthias Corvinus of Hungary, the Aragonese kings of Naples, Cardinal Bessarion in Venice and most espe-cially the popes at the Vatican followed the guidance of their humanist advisors and created repositories of ancient learning where anyone who could read these books (admittedly a small percentage of even the ver-nacular literate population) could freely consult them *in situ*. Almost all these great libraries – and those of individual humanists – were built and served a public *outside* the walls and conventions of academia.

Essential then to the role of the humanists and humanistic studies has always been the notion of public access that was free and open, in keeping with the essential role of the *studia humanitatis* to impart both knowledge and civic good. Central to this ideal was that of patronage: of the prince, either secular or religious, who funded their research and writing through both financial reward and position and who was recognized in the dedications of the humanists' texts. We possess many illustrations from manuscripts and early printed books showing the author on bended knee, offering his work to his powerful patron in exchange for financial support or position. Perhaps the best known is the fresco by Melozzo da Forlì in the Vatican portraying the humanist Bartolomeo Platina kneeling before Pope Sixtus IV as the pope appoints him prefect of the Vatican Library. In one important regard, therefore, open access always carried a notion of elite patronage and limited audience. Access to patronage set off bitter disputes among humanists at court. The diatribes written by Poggio Bracciolini against George of Trebizond, Bartolomeo Facio and Antonio Beccadelli, for example, are some of the more unsavory aspects of the history of humanism and the humanist as courtier.

At the same time, the humanist and then Enlightenment ideal of the public library as a civic good became a central focus of the emerging nation-state. The great national libraries of France, Italy, Spain, Germany and the United States, among others, were formed around these humanist goals enshrined in the inscriptions and symbolic statues along their grand facades, themselves modeled after the great public buildings of antiquity. These libraries became both focal points for connection to a cultural inheritance and a national past (often newly in the process of invention) and institutions dedicated to the public good for the preservation and dissemination of knowledge. The transition from a world defined by print to one defined by the digital would therefore become a natural concern for the library, both public and university. Harnessing the potential of the Internet to pool resources and to disseminate information and knowledge was a natural stage in the evolution of the library.

Simultaneously, the rise of printing as a commercial, industrial enterprise had laid out an alternative future. Erasmus had already dubbed his publishing with Aldus a "library without walls" (*Adagia* 2.1.1). Access to knowledge based on a widening ability to pay for books moved quickly away from the prince or religious patron, who alone could subsidize the cost of deluxe manuscript production. It also soon overcame the medieval urban scriptoria that were sustained by the need of the universities for multiple manuscript copies of text-books. From the late fifteenth century a reasonable amount of cash could purchase books produced by increasingly more rapid and ubiquitous technologies. By the nineteenth and early twentieth centuries, mass production was able to provide access to popular entertainment, literature and news at prices that almost anyone in the newly literate classes could afford.

The late twentieth century therefore inherited two vibrant models of access to information and knowledge: one the patronage model sustained by individual, institutional or governmental resources and the other the commercial model built on the ability to produce vast amounts of inexpensive print for the broadest market possible. By the mid-twentieth century these two models had come together briefly in the highly democratic movement of widespread higher education embraced by the Western democracies and the socialist world. "Access" to knowledge ceased to become an issue in a period when both J. D. Salinger's *Catcher in the Rye* or Paul Oskar Kristeller's *Renaissance Thought* were printed in thousands and tens of thousands of copies and sold in paperback for less than the cost of a Manhattan lunch.

The culture shocks of the later twentieth century, the rapidly diminishing place of the consensus "middlebrow" in Western life, the turning away from humanities disciplines in higher education after the 1960s, the consolidation of the book industry into the hands of a very few monolithic entertainment corporations and the beginning of the computer era and Internet began to change long-held notions of access to knowledge. In the 1960s a university press could expect to sell five thousand copies of a monograph. Between 1980 and 2000 average sales/title had plummeted in the key monograph market, the library, from about two thousand copies in 1980, to one thousand by the late 1980s, to five hundred by 1990, to two hundred in 2000[24] – often not even enough to cover publishers' overhead costs and often fewer copies than popular medieval books in manuscript. Prices of monographs – now restricted to an academic market – rose at times to more than $200 a copy, well out of reach of students and most specialists. According to a recent Harvard Humanities Report,[25] in 1966 humanities, including classics, languages, philosophy and history, had attracted 14 percent of BA degrees at the "average" university, by 2010 these numbers had dropped overall to 7 percent, and these very departments were being trimmed down, consolidated or eliminated.[26] In this situation the arrival of the digital was greeted either as a source of salvation or as further evidence of the rapid decline of humanistic culture. "Access" to knowledge in the digital era began to take on a highly contested nature as all stakeholders – scholars, libraries, publishers – began to set their own priorities and stake out their own positions.

One of the more important meta-issues that grew out of these developments was the question of how these various groups might establish and guarantee access in the digital era, especially in the face of commercially dominated publishing. Startled into action by the increasingly high subscription fees charged to university and public libraries by a small group of large commercial publishers for scholarly journals – most especially in the STM (science, technology and medical) fields – by the late 1990s the call was sounded and a movement began to coalesce around the idea of "open access."[27] Proponents rightly decried the ever-increasing percentages of library acquisitions budgets devoted to STM subscriptions to the detriment of humanities budgets for journals and monographs. After efforts to persuade the journal publishers to reduce fees or to scale services had essentially failed, librarians and other information specialists began to consider the possibilities that digital publication offered. If the digital eliminated printing, paper, storage and warehousing, transportation, receiving and inventory of journals and books, OA proponents began asking – often quite vociferously – why should digital publishers not drastically reduce subscription fees as well? In 1985 Stewart Brand, founder of the iconic countercultural *Whole Earth Catalog*, had already issued the call that "information wants to be free."[28] As the concept drifted into library and academic circles, it sometimes metamorphosed into the phrase, "knowledge wants to be free" and soon hardened into an ideology that often seemed to equate information with knowledge.

When applied to scholarly communication, one might argue that much of early OA ideology rested on a plethora of faulty assumptions about publishing: the cost of print, the value added by publishers, the collaborative nature of scholarship and the size of potential readership. OA ideology declared that printing costs were driving up the price of books, whereas in fact the cost of producing print is nowhere near as significant as the cost of editorial, peer review, copyediting, proofreading, formatting, sales, distribution and marketing – all of which have to be done whether the end product is a print or an electronic publication. These same ideologues declared that publishers did not create any value when they performed these functions, and in fact the community of scholars would be willing to work for "free" to add this value without the need for a publisher. Learned societies for their part were also blocking progress, as one librarian put it, using publications to fund their "vacations," that is, their annual meetings.[29] Finally, so the thinking went, there was a vast audience waiting to read the latest scholarly monograph, if only they did not have to pay for it. In truth, during this same period 60 percent of all monographs purchased by university libraries were being deaccessioned within three years, having never circulated. The average user at a university library checked out 80 percent fewer books in 2008 than in 1995.[30]

Nonetheless, once critical analysis, public discussion and governmental pressure began to be focused on the OA movement, a maturing of approach, attitude and expectation began to take firm hold. According to Peter Suber's recent, catholic definition, "Open-access (OA) literature is digital, online, free of charge, and free of most copyright and licensing restrictions."[31] OA is not for everyone and is not intended to replace traditional print publishing in most cases. But it certainly makes sense, according to Suber, for academic writers who, like the Renaissance humanists, are now subsidized through their teaching positions and their system of rewards: promotions, grants, prizes, travel funds, larger offices, book budgets, named chairs, graduate assistants, centers, institutes and similar soft money. Despite the fact that upward of 75 percent of humanities faculty are contingent and unlikely to gain tenure or even full-time academic work with all its perks, for the narrowly restricted class of academics who are tenured giving away one's work – again like Renaissance humanists – makes great sense: it eases distribution and audience access. The rewards are not immediately financial, as in the transaction inherent in publishing itself or in society at large, but they certainly are in the academic reward system where promotion and other advancement carry such a wide array of benefits.

When OA regulation reaches governmental levels, the rules and the compulsion to comply at times appear intolerable and have spawned widespread indignation and protest, as has recently been the case among scholarly societies in the United Kingdom in the face of government OA regulation. In response to protest, positions have hardened rapidly. As one European Commission funder recently declared: "if learned societies are a casualty of the move to OA, then so be it."[32] In the United States, similar legislation and mandates are now forcing open access in everything from science research funded by the federal government to the open access of dissertations in medieval art history in cases where a school or an individual receives government funds. Historians of the book, such as Robert Darnton,[33] have published widely on the effects of early modern governments' attempts to define what proper content is and on governmental interference with publishing. Can the humanities flourish in the face of ideological conviction and government compulsion? Desiderius Erasmus, the most famous of all humanists, was courted by both Catholics and Protestants in the widening ideological rifts of the Reformation. When he chose neither and sought a nonideological, open-ended path, relying on reason and humanist discourse, he ended his life reviled by many in both camps.

As the university becomes increasingly transformed under the corporate and research model, faculty research becomes not the intellectual property of the author but of the corporate institution, akin to laboratory research conducted for a pharmaceutical company. Under such regimes, OA mandates are viewed as further eroding the autonomy of humanities faculty and their rights to publish their work where and when they see fit. University and government mandates increasingly overlap with the OA movement's contention that individual scholarly work has no financial value. Its aggregate value to the corporation, however, continues to increase, ironically returning scholarly publishing to the very situation decried by the original OA movement: scholars produce their work for free, yet aggregators then capitalize on it in their monetization of its aggregate value. If the aggregator happens to be the research university rather than the corporate publisher, is the end result any better for the individual humanist?

Various solutions, commercial, not-for-profit and governmental, have been attempted now with various degrees of success. Issues of embargoes on dissemination of dissertations and articles, the question of "who pays" and its ramifications on the continuing hierarchization of scholarly work and on the people who produce it and the ultimate sustainability of OA models are still being debated, if not as hotly or as ideologically as a decade ago. Proponents have now begun to clearly distinguish two types of OA: gold, for OA articles delivered by journals, regardless of their business model; and green, for content served up through institutional repositories, that is, the work of university faculty and/or deposited dissertations. Within these two broad categories (developed by OA proponents in an attempt to respond to critics), there remains a wide range of schemes and models, including "libre" and "gratis," author-pays, institution pays, funding agency pays, reader's institution pays (similar to closed access): the most important consideration being that the commercial market does not pay, thus adhering to the venerable Renaissance patronage model. New rules are continuously being issued, and old ones

updated and reiterated to insure compliance. Like the Ptolemaic cos-
mologies of the later Middle Ages and Renaissance with their cycles and
epicycles, the complexity of the schemes, the variations and the subdivi-
sions within categories continues to grow.

Instead of reader pays – which is decried as an access barrier – most
OA models assume that author pays, author's institution pays, reader's
institution pays or some not-for-profit foundation pays. In this effort
to open access to readers, however, there arises the danger of actually
closing authors' access to publication, when publication is left in the
hands of corporatized institutions interested in promoting their own
brands and their own star products. Institution-pay schemes have raised
the criticism that just because someone teaches at a well-endowed institution it does not mean that person's ideas should be published while
those of others at less wealthy schools are left in bottom drawers. Thus
OA can tend to reconfirm what has long been an unspoken prejudice
within humanities academia: that the best scholars are those hired by
the richest institutions. Another outcome is that publication comes to
individuals with money to pay for it themselves. Again this favors certain
classes of academics: the more senior and tenured, those at more elite
schools, those with full-time positions, those whose resources do not
depend upon their academic salaries (either through personal circumstances or through lucrative commercial publishing or entertainment
contracts).

The OA movement has also managed to spawn a host of dubiously
ethical publishers who are willing to take payment to publish almost anything under a variety of imprints – mostly journals – and payment is
often available on a sliding scale. It has also spawned an equally vigilant
order of Internet monitors who trawl cyberspace hunting for specious
and fraudulent publishers and journals, calling them out in regularly
published listings and spreading the word that scholars should avoid
them: the digital equivalent of the *Index Librorum Prohibitorum* (Index of
Prohibited Books) of the Catholic Inquisition or of the pre-Revolutionary
French royal censors. As in late medieval manuscript culture, the gentle-
manly ideal of freely granting away one's work under the aegis of gen-
erous patrons has quickly dissolved into a situation that resembles the
earliest days of print and its numerous unauthorized and pirated editions before copyright and other intellectual rights were firmly established and spread. Revisionist histories of the book[34] have cast this as a
necessary phase of experimentation, and perhaps this is how one should
view OA publishing at this point.

Although the physical- and social-science models of publication lend themselves more easily to such OA models – given the currency of the research, its short shelf life and its more public sources of funding – experiments in humanities OA are also underway. These, however, must confront both the traditional culture and the intrinsic methodologies of the humanities: a publication and reception model that – whatever the elite academic rewards system – still values the individual author and her celebrity and compensation, provides far longer life to journal articles and relies more heavily on monographs. The sustainability of both human-ities journals and books relies primarily on individual scholarly presses, whose professional editorial and other staffs are funded largely through sales; and on learned societies, which are funded largely by the dues of members, most of whom are now contingent, junior or untenured faculty.

Again, one of the original impulses of the humanist movement in its creation of public libraries was its belief that the wisdom of the ancients, properly edited, presented and taught could change individual morals and society at large. This impulse remained the fundamental core of humanities faculties, teaching and publication into the late twentieth century, and the democratic impulse behind universal higher education was to instill these humanist ideals into the citizenry at large. The shocks of the late twentieth century, the impact of new critical theory, which often attacked the humanist Enlightenment agenda, and the changing economics of both higher education and of the American population at large have all but eliminated much of this impetus. As Peter Suber, cur-rently director of the Office for Scholarly Communication at Harvard University, says bluntly, "OA isn't primarily about bringing access to lay readers. If anything, the OA movement focuses on bringing access to professional researchers whose careers depend on access."[35] Can the OA movement therefore be seen as one more step in the retreat from the Western humanistic ideal of knowledge in the service of an informed cit-izenry and back to a patronage society?

Perhaps the most noteworthy experiments in OA publishing in the humanities were, appropriately, attempted by the American Historical Association (AHA), itself perhaps the most representative learned soci-ety in terms of its mission of outreach to the American people. The first experiment took place in 1999[36] when the *American Historical Review* offered open access through the History Cooperative. After one year that witnessed subscription income drop by 8.5 percent – the society's largest annual drop ever – the AHA decided that, although the model afforded great access to recent scholarship, it was unsustainable. In 2005, urged on by its then head of the research division, Roy Rosenzweig[37] and his supporters, the AHA decided to provide free open access to all the articles published in the *American Historical Review*, while retaining its book reviews behind a subscription wall. The theory went that such content should not be valued monetarily but solely for its scholarly worth. Issues of sustainability for the society and its staff and operations were secondary to this higher calling. After a further decline in subscriptions of 18 percent over the next thirty months (during which the AHA moved *American Historical Review*'s production and distribution to the University of Chicago Press), the association reversed its decision and reverted to an all-pay model through subscription, with provision for a moving wall access on back issues, using digital resources to expand services to members and initiating other, less formal forms of scholarly communication.

The debate over open access continued after more and more journals went OA and after the British government issued stringent new rules mandating OA. On September 24, 2012, the AHA issued a public "Statement on Scholarly Journal Publishing"[38] – unanimously approved by the AHA governing council – in which it severely criticized the rush toward OA, reminding readers that the humanities were far different from the STM fields, of the real value-added and costs of editing and peer review ($460,000/year) and of the dangers of a new, highly unfair structure that would favor scholars who could afford the hefty fees ($2,000/article) charged by OA journals.

A more recent survey of learned societies in the United Kingdom, United States, and European Union[39] found that most were marginally (55 percent) in favor of OA, citing its ability to lower barriers to current literature, most especially in the Global South and among those least able to pay for subscriptions. The majority of societies surveyed, however, continue to express concern over lost revenues from these journal subscriptions. It is important to note, moreover, that only thirty-three societies participated, and of these 75 percent were STM focused. While experimentation and dissent continues, the consensus remains that time, testing and flexibility of approach will be needed before working models emerge for OA in the humanities. Meanwhile huge projects such as Google Book and the digitization of resources at the Library of Congress, the Metropolitan Museum, New York Public Library, Bibliothèque nationale de France, the British Library, the Swiss national consortium and many other great institutions move forward, offering up millions of visual and verbal texts open access.

The Evolving Landscape
for the Digital Humanities

~

INTRODUCTION

Every landscape has two aspects to it: the perspective and other external points of view and the view obtained by the human agent moving in and through it. "What begins as undifferentiated space becomes place as we get to know it better, endow it with value."[1] With the new insights garnered from landscape studies and humanists' embrace of such fields as rural archaeology, we have begun to realize more fully and to understand better the human impact upon landscapes: everything from agriculture to the clearance of rivers and swamps and forests to massive land moving. Simon Schama's classic *Landscape and Memory*[2] is one example of how literary and historical studies have traced the changing understanding of the landscape – from ancient and medieval awe to Romantic idealization to industrial utilitarianism. Such new studies have provided deep insights into how we understand the world around us – the world through which we move and in which we work and live.

In the same way, throughout this book we have described the impact of the digital upon the humanities and how it has changed many aspects of research and disciplinary thought; but in this chapter we will first briefly discuss the impact of humanists as agents upon the world of computing. We began our discussion with Roberto Busa's request to Thomas Watson for help in building a search engine for the massive corpus of Thomas Aquinas's works. That collaboration remains paradigmatic of the way in which humanists have approached the world of the computer in its first stages.

The library world had been working for years on various computer solutions to issues raised by humanities research questions: cataloging, word and metadata searches, sorts and report formats. At the universities of Michigan, California and Virginia, for example, library and computing departments have set up various offices to accommodate the humanists' research agendas, and we have reviewed these in detail in many places throughout this book.

How else have the humanities impacted computer technologies and culture over the years? There are several broad categories, and one would need an entire other book to cover them in detail from this perspective. Here we want simply to emphasize that this is an ongoing process that the reader and the researcher should neither ignore nor underestimate: the active input of humanists' research agendas have had a profound impact on the digital era and is responsible for much of the digital's impact on the general public.

Everything from the footnote format in Microsoft Word to the indexing in InDesign to the use of TEI for digital art books to the Getty's use of NASA-style imaging to the harnessing of data mining for nineteenth-century literature collections have reflected humanists' role in the world of computing. Now, with active digital humanities programs and a generation of humanists familiar with all aspects of computing, that impact has become ongoing, profound and pervasive, so much so that, for example, it is humanists' interest in issues of mind[3] that helps researchers working in areas of cognitive science continue their work and receive campuswide funding. Many, in fact, see the interest in humanities computing among computer departments as strategic to maintaining IT and computing departments, depending upon the insights and prestige of humanist colleagues and departments to bolster their positions on campus.

Over the last two decades, the landscape for the digital humanities appears to have changed rapidly at first, and then the evolution has slowed as work concentrated on knotty problems. In 1996 a survey by the Modern Language Association (MLA) saw the digital landscape as one of word-processing applications, online public access catalogs (OPACs) and bibliographic databases. The growth of e-mail, mailing lists, listservs and news groups, it noted, were creating "major change from the stereotype of the isolated scholar."[4] These elements have all become so ubiquitous – what Vincent Mosco has characterized as "banal"[5] – that they no longer merit mention. By the middle of the first decade of the new millennium, the talk was all of digital tools, and now they can be accessed online with such ease that even they hardly merit mention. What is left to accomplish?

On the ground the digital humanities face two immediate challenges: the need to bring together all the disparate and excellent resources already created into a comprehensive system of scholarly communication – a cyberinfrastructure[6] – that facilitates the work of individuals, publishers, learned societies and all institutions of higher learning in the humanities, investigating and answering questions from the most specialized research focus to the broadest public interest. The second challenge is to provide frameworks that permit all scholars to take advantage of the available tools in their research fields.

While digital humanities centers and institutes are often set up within research universities to provide computing power, tools and applications, technical advice and inexpensive assistance for digital research projects (discussed in Chapter 6), other digital humanities organizations provide a forum for the exploration of future directions. They often host meetings and workshops, inviting experienced digital humanists to present their experiences while trying to attain a global perspective on the shifting priorities in higher education and the humanities. They focus on keeping their constituents up to date on current technology and on tracking the progress of the cutting edge as it moves rapidly toward the "banal" and as all things digital become a normal part of humanities research. But the issues of digital humanities cannot be divorced from the current situation in the humanities in general and particularly the academic humanities.

THE HUMANITIES IN ACADEMIA

The condition of the humanities in academia has recently and often been characterized as "a state of crisis," which has been tied directly to the reach of the humanities, the extent to which it is engaged with the public. The crisis in the humanities is not simply a matter of undergraduate enrollments, but is linked to the well-known and by now well-worn meme: the "crisis in scholarly communication." This crisis – if one can call a situation spanning fifty years a "crisis" – has been analyzed repeatedly to involve four elements: the audience for and fate of the print monograph, its role in professional assessment and advancement, the future of the university presses and the role of the library in collection development, access and preservation of scholarship.

The discussion has tended to focus on just one of these issues, which has become core: the declining reach, profitability and responsiveness of the university presses as the publishers of the primary vehicle of humanities research: the monograph. The litany of causes is often repeated, and it was succinctly formulated by Cathy Davidson (then of Duke University) at the 2003 ACLS Annual Meeting.[7] In the crisis in scholarly publishing, the problem is any combination of several menu items: the high cost of print manufacturing, the high cost of science journals, the greed and inefficiency of publishers, declining library budgets in the humanities, cutbacks in university funding for presses, the narrowing of focus among academic humanists to more and more esoteric specialties, lack of publishing subsidies for authors or the universal popularization of our culture. All of these topics are still covered almost weekly in the *Chronicle of Higher Education* or The Scholarly Kitchen[8] and remain the object of speculation, debate and a great deal of anecdotal description and categorical prescription.

By the late 1990s it was acknowledged that something had to be done. And the maturing of the electronic media touted by scholars like James O'Donnell (medievalist and author of *Avatars of the Word*), Robert Darnton (as president of the American Historical Association [AHA]), Jerome McGann (author of The Rossetti Archive) and Edward L. Ayers (author of The Valley of the Shadow) seemed to offer a solution. By the end of 1999, both Gutenberg-e and the ACLS History E-Book Project (HEB) were therefore conceived as a joint ventures among the ACLS, the AHA, the Mellon Foundation and a small consortium of major university libraries, additional learned societies and university presses as key partners in the expectation that turning around the economics of monograph publishing by using digital media would solve many of these problems. Meanwhile other projects, such as the California Digital Library, Project MUSE and JSTOR, had substantially expanded the scope of such publication schemes.

While there were tangible gains in most areas of e-publishing during the decade from 2000 to 2010, and the Mellon Foundation continued to fund various experiments through university presses and consortia,[9] many of the university presses continued to focus on only one model of e-book: the derivative, electronic version of print-first monographs. At the same time most university departments, deans and provosts continued to insist that the only coin of the realm for hiring, tenure and promotion (HTP) was the print monograph, and this published by a small circle of first-tier university presses. Simultaneously, libraries continued to report that budgets were stretched, readership down and mission adrift.

A BERMUDA TRIANGLE

How was this possible? At conference after conference, in publication after publication, humanists heard and read how the problems of scholarly communication were really an issue of the shifting balance between publishers and libraries. The litany went (and still goes) something like this: if we can use electronic publishing to change the economics of the publishers' manufacturing system things will get better. If we can persuade the publishers to make their books cheaper and distribute them more widely, things will get back to where they once belonged. If we can release libraries from the grip of greedy mega-national journal distributors, we can free up their budgets and give them the chance once again to buy our monographs. If we can subsidize first publications, second publications, publications series, individual university presses, the entire Association of American University Presses (AAUP) publishing network, "they" will once again publish the monographs "we" need them to. If we can just get the publishers out of the scene, remove them from the equation, we can do it all ourselves and then acquire, edit, schedule, clear rights, typeset and design, copyedit, proofread, publish, value, price and store, distribute, and then advertise, bill and pay royalties on our monographs ourselves, and we will then restore the system that "they" broke. Or even better, if libraries can take this over for us – and still take care of the library and its ever-growing collections and types of materials – they will surely solve this problem for us. If only "they" would solve this problem for "us."

Repeated over and over again: the problem for humanities scholars in scholarly communication was not "us" but "them." Despite years of statistics gathering and surveys, insightful analysis, advice and warnings from publishers and editors, changes in, and elimination of, publishing programs, and even the disappearance of some university presses, scholars and their deans and provosts remained almost universally uncommunicative on an essential truth about scholarly communication: humanist scholars are both its producers and its market, its writers and its readers, and scholars bear at least as much responsibility as do publishers and libraries for the success or failure of the humanities' broken system of scholarly communication.

Over the years it became apparent that the dynamic of scholarly communication is not a line of tension or opposition between publishers and libraries alone but a triangle that must include scholars: the "Bermuda Triangle of scholarly communication": a cultural space of lost opportunity, missing responsibility and unexplained inertia, much like the mysterious and unexplained disappearances of various forms of transportation reported in the 1950s and 1960s in one region of the western Atlantic. This triangle remains a shifting, uncertain and often perilous force field of alliance and friction among the three major nodes in scholarly communication within the humanities: the scholar, the university press and the library. Our discussion here omits the funding agencies because they have traditionally played an important but less visible role, supporting each of these in various forms and degrees. To understand the current situation, it is important to analyze briefly the three poles of this triangle and the dynamic among them, to discuss the impasse in scholarly communication that this has currently created, to highlight some attempts to break out of the triangle and to provide suggestions about some possible ways forward.

The varying analyses for this triangle have included the following positions. The fault lies with scholars: writing too narrowly and too densely, writing and publishing to serve only the needs of HTP committees. Alternatively, the fault is the publishers': seeking too much profit with too much short-sightedness and loss of mission focus, immobilized by fear of the changing landscape and disruptive technologies, clinging to their bibles and their canons. Last, it is the libraries' fault: cutting humanities budgets to please the sciences and social sciences, deaccessioning titles before they have a chance to fit into syllabi and research agendas, devising schemes like patron-driven acquisitions, setting off on their own to become "publishers" with open access, open peer review and large archival schemes, taking money away from real university press publishers.

This landscape has often been described – largely by The Mellon Foundation, drawing on cutting-edge cyber-theory by Jonathan Schull[10] among others – as an "ecology" gone astray, where large-scale funding or policy interventions from foundations might save the day. Such analysis offers a current, green, apparently benign social-scientific perspective for a system that is presumably governed by a set of natural laws and physical dynamics that could be understood and manipulated to good effect: an anthropologist's or an economist's model derived from social science, not humanities, precedent.

Yet another model of the changes being wrought with the ascendency of the digital is the almost ideological, zero-sum or Manichean approach to scholarly communication. Here, some contend, a digital tipping point has finally arrived to push one or the other of these three nodes to the fore: the scholar will become the new publisher (with websites, blogs, departmental collections); or the library will become the new publisher (with XML, vast archival strategies, mass digitization and data mining, open access, alliances with, or takeovers of, the university presses); or, even a more wildly visionary scenario: the university *press* will actually become a digital publisher. Rather than an ecological, science-based approach that manipulates environments, this is a faith-based approach, predicated on the thus-far unsupported hope in the final triumph of one or the other of these three forces over the rest. On the one hand, humanist research has demonstrated that such apocalyptic expectations have rarely been pleasant or productive, and, on the other hand, many humanists share a skepticism toward social-scientific impartiality.

Instead of this "ecology" or a faith-based rush to individual salvation, the humanist might draw on such theorists as Jürgen Habermas or Pierre Bourdieu to better emphasize the unique agency for each of these three players and seek to change the model to a public and social contract.[11] This acknowledges a constantly changing balance of power and interest among autonomous agents within a common field of endeavor, faced with the same problems of bringing humanities scholarship into the digital age while maintaining quality, reach and sustainability.

According to this alternative model, then, the current crisis in scholarly communication – exposed but not created by the digital – is not an "ecosystem" in disarray or a zero-sum race for final victory but a social contract, a "commons," that has broken down. This breakdown is the result of a series of conscious decisions and calculations by active agents with valid self-interests and rational motives, rather than the results of natural forces and unconsciously balanced systems. Only by attempting to re-establish the social contract – taking into account all competing or overlapping interests – can the humanities community hope to work toward common solutions. Even as it explores and develops new digital publishing tools, this means that it must reintroduce into the equation of these social contracts one element that such analysis seems to ignore: the role of the scholar in adhering to the social contract or attempting to rebuild it responsibly. The solution therefore lies not in focusing on any one of the nodes of this triangle, for neither the scholar, nor the library nor the university press can solve this problem alone. One alternative has therefore been to focus on the very structures of the university itself in the new digital age.

THE UNIVERSITY

A growing consensus has started to form that these well-known problems might be solved by policies set at the very highest levels of university administration: by deans', provosts', vice-presidents' and presidents' offices. It is, after all, the highest levels of administration that ultimately set the standards for the hiring, tenure and promotion (HTP) of scholars whose work the university presses publish and the libraries acquire, and for the departments who decide on such HTP issues; and it is ultimately the highest levels of administration that provide the policy goals and budgets for all three of these now competing agents.

In real terms the ultimate success of any form of scholarly communication – whether print or digital, whether curatorial, synthetic or analytical – will only be determined by policy decisions that see all three agents as part of a single approach to scholarship and its communication in the digital age in terms of highest quality scholarship; best technology suited to the subject matter and disciplinary approach; its peer review and broader validation; its replicability (both technological and scholarly); its scalability and wide dissemination through consistent standards and methods of publication; and of its accessibility and preservation. But despite a growing consensus on what needs to be done, there have as yet been few such initiatives at the highest levels of university administration.

LEARNED SOCIETIES

Recent attention has focused on whether learned societies – independent associations of scholars – could offer a way to break out of this Bermuda Triangle of scholarly communication. After all, the learned society has been known to offer the best assemblage of forces currently available to resolve many of the issues that concern the humanities. Michael Brintnall, former executive director of the American Political Science Association (APSA), has noted that because learned societies fulfill an essential role in the society as a whole, they are given autonomy and freedom to form and regulate themselves. As scholars, humanists enjoy a privileged position to create their own associations in exchange for the larger service that they provide: the advancement and evaluation of knowledge, whose usefulness can only be determined over time. To accomplish this, the scholarly society possesses a host of valuable assets: self-governance and self-sustainability and a long tradition of expert peer review. The learned society's independence from the university department, the library and the university press combine with self-financing and sustainability through membership dues and endowments, with the means of production, with a tried-and-true editorial system and with solid collegial alliances to seek innovative paths in scholarly communication.

Unlike the heretofore stalemated situation for the university presses and libraries, within the learned society the very concept of scholarly communication is constantly in flux, evolving to meet the changing needs and constituencies of its membership. The learned society offers a wide spectrum of such communication: everything from the conference panel and paper, to the article, to the online blog, grey publication, to member-mediated databases, bibliographies, image collections, listservs, newsletters, Twitter and Facebook groups that reflect real and core forms of scholarly communication. Most of these forms fall outside the university system and its budget and governance restrictions and lie fully within the purview of the learned society and its members.

But digitization remains virtually unchartered territory in terms of the mission of scholarly societies. There are obvious precedents, many of which we have already discussed in the previous chapters: websites, online delivery of journals and newsletters, wikis, blogs, social networking, online directories of members, online books, bibliographies and links to other online resources. These are all good starts, but where are societies in the digital age in terms of being positioned to fulfill their scholarly role vis-à-vis their memberships? How are their current systems serving the way humanists now do scholarly work? Societies still publish some books and articles in print, but how does a learned society respond to such dramatic digital changes in the field? Does the learned society let other organizations step in to fulfill its own mission? Or does it take strength from the digital turn and develop new ways to manage the digital landscape, to structure it and to communicate it to members? Can they give shape to a cyberinfrastructure for the verbal, visual and material elements of humanists' disciplines and resources, everything from the digital archive to the image collection, the HTML website to the born-digital article and monograph?

Could the learned societies create a framework of tools, publication options and communication venues to make themselves the center of the digital for each discipline or field? This remains one of the chief potentials of the learned society: to effectively marshal and leverage its ability to bring to bear the highest standards of expertise and peer review to the disparate digital resources currently available.

But are the scholarly societies prepared for this mission? Two major issues – aside from the usual ones of inertia and lack of resources – facing humanities societies have begun to emerge. The first, especially among the larger professional societies, such as American Historical Association (AHA), the College Art Association (CAA) and the Modern Language Association (MLA), is the splintering off of more specialized groups – social historians, architectural historians, sculptors or literary theorists, for example – both diminishing the overall effectiveness and influence of the scholarly society and concentrating digital efforts into subsidiary or affiliated groups. Frustration at the pace of digital innovation at one society might spur a subgroup to form a digital organization and to apply for government or private foundation funding outside the contexts of the larger society, thus slowing the pace of innovation even further and diverting needed resources – both financial and human – from digital programs.

Another major trend in learned societies is the offloading of journal and book publishing to larger entities: usually large university or commercial presses. Oxford, Cambridge, California, HighWire, Chicago, Hopkins, Routledge and a host of other publishers now account for an increasing number of scholarly journals. While this can save a society many expenses of staff and scale and broaden out subscription bases while leveling risk cycles, most large publishers, university or commercial, have proven highly risk averse to innovative forms of digital publishing, for many reasons already discussed in the preceding chapters. Authors and editors who had planned innovative digital articles have therefore often been left with a simple, enhanced PDF or a minimally functional HTML version of digital articles that is fit into the simplified coding systems and the least-common denominator publishing strategies of large corporations. For many obvious reasons of finance, staffing, skill levels and structural limitations, many societies find such arrangements well worth the trade-offs. Are other emerging organizations therefore capable of fulfilling the mission of the scholarly society in the digital age?

OUTSIDE ACADEMIA

It is difficult to ignore the fact that the organization of scholarly resources online relies on entities outside the control of the academy.

The best example is Google and other search engines that filter and deliver results based on algorithms with little or no input from academia itself. It is also apparent that the efforts at tool building (see Chapter 5) have also moved outside academia where companies devoted to software development can apply skill, personnel, experience and proven code to multiple problems. These companies have sometimes made these tools available free for academic use without negatively effecting product development or corporate profits. Parallel efforts to fund small-scale tool development within academia have often resulted in duplication of efforts, followed by abandoned projects or products that no longer function on new systems.

Many large-scale content projects have succeeded outside academia. One example here will suffice. Wikipedia, which started in 2001, has more than 4.7 million articles on the English-language site – one of more than 287 editions – 73,000 active editors, 18 billion page views and 500 million unique monthly visitors. It is free. It is reviewed and edited. It is open to contributions from everyone. Scholars, scientists, specialists, hobbyists and fans contribute. When looking for information on Galileo, a student is more likely to start at Wikipedia than, for instance, at the Galileo Project[12] at Rice University, but the Wikipedia article will bring the user to that website and to about twenty-five others as well as almost one hundred resources in print. It is hard to ignore, argue or compete with these sorts of statistics. Most recently a series of "edit-a-thons"[13] have used crowdsourcing and other collaborative methods to create, edit and curate new content on the Wikipedia site with the active participation of academics. They have also set out to correct gender and other imbalances among topics and contributors. Such efforts bridge the gap between academia and the public in both creation and reception and may point toward one way of breaking down old walls.

More broadly, as academic humanists turn more and more to questions and concerns of interest only to themselves and a handful of other humanists (and tenure committees), have the humanities as a whole already begun to move beyond the academy? When the most profound – and widely discussed – reflections on the past come to us through film, television, websites and popular fiction and nonfiction books, have the academic humanities lost their hold on the public? Simultaneously is the digital freeing the humanities from the monopoly of academia? Are the digital humanities only a small subset of a vastly larger transformation that has already taken place outside academia? Are academic humanities a footnote to the vast digitization – and oftentimes concomitant com- modification – of information?

In addition to the challenges of building a cyberinfrastructure for digital scholarly communication, there is also an important opportu- nity, one of the most profound possible outcomes of this new digital turn of the humanities. This is the chance that the digital provides for humanists to reengage with a broader public in an effort to col- lectively understand our past and point toward our future. Are most academic humanists ready to embrace it? Or will the survival of the historical humanities as a force in our culture and intellectual life require their divorce from the academy, and has the digital already begun the separation?

Epilogue: The Half-Life of Wisdom

⌇

In the Werner Herzog film, *Cave of Forgotten Dreams*,[1] investigators examine the cave of Chauvet in southern France where they discovered what proved to be the oldest cave art known, dating from thirty-two thousand years ago. The cave's mouth had been closed by a landslide about twenty thousand years ago; and so the exquisite paintings of horses, rhinos, ibex, bison, mastodons, lions and bears remained pristine through the millennia. The cave was closed to the public immediately so that scientific analysis by archaeologists, paleontologists, art historians and computer scientists could begin. A detailed three-dimensional digital map covering every point of the cave was created and has become the standard reference point for all further investigators. Radio carbon analysis traced various painting campaigns over the cave's long use, and very careful, if old-fashioned, visual analysis also identified one of the cave's painters: the six-foot-tall, probable male with the crooked pinky finger who left his positive hand prints throughout the cave's chambers.

One of the most intriguing sequences in the film was the brief discussion of how one set of paintings was revisited and overdrawn with another set of images that enhanced the first. This second painter used the same techniques, at the same spot – but five thousand years later. The brief mention was astounding: what kind of cultural memory would have to be enshrined in physical retracing, mapping, secret sharing, ritual initiation, artistic tradition, song, dance or other cultural referents so that one could retrace the steps of long-dead ancestors during a time when most life spans must have been little more than a single human generation? We know that Australian Aboriginals have handed down similar memories and artistic traditions, and we do have some idea of the methods by which such deep cultural memory is transmitted in both spiritual and physical memory.

But think of this in contrast with our own civilization's cultural memory. Of course we do gather and preserve the deep records of ancient, long destroyed civilizations. That is the job of the historian, archaeologist and art historian. But that is precisely the point: to record the remains of long-destroyed civilizations, to gather the fragments of the past. Quite different was the cultural enterprise of these cave painters who preserved a living form that went beyond heritage and made the past alive in the present and the present a continuation of the past. As an Aboriginal artist told one investigator, it was not he who was retouching the fading art of his ancestors but their own spirit actively working through him.

What is the cultural half-life of wisdom in our own civilization? Presentism, education for the job market, the increasingly ephemeral nature of contemporary arts driven by technology, finance and theory privilege the new and the changing, as do our commercial, consumption-driven lives. Our arts and our thought reflect our material culture as surely as the unchanging artistic modes of thirty-two thousand years ago reflected a world where cycles replaced change and wisdom lived on through the collective traditions of peoples and was made manifest in the bodies – the hearts, hands and eyes – of individuals.

The very first humanists who wrote of themselves – Petrarch and followers – shared the same sense of the past living again through them: through their pens, their brushes and their buildings. When Petrarch conversed with Cicero through his letters, or later when Machiavelli did the same with other ancients, alone in their studies as they contemplated the world of power and politics, they were creating both a highly self-conscious literary conceit and what for them was a true engagement with a living tradition. "Living" not in the sense that we use this flippant cliché, but in a sense far more akin to that of the second cave artist or Aboriginals: the spirit of the past actually – literally – living through us. The humanism that these first generations brought to the forefront of Western culture retained this sense of living recreation of the past. In their Latin style and their new works and editions, humanists saw themselves as enshrining and carrying forward the spirit of the past as their very present and devoted themselves to uncovering the traces of this past so that they too could retrace, overdraw the living work of their ancestors. As much as we like to claim that Petrarch was the "first modern man of letters," he was perhaps one of last of the premoderns who lived fully conscious of the same sorts of cultural memories of the ancient past as *present* that kept alive the Chauvet paintings for millennia.

When humanist architects rediscovered and reused the forms and materials of ancient Rome in their new churches, palaces and public buildings, they consciously set out to recreate not mere formal styles but the spirit of the past that spoke through formerly mute stones. A Renaissance procession flowing through the triumphal spaces of St. Peter's Basilica was not merely carrying on ancient religious tradition but reenacting the triumphs of the Roman emperors and high priests. Raphael's placing his philosophers and religious leaders of *The School of Athens* into the very same architectural setting as the new St. Peter's was not merely following or improving on a Renaissance form book: he was offering the metadata of stone and space to his proposition that the thinkers and artists of his own time were reliving and reviving the spirit and wisdom of antiquity. The humanities were born of this sense, not only of recapturing but of reliving the past and attaining both its formal and its moral content. They made literature, history and the arts a virtual replication of the past in order for citizens of the present to actually feel and think like the ancients. Grace and will could span the centuries of darkness dividing the modern from the ancient worlds of forebears.

What then do we make of the humanities in the digital age? We have accumulated and can now analyze millions of pieces of information, and we call it knowledge. But what is now the half-life of wisdom when all our works come and go through the ether and have abandoned materiality and the body, when individuality and corporality are disappearing from our discourse, our methods of communication? What remains of our deepest cultural memory, when our methods of recording our digital dreams become obsolete within a decade, when our words, our images and songs leave the confines of both time and space, when we have replaced the recognizable digit of that cave painter's handprints – his twisted pinky – with the utterly interchangeable "o" and "1" digits of the computer? How then do the humanities, born of a generation's desire to live the past through their bodies – their hands, eyes, breath – remain truly human?

What does it mean in our own age to create the renewed person of whom Petrarch and the first humanists spoke? What is our postmodern equivalent of the spiritual renewal achieved through the rigorous application of our ancient, inherited learning and wisdom? Are we now merely information hunters and gatherers, as some cutting-edge digital theorists would assert? Or do we humanists seek an ideal through a new model of citizenship: a spiritual opening to the world and creation? Are

there modern equivalents of these historical models in our digitally satu-
rated culture? Are the humanities and such questions still relevant?

We are now living at the outset of the semantic web when the digital
has replaced not only the publisher and the library but now promises to
remove the author herself from the dynamic of what we have come to see
as humanistic discourse. Will the digital humanities become what some
specialists have long hoped for and planned: a dead corpus subjected
to the analysis of various computer processes, mined and harvested for
computational studies and mind-sets? If indeed our answer is that, yes,
the digital humanities are nothing more than a narrow set of academic
specializations and methodologies, are academic life and the humanities still a useful and creative marriage? If, however, the humanities,
even in the digital age, remain a path toward freeing and renewing the
spirit, then perhaps Petrarch's own contempt for the "Schoolmen" must
also guide a new humanist movement in the twenty-first century, and
this movement must be supported and spread by our new digital technologies, but outside the university and its increasingly self-referential
rewards system.

Will humanistic studies become like the dead and mute bones strewn
across the floor of Chauvet: distant memories of life inhabiting a sacred
space and time, now carefully pried out of context and studied as artifacts? Or will there remain the hope that these dry bones shall live, that
the spirits of our ancestors will again speak through us, lead our hands,
our eyes and our breath to rediscover the wisdom of the past and make
it live again? The humanities are nothing if not born of humanity's past,
to explain to us what it is to be human now, to lead us to imagine what it
might mean to be even more fully human in the future.

Appendix: Digital Tools

As we have stressed throughout this book, most humanists continue to use a limited tool kit of digital tools for most work in their disciplines and research agendas. As the corpus of digital work grows and potential and expectations begin to evolve, the importance of many of the tools in this section will become increasingly acknowledged. The following list is not meant to be complete or exhaustive and does not imply any recommendation on the part of the authors. However, it is a detailed sampling of what was available and supported at the time of writing. In terms of testing, in most cases we have verified only that the websites were still functioning and the products still available. The descriptions are taken from the product information available online. DiRT[1] (digital research tools), TAPoR (Text Analysis Portal for Research)[2] and SPARC (Scholarly Publishing and Academic Resources Coalition)[3] have been major resources used to identify these tools. While most tools listed have been put into single categories, many perform multiple functions in addition to the one assigned here.

1. 3D MODELING AND PRINTING

3DCrafter (http://amabilis.com/products) is a real-time 3D modeling and animation tool that incorporates an intuitive drag-and-drop approach to 3D modeling.

After Effects (http://www.adobe.com/products/aftereffects.html) is digital motion graphics and compositing software from Adobe that allows users to animate, alter and composite media in 2D and 3D space with various built-in tools and third-party plug-ins.

Amira (http://www.vsg3d.com/amira/overview) is a multifaceted tool that allows for integration, manipulation and visualization of large sets of data. Automatic and interactive segmentation tools support processing of 3D image data.

Art of Illusion (http://www.artofillusion.org) is a free, open-source 3D modeling and rendering studio.

Autodesk 3ds Max (formerly 3D Studio MAX, http://www.autodesk .com/products/autodesk-3ds-max/overview) is an open-source graphics software tool for modeling and animation projects.

Blender (http://www.blender.org) is a free and open-source 3D animation suite. It supports the entirety of the 3D pipeline: modeling, rigging, animation, simulation, rendering, compositing and motion tracking, even video editing and game creation.

BRL-CAD (http://brlcad.org) is a cross-platform, open-source, solid modeling system that includes interactive geometry editing, high-performance ray-tracing for rendering and geometric analysis, image and signal-processing tools, a system performance analysis benchmark suite and libraries for robust geometric representation.

netfabb Basic and Professional (http://www.netfabb.com) provide mesh edit, repair and analysis capabilities for 3D-printing data.

OpenSCAD (http://www.openscad.org) is a free software application available for Linux/UNIX, Windows and Mac OS X for creating solid 3D CAD models.

SketchUp (http://www.sketchup.com) is a free 3D modeling and image editing software tool.

Tinkercad (https://www.tinkercad.com) is a tool for creating digital designs that are ready for 3D printing into physical objects.

TurnTool (http://www.turntool.com) is a suite of web-based tools that enable 3D models to be created and viewed in a low-bandwidth environment.

Wings 3D (http://www.wings3d.com) is a free, open-source set of modeling tools with a customizable interface, support for lights and materials and a built-in AutoUV mapping facility.

2. AUDIO AND VIDEO PROCESSING

Advene (http://liris.cnrs.fr/advene) is a free, cross-platform application from the LIRIS Laboratory at the University of Lyon for creating comments on and analyses of video documents through the definition of time-aligned annotations and their mobilization into automatically generated or user-written comment views (HTML documents).

Anvil (http://www.anvil-software.org) is a free video annotation tool.

EchoDamp (http://echodamp.com) is a free, multiplatform, multi-channel audio mixer and echo controller designed primarily for the high-bandwidth musical video-teleconference environment.

ELAN (http://tla.mpi.nl/tools/tla-tools/elan) is a free, multiplatform tool from the Max Planck Institute for Psycholinguistics for creating annotations on multiple layers of audio and video resources.

Final Cut Pro (http://www.apple.com/final-cut-pro) is a Mac software application for video organization and processing.

Pro Tools (http://www.avid.com/US/products/family/Pro-Tools) is a collection of proprietary software packages for composing, recording, editing and mixing music or sound for pictures and video.

ScreenFlow (http://www.telestream.net/screenflow/overview.htm) is screen recording and editing software for the Mac that facilitates recording, editing and sharing of audio and video.

Screenr (http://www.screenr.com) is a free web-based screen recording program for creating and sharing screencasts on the web.

Snagit (http://www.techsmith.com/snagit.html) is a screencasting and image-capture tool.

Vertov (http://digitalhistory.concordia.ca/vertov), from the Concordia University Digital History Lab, is a free, multiplatform media annotating plug-in for Zotero that allows cutting audio and video files into clips, annotating the clips and integrating annotations with other research sources and notes stored in Zotero.

VideoANT (http://ant.umn.edu), from the University of Minnesota, is a free online environment that synchronizes web-based video with timeline-based annotations.

3. BLOGGING

Blogger (https://www.blogger.com) is free blog publishing software from Google.

Edublogs (http://edublogs.org) is free cloud hosting for educational WordPress sites with an option for a simplified interface.

LiveJournal (http://www.livejournal.com) is a free blogging/personal journal platform.

Open Attribute (http://wordpress.org/plugins/openattribute-for-wordpress and https://chrome.google.com/webstore/search/openattribute) is a suite of tools for adding licensing information to WordPress sites and Google blogs.

Open Salon (http://open.salon.com/cover) by Salon is a simple, plain blog service focused on content rather than design and features.

Squarespace (http://www.squarespace.com/stories) is a cloud-based blogging platform for setting up a blog or a full website that can be managed remotely with interfaces for designing, customizing and personalizing a blog without programming language.

Tumblr (https://www.tumblr.com) is a free blogging/microblogging platform with a focus on data sharing between individual blogs.

Tweetster (http://corybohon.com/tweetster) is a free, web-based plug-in for Omeka and WordPress that allows for automatic tweeting of new additions to Omeka archives or WordPress blogs.

Twitter (https://twitter.com) is free, web-based microblogging software for messages of 140 characters or fewer.

TypePad (http://www.typepad.com) is a commercial blogging platform.

WordPress (http://wordpress.com/website) is a free web publishing platform originally designed around blogging, with many themes and plug-ins for extra functionality.

Zotpress (http://wordpress.org/plugins/zotpress) is a free, web-based application for adding Zotero citations to blogs using in-text citations and bibliographies.

4. BRAINSTORMING

Aeon Timeline (http://www.scribblecode.com) is a multiplatform, temporal entity management program that uses a visual timeline for brainstorming and collecting through input and export.

Basecamp (https://basecamp.com) is multiplatform project-management software for sharing files, messages and task management, including options for daily update e-mails and real-time document editing.

bubbl.us (https://bubbl.us) is a free web-based mind mapping/brainstorming software application.

CMAP (http://cmap.ihmc.us) is a free, web-based application for creating, navigating and sharing concept maps that can be displayed online using HTML and JavaScript.

Coggle (http://coggle.it) is a free, web-based application for structuring information for real-time collaboration.

Exploratree (http://www.exploratree.org.uk) is a free, web-based database of downloadable and editable templates for brainstorming.

FreeMind (http://freemind.sourceforge.net/wiki/index.php/Main_Page) is a free software application for brainstorming and mind mapping.

Instaviz (http://instaviz.com) is an iOS mind-mapping/brainstorming app that transforms sketching into diagrams.

Mindjet MindManager (http://www.mindjet.com/mindmanager) is a Windows-based visual brainstorming software application.

MindMeister (http://www.mindmeister.com) is an inexpensive, web-based brainstorming and mind-mapping tool.

MindMup (http://www.mindmup.com) is a free browser-based brainstorming tool for creating mind maps.

NovaMind (http://www.novamind.com) is multiplatform mind-mapping software.

Padlet (http://padlet.com) is a free online sticky-note tool for collaboration, brainstorming, planning and organizing projects.

Popplet (http://popplet.com) is a free web and iOS mind-mapping and collaborative brainstorming tool.

VUE (Visual Understanding Environment, http://vue.tufts.edu) is a free, web-based application from Tufts University that provides a visual environment for structuring, presenting and sharing digital information.

5. CHARACTER RECOGNITION (*SEE ALSO* MUSIC RECOGNITION)

ABBYY Fine Reader (http://finereader.abbyy.com) is a commercial OCR engine that creates electronic files from scanned documents, PDFs and digital photographs. It operates on Mac and Windows systems and is also available online and as a mobile app.

DocScanner (http://www.docscannerapp.com) is an inexpensive Android and iOS app that uses the built-in cameras of hand-held devices to scan documents, optimize images, perform OCR and create and send PDFs, text files and jpegs.

OmniPage (http://www.nuance.co.uk/for-individuals/by-product/omnipage/index.htm) is a proprietary OCR software that enables text on physical objects to be scanned, processed and exported to a document file format. It runs on both Mac and Windows.

Tesseract (https://code.google.com/p/tesseract-ocr) is a Google-sponsored open-source OCR engine that works on Linux, Windows and Mac OSX and can read a wide variety of image formats and convert them to text in more than sixty languages.

6. COLLABORATION

Co-ment Pro (http://www.co-ment.com) is a free, online text annotation and collaborative writing tool.

Conference Maker (http://editorialexpress.com/conference/confmaker.html) is web-based software for creating programs for international conferences, handling the submission process in a decentralized fashion.

ConfTool (http://www.conftool.net) is a conference management system (free for noncommercial events with fewer than 150 participants) from the University of Hamburg that helps users register participants, submit and review contributions and schedule conference programs.

Edit Flow (http://editflow.org) is a free tool for organizing collaboration within WordPress.

Github (https://github.com) is a free environment for public software code repositories, collaborator management, issue tracking, wikis, downloads, code review and graphs. Private repositories are also available for a monthly fee.

Google Docs (http://docs.google.com) is a free, online environment for editing and sharing documents, spreadsheets, presentations, forms, drawings and tables.

LaTeX Editor (https://www.sharelatex.com) is a text-editing tool for collaborating on shared documents.

nb (http://nb.mit.edu) from the Haystack Group at MIT is a free, online environment for collaboratively annotating PDFs.

Open Conference Systems (OCS, http://pkp.sfu.ca/ocs) is a free, web-based tool, developed by the Public Knowledge Project, for creating a conference website, sending a call for papers, accepting paper and abstract submissions, posting conference proceedings and data sets, registering participants and enabling postconference online discussion.

Participad (http://participad.org) is a free, web-based plug-in, developed by the Roy Rosenzweig Center for History and New Media, that allows multiple people to edit the same WordPress content at the same time.

Pundit (http://www.thepund.it) is a free, web-based semantic annotation and augmentation tool for sharing annotations and collaboratively creating structured knowledge.

Sched (http://sched.org) is a web-based software application for organizing conferences.

SepiaTown (http://sepiatown.com) is a free, web-based cultural history platform that merges photography, geography and technology and that provides a forum for institutions and individuals to share and map historical images.

Snapzen (https://snapzen.com) is a free, Chrome-based tool for collaborating on the information on any web page.

Trello (https://trello.com) is a free, web-based tool for organizing projects.

Yutzu (http://www.yutzu.com) is a free, web-based tool that allows collaborative collecting, sharing and publishing of multimedia content.

7. COMMUNICATION

Doodle (http://www.doodle.com) is a free online scheduling tool to help set up meetings.

Google+ (https://plus.google.com) is a free, web-based, social networking platform that interacts with other Google services.

GoToMeeting (https://www4.gotomeeting.com) is proprietary web-based online meeting, desktop-sharing and video-conferencing software.

Piazza (https://piazza.com) is a free, web-based discussion tool used particularly for course communication.

Skype (http://www.skype.com) is a web application that facilitates free voice and video computer-to-computer calls (with calls to phone numbers for a fee).

Wiggio (http://wiggio.com) is a free, web-based service that allows users to create groups, host virtual meetings and conference calls, manage events, create to-do lists, poll members, send messages and upload and manage folders.

8. DATA ANALYSIS

ANTHROPAC (http://www.analytictech.com/anthropac/apacdesc.htm) is a free DOS program for collecting and analyzing data on cultural domains. The program assists with the collection and analysis of structured qualitative and quantitative data and provides analytical and multivariate tools.

ATLAS.ti (http://www.atlasti.com/index.html) is a software application for analyzing phenomena in text and multimedia data.

Bookworm (http://bookworm.culturomics.org) is a web-based application, developed at Harvard University, that visualizes trends in repositories of digitized texts. It has been used in several high-profile projects, including the Library of Congress's Chronicling America collection of historical newspapers (http://chroniclingamerica .loc.gov).

CATMA (http://www.catma.de) is a free text-analysis tool for literary research from the University of Hamburg that also facilitates the collaborative exchange of analytical results using the Internet.

Collin's Parser (http://people.csail.mit.edu/mcollins/code.html) is a free, Windows, Mac and Linux statistical natural language parser for analyzing text to determine its grammatical structure.

cue.language (https://github.com/jdf/cue.language) is a free Java-library application for data analysis and linguistic research with natural language processing abilities.

CulturalAnalytics (http://r-forge.r-project.org/projects/rca) is a free R-based package containing functions for data analysis and visualization.

Cytoscape (http://www.cytoscape.org) is a free platform (Windows, Mac, Linux) for complex network analysis, visualization and annotation.

Data Desk (http://www.datadesk.com/products/data_analysis/datadesk) is a Mac and Windows data visualization and analysis tool.

Dataplot (http://www.itl.nist.gov/div898/software/dataplot/homepage .htm) is a free, public-domain multiplatform (Unix, Linux, Mac OS X, Windows XP/VISTA/7/8) software system for statistical analysis and nonlinear modeling.

Dataverse (http://thedata.org) is a free, open-source application developed at Harvard University to publish, share, reference, extract and analyze research data. This application is being used by the Data Preservation Alliance for the Social Sciences (Data-PASS, http://www.data-pass.org), a partnership of organizations that are archiving, cataloging and preserving social-science research data, such as opinion polls, voting records, surveys on family growth and income, government statistics and indices and geographic information system (GIS) data measuring human activity.

Dedoose (http://app.dedoose.com) is a cross-platform application for quantitatively and qualitatively analyzing text, video and spreadsheet data (analyzing qualitative, quantitative and mixed methods research).

E-Net (https://sites.google.com/site/enetsoftware1) is a free Windows application for analyzing ego (as in individual persons, groups, organizations or whole societies) network data.

Ethno Event Structure Analysis (http://www.indiana.edu/~socpsy/ ESA) is free data analysis Java program for sequential events involving agent, action, object and other event characteristics. This software was used, for example, in John G. Richardson's "Mill Owners and Wobblies: The Event Structure of the Everett Massacre of 1916." *Social Science History* 33 (2009): 183–215.

GeoParser (http://edina.ac.uk/projects/geoxwalk/geoparser.html) is a free web-based text analysis tool developed at the University of Edinburgh. It allows users to upload web pages, text files, metadata records, XML and so forth, which can then be parsed for geographical names. It has been used as part of the Archaeology Data Service (http://archaeologydataservice.ac.uk) at the University of York.

MATLAB (http://www.mathworks.com/products/matlab) is an interactive environment for numerical computation and visualization.

MAXQDA (http://www.maxqda.com) is a tool for qualitative data analysis, evaluation and text analysis.

Minitab (http://www.minitab.com/en-US/products/minitab) is a set of tools for statistical analysis and visualization.

Observer XT (http://www.noldus.com/human-behavior-research/ products/the-observer-xt) is a Windows-based, event-logging software application for the collection, analysis and presentation of observational data.

Philologic (https://sites.google.com/site/philologic3) is a free, full-text search, retrieval and analysis tool with support for TEI-Lite XML/SGML, Unicode encoding, plaintext, Dublin Core/ HTML and DocBook. It was produced by the ARTFL Project of the Department of Romance Languages and Literatures at the University of Chicago.

Publish or Perish (http://www.harzing.com/pop.htm) is a free software program that retrieves and analyzes academic citations.

QDA Miner (http://provalisresearch.com/products/qualitative-d ata-analysis-software) is a commercial software package for the qualitative data analysis used for coding, annotating, retrieving and analyzing collections of texts and images.

Science of Science Tool (Sci², https://sci2.cns.iu.edu/user/index .php) is a free modular tool set supporting temporal, geospatial, topical and network analysis and visualization of data sets at the micro (individual), meso (local) and macro (global) levels. It was developed at the School of Library and Information Science at Indiana University. Although developed as a tool for scientific research, it can also be used for humanities applications.

Siena (http://www.stats.ox.ac.uk/~snijders/siena) is a free package for the statistical analysis of network data – focused on social, not ego, networks – including longitudinal network data, longitudinal data of networks and behavior and cross-sectional network data. RSiena is an R-language package. Both were developed at the Department of Statistics, University of Oxford.

SPSS Statistics (http://www-01.ibm.com/software/analytics/spss/ products/statistics) is a commercial package of software products from IBM for data collection, analysis, reporting and deployment.

StatCrunch (http://www.statcrunch.com) is web-based statistical analysis and data-sharing software from Pearson Education.

SwiftRiver (http://www.ushahidi.com/contribute/swiftriver) is a free, open-source web-based application for real-time filtering, curation and qualitative analysis of social media.

VassarStats (http://vassarstats.net) is a free web-based tool, originally developed at Vassar College, for performing statistical computation. It works with Firefox, Safari and Chrome.

9. DATABASE MANAGEMENT SYSTEMS

FileMaker Pro (http://www.filemaker.com) is a proprietary, cross-platform relational database application.

IBM DB2 (http://www-01.ibm.com/software/data/db2) is a proprietary, cross-platform family of database server products developed by IBM that supports the relational model, with some products extended to support object-relational features and nonrelational structures, such as XML.

LibreOffice Base (https://www.libreoffice.org) is a free, cross-platform open-source office suite, developed by The Document Foundation. In addition to a database, it also includes programs to do word processing, spreadsheets, slideshows, diagrams and math formulae. It is available in 110 languages.

MDID (Madison Digital Image Database, http://sites.jmu.edu/ mdidhelp) is a freely distributed, open-source, digital media management system, developed at James Madison University, offering tools for discovering, aggregating and presenting digital media in a wide variety of learning spaces.

MySQL (http://www.mysql.com) is a free, open-source, cross-platform relational database management system from Sun Microsystems.

Oracle (http://www.oracle.com/us/products/database/overview/ index.html) is a proprietary, object-relational database management system.

PostgreSQL or Postgres (http://www.postgresql.org) is a free, open-source, object-relational database management system (ORDBMS) available for a number of different operating systems. It emphasizes extensibility and standards compliance.

SQLite (http://sqlite.org) is a free, public domain, relational database management system contained in a small C programming library.

SQL Server (http://www.microsoft.com/en-us/sqlserver/default.aspx) is a proprietary relational database management system developed by Microsoft for the Windows platform used primarily to store and retrieve data as requested by other software applications.

10. DATA COLLECTION

Altmetric (http://www.altmetric.com) is a fee-based web app that tracks the conversations around articles online.

Blog Analysis Toolkit (BAT, http://www.ibridgenetwork.org/ university-of-pittsburgh/blog-analysis-toolkit) is a free, web-based system, from the University of Pittsburgh, for capturing, archiving and sharing blog posts.

CoCoCo (http://projects.oucs.ox.ac.uk/runcoco/resources/cococo .html) is a Ruby on Rails web application for collecting, cataloging and assessing the quality of user-submitted text or uploaded-file contributions. The Great War Archive (http://www.oucs.ox.ac.uk/ ww1lit/gwa) was assembled at the University of Oxford using this software.

Constant Contact (http://www.constantcontact.com) is best known as a communications and marketing package, but it also features an easy-to-use survey platform.

Data for Research (DFR, http://dfr.jstor.org) is a free, web-based, text-mining tool for research in JSTOR.

KORA (http://sourceforge.net/projects/kora) is a database-driven, online digital repository that allows institutions to ingest, manage and deliver digital objects and their corresponding metadata.

LimeService (https://www.limeservice.com) is a free, web-based application that enables users to prepare, run and evaluate online surveys in fifty languages.

LimeSurvey (http://www.limesurvey.org) is a free, web-based survey application. Ars Electronica (http://www.aec.at/festival) uses this software to gather feedback from visitors to its annual festival.

Pdf-extract (https://github.com/CrossRef/pdfextract) is an open-source set of tools and libraries from CrossRef for identifying and extracting semantically significant regions of a scholarly journal article or conference proceeding formatted as a PDF.

Polldaddy (https://polldaddy.com) is a web-based poll and survey application. A basic, free package is available, as are several other inexpensive options with additional features.

Sample Size Calculator (http://www.macorr.com/sample-size-calculator.htm) is a free online tool for calculating sample size according to different variables.

Survey Monkey (https://www.surveymonkey.com) is a web-based, survey software application that facilitates the design, collection and analysis phases of surveys. A basic, free package is available, as are several other inexpensive options with additional features.

11. DATA MANAGEMENT (INCLUDING DATA MIGRATION AND DATA STORAGE)

Asset Bank (http://www.assetbank.co.uk) is a digital asset management system for the storage, management and delivery of raster images, audiovisual content, documents and other resources.

DSpace (http://www.dspace.org) is a free, open-source software application for building open digital repositories.

Dundas (http://www.dundas.com/dashboard) is a web-based platform for developing custom interactive dashboards.

Fedora Commons (Flexible Extensible Digital Object Repository Architecture, http://fedora-commons.org) is a free, creative-commons-license set of software tools to migrate, ingest, manage and deliver digital objects.

FieldWorks Data Notebook (http://fieldworks.sil.org) is a free data-management tool developed primarily for managing observations, texts and similar types of data in language and cultural fieldwork.

Google Scholar Citations (http://scholar.google.com/citations) is a free, web-based application that tracks, graphs and computes a user's publication citations.

MicrOsiris (http://www.microsiris.com) is a free Windows-based statistical and data management package that can accept data from Excel. It is derived from a package developed at the University of Michigan.

Netvibes (http://www.netvibes.com) is a web dashboard for connecting, comparing and automating data with options for analytics, tagging, curation, alerts, sentiment analysis and search. Free and paid versions are available.

Open Harvester Systems (OHS, http://pkp.sfu.ca/ohs) is a free metadata indexing system developed by the Public Knowledge Project that facilitates the creation of searchable indexes of metadata from Open Archives Initiative (OAI)-compliant archives.

Qualrus (http://www.ideaworks.com/qualrus) is a commercial qualitative data-analysis tool to manage unstructured data.

Subversion (SVN, http://subversion.apache.org) is a free, multiplatform version control system for controlling and managing multiple versions of data objects.

TerraSurveyor (http://www.dwconsulting.nl/TerraSurveyor.html) is a package for downloading, assembling, enhancing, publishing and saving the geophysical data from a range of instruments. It was designed originally as ArcheoSurveyor to meet the needs of archaeologists.

12. DATA VISUALIZATION

ANNIS3 (http://annis-tools.org) is an open-source, web browser-based search and visualization architecture for complex multilevel linguistic corpora with diverse types of annotation.

Circos (http://circos.ca) is a free, web-based and downloadable (Mac, Windows and Linux) software application for visualizing data and information in a circular layout and creating publication-quality infographics and illustrations.

Gephi (https://gephi.github.io) is free and open-source graphing software for Windows, Mac and Linux that provides an interactive visualization and exploration platform for all kinds of networks and complex systems and dynamic and hierarchical graphs.

Graphviz (http://www.graphviz.org) is free, open-source software for graph visualization, representing structural information as diagrams of abstract graphs and networks.

myHistro (http://www.myhistro.com) is a free iOS and web-based tool for combining maps and timelines into presentations, PDF files, Google Earth format, blogs and websites.

NetDraw (https://sites.google.com/site/netdrawsoftware/home) is a free Windows program for visualizing social network data.

NewRadial INKE (http://inke.acadiau.ca/newradial) is a web-based collaborative visualization tool for annotative commentary and discussion. It is a prototype scholarly edition environment for creating and sharing secondary scholarship relating to primary text databases and archives.

NodeXL (http://nodexl.codeplex.com) is a free, open-source Windows template from Microsoft that works in conjunction with Microsoft Excel to create network graphs.

Processing (http://processing.org) is a free, open-source programming language and environment for people who want to create images, animations and interactions.

Project Quincy (http://projectquincy.org) is a free application that visualizes information about people, places and organizations to trace how social networks and institutions develop over time and through space. It is implemented in the Early American Foreign Service Database (EAFSD, http://www.eafsd.org), which traces the U.S. Foreign Service from the American Revolution (1775) through the establishment of U.S. embassies in South America (1825).

Ptolemaic (http://ptolemaic.lander.edu) is a free Java application developed at Lander University for music visualization and analysis of all types of Western music, including tonal functional analysis, pitch-class set analysis, hierarchical linear analysis, tonal pitch-space analysis and transformation analysis.

Quadrigram (http://www.quadrigram.com) is a tool for data visualization that allows the user to create custom, interactive visualizations along a range of different types of live data.

Silk (http://www.silk.co) is a free platform for visualizing and filtering data from websites.

Statistical Lab (http://www.statistiklabor.de/en) is a free user interface for R from the Free University of Berlin and the University of Vienna designed for statistical analysis and visualization.

Statwing (https://www.statwing.com) is free, web-based data analysis and visualization application.

TimeRime (http://www.timerime.com) is a free web application for creating, viewing and comparing interactive timelines.

Viewshare (http://viewshare.org) is a free web application from the Library of Congress for creating interfaces and visualizations – maps, timelines, facets, tag clouds, histograms and image galleries – of cultural heritage collections.

VisualEyes (http://www.viseyes.org) is a free, web-based tool developed at the University of Virginia for incorporating images, maps, charts, video and data into dynamic visualizations.

visual.ly (http://visual.ly) is free web-based software for creating and sharing infographics and data visualization.

Weave (http://oicweave.org) is a free visualization platform from the University of Massachusetts Lowell.

13. HANDWRITING RECOGNITION

Evernote (http://evernote.com) is free, cloud-based, note-taking software that uses built-in OCR to allow users to take text notes and upload files to attach them to notes. Extra features include offline notebooks, additional storage, embedded PDF search and private and shared notebooks.

14. IMAGE CREATION

Adobe Illustrator (http://www.adobe.com/products/illustrator.html) is a commercial vector-drawing environment.

OmniGraffle (http://www.omnigroup.com) is a Mac-based, graphics editing and styling program for creating flow charts, diagrams and user-interface and user-experience interactions.

Painter 2015 (http://www.painterartist.com/us/product/paint-program) is design software from Corel for Mac and Windows with a focus on drawing, including a variety of tools, textures and media.

15. IMAGE PROCESSING, INCLUDING EDITING,
ANNOTATION AND MARKUP

Aperture (https://www.apple.com/aperture) is a Mac image processing software application for organizing, editing and sharing photos.

Clarify (http://www.clarify-it.com) is a free Mac tool for taking multiple screenshots, annotating them and combining them into a single document.

Clipping Magic (http://clippingmagic.com) is a free image-editing and mark-up software application.

digilib (http://digilib.sourceforge.net/index.html) is a free, open-source image viewing environment for the Internet with elaborate viewing features that enable very detailed work on images.

DM (http://schoenberginstitute.org/dm-tools-for-digital-annotation -and-linking) is an environment for the study and annotation of images and texts and includes a suite of tools for gathering and organizing evidence based in digitized resources. It is hosted at the Schoenberg Institute for Manuscript Studies at the University of Pennsylvania,

FotoFlexer (http://fotoflexer.com) is a free, web-based image-editing application.

GIMP (http://www.gimp.org) is freely distributed software for such tasks as photo retouching, image composition and image authoring. It works on many operating systems, in many languages.

Greenshot (http://getgreenshot.org) is a screenshot software tool for Windows that allows for editing and annotation.

HyperImage (http://www.uni-lueneburg.de/hyperimage/hyperimage/idee_E.htm) is a free platform from Humboldt University, Berlin, and Leuphana University, Lüneburg, that enables the capturing of digital objects, adding of layers, linking, editing of metadata and compiling of annotations.

ImageJ (http://rsb.info.nih.gov/ij/index.html) is a free image-processing program that can display, edit and analyze images and perform simple transformations like scaling and rotating. It runs as an online applet or as a downloadable application.

ImageMagick (http://www.imagemagick.org/script/index.php) is a free software suite to create, edit, compose or convert bitmap images. It can read and write images in a variety of formats.

iPhoto (http://www.apple.com/mac/iphoto) is a Mac application that supports image editing, tagging, display and publication.

Irfanview (http://www.irfanview.com) is a free, Windows-based image viewer and converter with simple editing features.

iShowU Studio (http://www.shinywhitebox.com) is a series of screen and camera image-capture and editing tools for the Mac.

Kaleidoscope (http://www.kaleidoscopeapp.com) is a Mac tool for detecting and comparing differences in images and text.

Mediathread (http://mediathread.ccnmtl.columbia.edu) is a free open-source platform from the Columbia Center for New Media Teaching and Learning (CCNMTL) for the exploration, analysis, annotation and organization of web-based multimedia content.

Photoshop (http://www.adobe.com/products/photoshopfamily.html) is digital-imaging software from Adobe.

Picasa (http://picasa.google.com) is free, simple photo-editing software that integrates with online Picasa Web Albums for photo sharing.

Skitch (http://evernote.com/skitch) is a Mac-based software tool for annotating, editing and sharing images.

SumoPaint (http://www.sumopaint.com) is a web-based image editor with photo editing and drawing features. Sumo Pro is a download-able, subscription-based version.

UVic Image Markup Tool (http://tapor.uvic.ca/~mholmes/image_markup/index.php) is a free tool for describing and annotating images and storing the resulting data in TEI XML files. Runs primarily on Windows but can run on Linux.

XnViewMP (http://www.xnview.com/en/index.php) is a free Windows, Mac and Linux tool for viewing and converting a wide variety of image formats.

Zoomify (http://www.zoomify.com) is a suite of Windows, Mac and Linux products for converting large images into a form that can be zoomed and panned.

16. MAPPING

ArcGIS (http://www.esri.com/software/arcgis) is a suite of soft-ware for building a geographic information system (GIS). It provides tools for creating, editing and analyzing geographic data on the desktop and publishing data, maps, globes and models to a geographic information system (GIS) server or for sharing them online.

BatchGeo (http://batchgeo.com) is a proprietary, web-based tool that converts addresses into coordinates and that maps the results.

Crowdmap (https://crowdmap.com/welcome) is a simple, free map-making tool, built on an open application programming inter-face (API) with cloud storage.

ERDAS Imagine (http://geospatial.intergraph.com/products/ERDASIMAGINE/ERDASIMAGINE/Details.aspx) is a free suite of geospatial authoring tools that perform advanced remote sensing analysis and spatial modeling and also visualize results in 2D, 3D and movies and on cartographic quality map compositions.

GapVis (http://nrabinowitz.github.io/gapvis/#index) is a free, web-based interface for exploring and reading a set of specific uploaded texts, including maps and data visualizations, that reference ancient places.

GeoCommons (http://geocommons.com) is a free, web-based open repository of data and maps that includes a large number of features to easily access, visualize and analyze data.

GeoNames (http://www.geonames.org) is a free, web-based tool for identifying and tagging references to geographical locations. It contains more than eight million entries with the geographic name (in various languages), latitude, longitude, elevation, population, administrative subdivision, postal codes and information on unique features.

Google Maps (https://maps.google.com) is a free, web-based mapping application that facilitates tagging, publishing and sharing maps online.

GPS Visualizer (http://www.gpsvisualizer.com) is a free, easy-to-use online utility that creates maps and profiles from global positioning system (GPS) data.

GRASS GIS (http://grass.osgeo.org), commonly referred to as GRASS (Geographic Resources Analysis Support System), is free, multiplatform, geographic information system (GIS) software for geospatial data management and analysis, image processing, graphics/map production, spatial modeling and visualization.

Kartograph (http://kartograph.org) is a free, web-based framework for building interactive map applications. Kartograph.py is a Python library for generating Illustrator-friendly scalable vector graphics (SVG maps). Kartograph.js is a JavaScript library for creating interactive maps based on Kartograph.py SVG maps.

Leaflet (http://leafletjs.com) is a free, web-based, open-source JavaScript library for creating mobile-friendly interactive maps.

Map Box (https://www.mapbox.com) is a subscription-based, open-source map-building tool.

Maphub (http://maphub.github.io) is a free, web-based application from Cornell Information Science for exploring and annotating digitized, high-resolution historic maps.

Mapline (http://mapline.com) is a free online service for capturing and geocoding spatial data from spreadsheets and creating point, territory and heat maps. There is also a pay version available.

Mapstraction (http://mapstraction.com) is a free, web-based Java-Script mapping abstraction library that supports mapping providers with dynamic switching from one map's application programming interface (API) to another's, showing markers, points, lines and polygons and adding image overlays and base map tiles.

Map Warper (http://mapwarper.net) is a free, open-source, web-based, map-warping, geo-rectifying service supported by the New York Public Library.

Modest Maps (http://modestmaps.com) is a free small, extensible library of tools from the University of California for creating interactive maps.

OpendTect (http://opendtect.org/index.php) is a proprietary, multiplatform software application for analyzing and visualizing multi-volume seismic data. Free and commercial versions are available.

OpenLayers (http://openlayers.org) is a free, web-based, JavaScript library for displaying map tiles and markers from any source.

ORBIS (http://orbis.stanford.edu) is the online Stanford Geospatial Network Model of the Roman World, which includes a free tool for reconstructing the time and expense associated with a wide range of different types of travel in antiquity.

Polymaps (http://polymaps.org) is a free, web-based JavaScript library for making interactive maps in web browsers, providing for the display of multi-zoom data sets over maps and supporting a variety of visual presentations for tiled vector data.

QGIS (QGIS, http://www.qgis.org) is a free, web-based open-source geographic information system (GIS) licensed under the GNU General Public License from the Open Source Geospatial Foundation (OSGeo).

RivEX (http://www.rivex.co.uk) is a proprietary geographic information system (GIS) tool designed to process vector river networks.

TileMill (https://www.mapbox.com/tilemill) is a proprietary, multi-platform, open-source map design studio for creating custom web tile maps that use MapBox's data.

timemap (https://code.google.com/p/timemap) is a free, web-based, JavaScript library for producing web-based maps with timelines.

*Time*Map (http://sourceforge.net/projects/timemap) is a free map-ping application for generating interactive maps. It was developed at the Archaeological Computing Laboratory of the University of Sydney.

UMapper (http://www.umapper.com) is a free/paid, web-based tool for creating embeddable, interactive Flash maps and geo-games from within a browser.

Ushahidi (http://ushahidi.com/products/ushahidi) is a free, web-based, Android/iOS platform for collecting and displaying information with a geographical component. See also **Crowdmap.**

WorldMap (http://worldmap.harvard.edu) is a free web-based mapping tool (a customized version of GeoNode from Harvard College) that allows users to visualize, edit, collaborate and publish geospatial information, either uploaded or from the existing library.

ZeeMaps (http://www.zeemaps.com) is a free, web-based tool for creating custom interactive maps with customized markers that can be embedded into websites.

17. MUSIC RECOGNITION

Aruspix (http://www.aruspix.net) is a software application that acts as a music scanning software for early music prints. It is supported by a grant from the National Endowment for the Humanities and in collaboration with the Music Encoding Initiative (MEI, http://www.music-encoding.org/home). It includes superimposition and collation features to facilitate comparing early music editions and reeditions for compiling comprehensive critical modern editions. One of its major projects is to create the Marenzio Online Digital Edition (MODE, http://www.marenzio.org), a complete critical edition of the secular music of Luca Marenzio (c. 1553–99), one of the most important composers of the European Renaissance.

capella-scan (http://www.capella.de/us/index.cfm/products/capella-scan/info-capella-scan) is scanning software that facilitates the OCR of music scores from PDF or common image formats and outputs the results in MusicXML for use with common music editing software.

SharpEye (http://www.visiv.co.uk) is music scanning/OCR software that can convert an image of a score into an editable format such as MusicXML.

SmartScore (http://www.musitek.com) is a commercial software application for Mac and Windows that takes an image of a music score and converts it into an editable format, including MusicXML.

18. ORGANIZATION

Durationator (http://www.durationator.com) is a free web-based tool that provides information regarding the copyright term of any given cultural work.

Mendeley (http://www.mendeley.com) is a free reference management tool for generating bibliographies, finding and importing papers, accessing them online and collaborating with other researchers online. An iPhone app is available.

Notational Velocity (http://notational.net) is a Mac open-source software application that can search across notes or create and edit notes.

OneNote (http://office.microsoft.com/en-us/onenote) is a Windows-based, digital notebook for gathering notes and information in a central environment and searching across shared notebooks.

Pear Note (http://www.usefulfruit.com/pearnote) is an application that records audio, video, typed notes and slideshows on a timeline.

Pliny (http://pliny.cch.kcl.ac.uk/index.html), from the Center for Computing in the Humanities, King's College London, is free, open-source software for note taking and annotation with tools for incorporating these into a developing interpretation.

Projects (https://projects.ac) is a Mac application for organizing and managing research outputs in a structured way.

Qiqqa (http://www.qiqqa.com) is research management software for organizing large numbers of papers, finding new papers to read, reviewing materials and creating annotation reports.

Scribe (http://echo.gmu.edu/toolcenter-wiki/indexphp?title= Scribe) from the Roy Rosenzweig Center for History and New Media is a free, cross-platform note-taking program for creating, organizing, indexing, searching, linking and cross-referencing research notes, quotes, thoughts, contacts, published and archival sources, digital images, outlines, timelines and glossary entries.

VoodooPad (https://plausible.coop/voodoopad) is a Mac iOS annotation and organization tool for folders, PDF files, applications and URLs with full screen editing and export and search capabilities.

Zotero (http://www.zotero.org), from the Roy Rosenzweig Center for History and New Media, is a free, multiplatform tool for collecting, organizing, citing and sharing research sources.

19. PUBLICATION AND SHARING, INCLUDING WEBSITE DEVELOPMENT

Academia.edu (https://www.academia.edu) is a social networking website for scholars that facilitates sharing papers, monitoring their impact and following research in specific fields.

Annotum (http://annotum.org) is a free, web-based, open-source, open-process, open-access scholarly authoring and publishing platform based on WordPress.

Anthologize (http://anthologize.org) is a free, web-based WordPress plug-in, developed at the Roy Rosenzweig Center for History and New Media, for outlining, ordering and editing content into a single volume that can be exported as PDF, TEI or EPUB.

Bluefish (http://bluefish.openoffice.nl) is a free, multiplatform editing tool for programmers and web designers for dynamic and interactive websites.

Bricolage (http://bricolagecms.org) is an open-source, content management, workflow and publishing system for creating, managing and publishing content.

chronam (https://github.com/libraryofcongress/chronam) is a free, web-based, public domain Django open-source web application developed by the Library of Congress for modeling newspaper data according to a set of technical guidelines to facilitate online publication.

Drupal (https://drupal.org) is an open-source content-management platform for websites and applications.

EPrints (http://www.eprints.org) is a free digital-repository software package, developed at the University of Southampton, that may be used to accept, manage and publish digital objects. It is widely used in academia as a system to manage academic research papers, electronic theses and other distinct digital resources.

ExpressionEngine (http://ellislab.com/expressionengine) is a modular content management system developed by EllisLab with a free "core" version available for personal and nonprofit websites.

Figshare (http://figshare.com) is a free, web-based tool for publishing research outputs, including videos and data sets, in a citable, sharable and discoverable manner.

Flickr (http://www.flickr.com) is an online service developed by Yahoo that enables registered users to upload, tag, group, comment, share and rate photographs, artwork, illustrations, screenshots and videos.

HUBzero (http://hubzero.org) is a web publication platform from Purdue University for research software and educational materials and includes a built-in environment for running software and a tool development area.

InDesign (http://www.adobe.com/products/indesign.html) is a desktop-publishing software application from Adobe for creating periodical publications, posters, flyers, brochures, magazines and books. Files can be exported to EPUB, XML, HTML, Flash and (with a plug-in) Kindle.

Jing (http://www.techsmith.com/jing.html) is a free Windows and Mac application for recording and sharing screenshots and screencasts.

Joomla (http://www.joomla.org) is a free, open-source content management system for building websites and online applications.

Legend Maker (http://www.zapptek.com/legendmaker) is a Mac tool for creating EPUB, MOBI and other e-book formats.

Movable Type (http://www.movabletype.com) is a creation and content management system for websites and blogs.

Omeka (http://www.omeka.org) is a free open-source web publishing platform for the display of library, museum, archival and scholarly collections and exhibitions.

OpenETD (http://rucore.libraries.rutgers.edu/open/projects/openetd) from Rutgers University is an open-source, web-based software application for managing the submission, approval and distribution of electronic theses and dissertations (ETDs).

Open Journal Systems (OJS, http://pkp.sfu.ca/ojs) is a journal management and publishing system that has been developed by the Public Knowledge Project through its federally funded efforts to expand and improve access to research.

Open Monograph Press (OMP, http://pkp.sfu.ca/omp) is a free open-source software platform, developed by the Public Knowledge Project, for managing the editorial workflow for monographs, edited volumes and scholarly editions through internal and external review, editing, cataloguing, production and publication. OMP can operate, as well, as a press website with catalog, distribution and sales capacities.

PressBooks (http://pressbooks.com) is a free, web-based tool for authoring and producing books in multiple formats, including EPUB, Kindle, print-on-demand-ready PDF, HTML and InDesign-ready XML.

Prezi (http://prezi.com) is free, cloud-based presentation software.

QuarkXPress (http://www.quark.com) is desktop publishing software commonly used to create page layouts for a variety of print and digital publications such as books, newspapers, magazines, posters and brochures.

Recollection (http://sourceforge.net/projects/loc-recollect) is a free web application, developed for the Library of Congress, that allows users to create and share embeddable interfaces to digital cultural heritage collections.

ReDBox (Research Data Box, https://sites.google.com/a/redbox researchdata.com.au/public) provides the ability to describe research data and make these descriptions (metadata) available to national/global registers. These registers allow researchers from around the world to locate and access research data.

Roambi Flow (http://www.roambi.com/flow) is an online service for publishing and distributing data in a mobile environment.

Scalar (http://scalar.usc.edu/scalar) is a free, web-based authoring and publishing platform from the Alliance for Networking Visual Culture for writing long-form scholarship online.

Scholastica (https://scholasticahq.com) is a web-based tool for journal collaboration, management and publication.

Sigil (https://github.com/user-none/Sigil) is a free, WYSIWYG, open-source, multiplatform XML-based EPUB editor for creating e-books.

Sophie (http://sophie2.org/trac) is an electronic tool from the Institute for the Future of the Book for authoring, collaborating, reading and publishing rich media documents in networked environments.

Storify (http://storify.com) is a free, web-based application for collecting, arranging and editing social media to create stories.

StoryKit (https://itunes.apple.com/us/app/storykit/id329374595) is a free iOS app from the International Children's Digital Library for creating electronic storybooks.

Substance Composer (http://substance.io/composer) is a free, web-based document authoring and publishing platform for the web.

Tackk (http://tackk.com) is a free, web-based service for publishing content on the web.

WebSlides (http://slides.diigo.com/help.html) is a free, web-based application for converting bookmarks and feeds to present them as live web pages in an interactive slideshow.

Wink (http://www.debugmode.com/wink) is a free Windows and Linux tutorial- and presentation-creation application that captures screenshots, mouse movements and accompanying audio.

Yana (https://osc.hul.harvard.edu/yana), from Harvard University, provides a free, open-source template that open-access journals can use as the basis of their own multiplatform mobile applications.

20. PEER REVIEWING

BenchPress (http://highwire.org/publishers/benchpress.dtl) from HighWire is an online manuscript management system that includes the facilitation of peer review. It is customizable for each journal and will generate reports and statistics on the editorial process. It can prepare manuscripts for print or online publication.

Commentpress Core (http://wordpress.org/plugins/commentpress -core) is a free, web-based, open-source plug-in for WordPress developed by the Institute for the Future of the Book. It enables granular public commenting on texts.

Digress.it (http://digress.it) is a free WordPress plug-in for paragraph-level commenting in the margins of a text and can be used collaboratively for blog-style comment threads off individual paragraphs.

EdiKit (http://www.bepress.com/aboutbepress.html) is a web-based management system from Berkeley Electronic Press for all aspects of the editorial process for print or online journals, dissertations, monographs and conference proceedings. It handles from submission to e-publication, including reviewer identification and tracking, correspondence management and reminders, revisions and resubmits, publication layout and oversight of multiple issues.

Editorial Manager (http://www.editorialmanager.com/homepage/ home.htm) is an online manuscript submission and tracking system. It provides a suite of customizable manuscript tracking and reporting tools for authors, reviewers, editors and journal office staff from submission to peer review and production.

EPRESS (http://www.epress.ac.uk) from the University of Surrey is an online manuscript tracking and journal production system that provides access to reports on the process. It was funded by JISC's Electronic Libraries Programme (eLib).

Open Journal Systems (http://pkp.sfu.ca/ojs) is an open-source journal management and publishing software system developed by the Public Knowledge Project for each stage of the refereed publishing process.

PaperCritic (http://www.papercritic.com) is a free, web-based open peer review tool for items with Mendeley, a reference manager and academic social network.

Scholarly Exchange (http://www.scholarlyexchange.org) is a free e-publishing platform that combines Open Journal Systems public-domain software with hosting and support to produce academic journals priced to foster open access. It offsets costs with on-screen advertising.

ScholarOne (http://scholarone.com) provides comprehensive workflow management for journals, books and conferences.

Scholastica (https://scholasticahq.com) is a cloud-based journal management platform that includes built-in analytics, file versioning, integrated e-mail, customizable reviewer feedback forms, customer support and single/double peer review blindness.

21. SEARCHING (INCLUDING VISUAL SEARCHING)

Bing (http://www.bing.com) is a free search engine from Microsoft.

Carrot2 (http://search.carrot2.org) is a free, open-source search-results clustering engine that automatically organizes small collections of documents into categories.

Cluuz (http://www.cluuz.com) is a free search engine that shows links to related pages, as well as entities and images that are extracted from within the search results, and displays a tag cloud of the most relevant entities from returned results, as well as a semantic graph view of a cluster of terms.

Gnod (http://www.gnod.net) is a free cultural search tool that generates search results for books, music, movies and people in floating tag clouds.

Google (https://www.google.com) is the free web browser that dominates the U.S. market.

Kartoo (http://www.kartoo.com) is a free search engine that works across many different languages.

Yahoo! (http://search.yahoo.com) is the free web browser that is second behind Google in the U.S. market.

22. SPEECH RECOGNITION

Dragon Dictate (http://www.nuance.com/for-individuals/by-product/dragon-for-mac/index.htm) supports a variety of audio file formats to allow automatic speech-recognition-based transcription from spoken-word audio recordings made on Mac, iPhone and digital recorders.
Voxcribe (http://www.voxcribe.com) uses speech recognition software to provide an editable basic text of audio or video files. It is a commercial product that operates on the Windows platform.

23. SPEECH TO TEXT TRANSCRIPTION

EXMARaLDA (Extensible Markup Language for Discourse Annotation, http://www.exmaralda.org/en_index.html) includes a suite of tools for the computer-assisted transcription and annotation of spoken language and for the construction and analysis of spoken-language corpora.
Express Scribe Transcription Software (http://www.nch.com.au/scribe/index.html) facilitates the transcription of a wide variety of audio and video file formats (mp3, .mov or .wav) without alternating between an audio player and a text editor. Working on both Mac and Windows platforms, it features variable speed playback, multi-channel control, playing video and file management.
F4 (http://www.audiotranskription.de/f4.htm) is a commercial transcription tool for audio or video recordings.
InqScribe (http://www.inqscribe.com) is commercial transcription and subtitling software for Mac and Windows.
Scripto (http://scripto.org) integrates crowdsourcing with transcription, allowing multiple users to transcribe files. The downloadable program is free and open source. The Papers of the War Department 1784–1800 (http://wardepartmentpapers.org/transcribe.php) uses Scripto as the basis for its crowdsourcing transcription endeavor.
Soundscriber (http://www-personal.umich.edu/~ebreck/code/sscriber) is a free Windows-based software application for transcribing digitized sound files. It was originally developed for the Michigan Corpus of Academic Spoken English (MICASE) project.

Transana (http://www.transana.org/about/index.htm) is a fee-paid, computer program from the University of Wisconsin, Madison for transcribing and analyzing large collections of video and audio data.

Transcribe (https://transcribe.wreally.com) is a browser-based writing environment that is tightly integrated with an audio player and allows users to transcribe audio in a single screen without switching between a media-player and a text editor. Works with Google Chrome.

Transcriber (http://sourceforge.net/projects/trans/files) is open-source software for the transcription and qualitative analysis of audio and video.

Transcriva (http://www.bartastechnologies.com/products/transcriva) is a fee-paid, transcription software for audio and video files on the Mac.

VoiceWalker (http://www.linguistics.ucsb.edu/projects/transcription/tools) is a free download, available for Windows only, that plays back sound in a controlled way, with the benefit of being able to systematically step (or "walk") through a recording while transcribing. It is a project of the Department of Linguistics, University of California, Santa Barbara.

Text Analysis, *See* 17. Text Mining

24. TEXT ANNOTATION

AGTK: Annotation Graph Toolkit (http://agtk.sourceforge.net) is a free framework for representing linguistic annotations of time series data.

A.nnotate.com (http://a.nnotate.com) is a free, web-based annotation tool for documents and images.

Annotator (http://annotatorjs.org) is a free, open-source JavaScript library for website developers to facilitate page content annotation.

Brat Rapid Annotation Tool (http://brat.nlplab.org) is a free, online environment for collaborative text annotation, including entity mention detection, event extraction, coreference resolution, chunking, dependency syntax, meta-knowledge and corpora annotation.

Domeo Annotation Toolkit (http://swan.mindinformatics.org) is a free, extensible web application for creating and sharing ontology-based, stand-off annotation on HTML or XML document targets.

iAnnotate (http://www.branchfire.com/iannotate) is an iOS tool for reading, marking up and sharing PDFs, Word documents, PowerPoint files and images.

Skim (http://skim-app.sourceforge.net) is a Mac OSX PDF reader and note-taking software.

TILE (Text-Image Linking Environment, http://mith.umd.edu/tile) is a web-based tool for creating and editing image-based electronic editions and digital archives of humanities texts. It is a project of the Maryland Institute for Technology in the Humanities (MITH) and Indiana University.

UAM CorpusTool (http://www.wagsoft.com/CorpusTool/contact .html) is a free multiplatform tool for annotating a corpus as part of a linguistic study.

WebLicht (http://clarin-d.net/index.php/en/language-resources/ weblicht-en) is a web-based tool from the German Federal Ministry for Research and Education to semiautomatically annotate texts for linguistics and humanities research.

Wmatrix (http://ucrel.lancs.ac.uk/wmatrix) is web-based software for corpus analysis and comparison providing a web interface to other corpus annotation tools and standard corpus linguistic methodologies, such as frequency lists and concordances.

WordFreak (http://sourceforge.net/projects/wordfreak) is a free, multiplatform, Java-based linguistic annotation tool designed to support human and automatic annotation of linguistic data.

Word Hoard (http://wordhoard.northwestern.edu/userman/index .html) is a free, text-annotation software tool from Northwestern University.

25. TEXT CONVERSION AND ENCODING

Abbot (https://github.com/CDRH/abbot) is a tool for undertaking large-scale conversion of XML document collections in order to make them interoperable.

Markdown (http://daringfireball.net/projects/markdown) is a free text-to-XHTML or text-to-HTML conversion tool.

Online-Convert (http://document.online-convert.com) is a free online converter that will convert documents to doc, docx, FLASH, HTML, ODT, PDF, RFT and txt formats.

TEI Boilerplate (http://dcl.slis.indiana.edu/teibp) is a free conversion application from Indiana University that converts styled TEI P5 material into documents that are simplified for browser delivery by using the built-in XSLT capabilities of browsers to embed the TEI XML, with minimal modifications, within an HTML5 shell document. It is used in the Algeron Charles Swinburne Project (http://webapp1.dlib.indiana.edu/swinburne). It works on Windows, Mac and Linux and depends on Firefox, Chrome, Safari and Internet Explorer 9 browsers.

Text Fixer (http://www.textfixer.com) is a free, web-based converter for .doc or .docx files to HTML.

TextPipe (http://www.datamystic.com/textpipe.html) is a commercial application from Datamystic that makes it possible on a single workbench to quickly transform, convert, clean and extract data from large documents in a wide variety of text formats.

Word2cleanHTML (http://word2cleanhtml.com) is a free, web-based converter for Word files to HTML. It also includes some automatic editing features to clean the HTML.

26. TEXT EDITING AND PROCESSING

Classical Text Editor (http://cte.oeaw.ac.at) is a fee-based, Windows word processor for critical editions, commentaries and parallel texts developed by the CSEL (Corpus Scriptorum Ecclesiasticorum Latinorum) at the University of Salzburg. It facilitates publication by generating camera-ready copy or electronic files.

Editors' Notes (http://editorsnotes.org) from the Electronic Cultural Atlas Initiative at the University of California, Berkeley, is an open-source, web-based tool for recording, organizing, preserving and opening access to research notes.

elaborate (https://www.elaborate.huygens.knaw.nl/login) is a free, online tool developed at the Huygens Instituut of the Royal Netherlands Academy of Arts and Sciences for the preparation of digital text editions, using Google Chrome and Mozilla Firefox.

GATE (General Architecture for Text Engineering, https://gate .ac.uk), from the University of Sheffield, is a free multiplatform framework for text processing and annotation.

Mellel (https://itunes.apple.com/us/app/mellel/id415467848) is a Mac-based word processor for long and complicated documents, such as books, manuscripts and dissertations.

NoodleTools (http://www.noodletools.com) is a suite of integrated tools for note taking, outlining, citation, document archiving/annotation and collaborative research and writing.

OpenOffice (http://www.openoffice.org/product/index.html) is a free, multiplatform, open-source office software suite for word processing, spreadsheets, presentations, graphics and databases.

Scrivener (http://www.literatureandlatte.com/scrivener.php) is software for writing long, complex documents and includes virtual index cards, outlining, version control, import/export options and scriptwriting features.

TextExpander (http://smilesoftware.com/TextExpander/index.html) is a Mac application for customizing abbreviations and inserting "snippets" for frequently used text strings or images.

VARD 2 (http://ucrel.lancs.ac.uk/vard/about) is a free, multiplatform application to assist with spelling variation in historical corpora, particularly in Early Modern English texts. It is designed as a preprocessor to other corpus linguistic tools.

WorkTop (http://cs.brown.edu/research/ptc/worktop/about.html) is a free, integrated environment developed by Brown University for capturing, displaying and linking heterogeneous documents or document fragments, including images, videos, notes, PDFs and web pages.

WriteRoom (http://www.hogbaysoftware.com/products/writeroom) is a full-screen writing environment for the Mac.

Text Encoding, *See* **25. Text Conversion and Encoding**

27. TEXT MINING OR TEXT-DATA MINING OR TEXT ANALYSIS

Claws Tagger (http://ucrel.lancs.ac.uk/claws) is a multiplatform parts-of-speech (POS) tagging software developed by the University Centre for Computer Corpus Research on Language (UCREL) at the University of Lancaster.

Collation Works (http://interedition-tools.appspot.com) is a free, web-based text collation tool.

Concordance (http://www.concordancesoftware.co.uk) is Windows proprietary software for performing text analysis and concordance.

DocumentCloud (http://www.documentcloud.org/home) is a free, multiplatform, web-based service for searching and analyzing primary sources, featuring highlighting, annotation and document sharing.

Juxta (http://juxtacommons.org) is a free online tool for comparing
and collating versions of the same textual work. It was developed by
NINES at the University of Virginia.

Lexomics (http://wheatoncollege.edu/lexomics) is a free, downloadable tool developed at Wheaton College for the analysis of the
frequency, distribution and arrangement of words in large-scale patterns. This tool works optimally on Old English and Latin texts but
can be used for others as well. An online tool, Lexos, helps with text
management.

LIWC Linguistic Inquiry and Word Count (http://www.liwc.net/
index.php) is a text analysis software program that calculates the
degree to which people use different categories of words across a
wide array of text, including e-mails, speeches, poems or transcribed
daily speech.

MALLET (http://mallet.cs.umass.edu/index.php) is free, open-
source software, developed at UMass Amherst, for statistical natural language processing, document classification, clustering, topic
modeling, information extraction and other machine learning
applications to text.

Meld (http://meldmerge.org) is a free tool that works on Mac and
Windows to compare files, directories and version-controlled projects with two- and three-way comparison.

Pattern (http://www.clips.ua.ac.be/pages/pattern) is a free
(Windows, Mac and Linux) Python, web-mining module with tools
for data retrieval, text analysis and data visualization from CLiPS
(Computational Linguistics & Psycholinguistics), a research center
associated with the Linguistics Department of the Faculty of Arts of
the University of Antwerp.

PDFMiner (http://www.unixuser.org/~euske/python/pdfminer/
index.html) is a free Python tool for extracting information about
text, fonts, encoding and layout from PDFs.

Prism (http://prism.scholarslab.org) is a free online tool for crowdsourcing the interpretation and visualization of variant readings
of texts.

SAS Analytics (http://www.sas.com/technologies/analytics) is an
environment for predictive and descriptive modeling, data mining,
text analytics, forecasting, optimization, simulation, experimental
design and other statistical functions.

SEASR (http://www.seasr.org) is free, open-source mining software, developed at the University of Illinois, that enables visualization, adjustment, querying and validation of text and data.

TAPoR Portal (http://tada.mcmaster.ca/Main/TAPoR) is an online environment developed at McMaster University for textual analysis.

Tesserae (http://tesserae.caset.buffalo.edu/index.php), from the University at Buffalo's Department of Classics and Department of Linguistics and the VAST Lab of the University of Colorado at Colorado Springs, provides a free web interface for exploring intertextual parallels.

Textalyser (http://textalyser.net) is a free, online text tool that provides detailed statistics of text, including word-group analysis, keyword density and word or expression prominence.

textpresso (http://www.textpresso.org) is a free, text-mining system, from the California Institute of Technology, designed for scientific literature.

Text Variation Explorer (TVE, http://www.uta.fi/sis/tauchi/virg/projects/dammoc/tve.html) is a free, interactive Java tool from the University of Tampere for exploring linguistic measures.

Topic Modeling Tool (http://code.google.com/p/topic-modeling-tool) is a graphical user interface tool for topic modeling.

TXM (http://sourceforge.net/projects/txm) is a free and open-source, cross-platform Unicode-XML-TEI-based text/corpus analysis environment.

Voyant (http://voyeurtools.org) is a free, web-based, text-analysis environment for user-uploaded text.

Weka (http://www.cs.waikato.ac.nz/ml/weka) is a free, web-based collection of machine learning algorithms from the University of Waikato for data mining tasks. It includes tools for data preprocessing, classification, regression, clustering, association rules and visualization.

28. TEXT TO TEXT TRANSCRIPTION

Crowdcrafting (http://crowdcrafting.org) is a free, open-source platform for creating and running crowdsourcing applications for image classification, transcription, geocoding and so forth.

FromThePage (http://beta.fromthepage.com) is free software for crowdsourced transcriptions of online, handwritten documents. Southwestern University is using this application for transcribing the Mexican War Diary of Zenas Matthews (http://beta.fromthepage .com/ZenasMatthews).

Proofread Page (https://www.mediawiki.org/wiki/Extension:Proof read_Page), a free extension for MediaWiki, facilitates editing OCR'd transcriptions side by side with the original page images.

T-PEN (Transcription for Paleographical and Editorial Notation, http://t-pen.org/TPEN) is an extensive set of web-based tools that allow collaborative transcription of manuscript pages in TEI-compliant XML. It now contains more than four thousand manuscripts. The Center for Digital Theology at Saint Louis University makes this collaboration tool available free. There are currently, for instance, almost 450 medieval manuscripts from the Houghton Library at Harvard University available at T-PEN for transcription.

Transcript 2.4 (http://www.jacobboerema.nl/en/Freeware.htm) is a Windows program designed to help transcribe the text on digital images of documents. It is free for private, noncommercial use.

29. TEXT VISUALIZATION

Leximancer (https://www.leximancer.com) is text analysis software that can create topic- and concept-based network visualizations. It includes a sentiment analyzer.

Lexipedia (http://www.lexipedia.com) is a free, online metadictionary displaying a semantic map of parts of speech related to the word of inquiry.

Neatline (http://neatline.wordpress.com), from the University of Virginia Scholars' Lab, is a free, online tool for creating interlinked timelines and maps as interpretive expressions of the literary or historical content of archival collections.

NewRadial (INKE, http://inke.acadiau.ca/newradial) is a free, web-based interactive visualization environment that displays and combines content from remotely served or locally situated databases.

Orange (http://orange.biolab.si) is a free, open-source, Windows and Mac, data-visualization and analysis application that also provides for data and text mining and machine learning.

TagCrowd (http://www.tagcrowd.com) is a free, web-based word cloud generator that accepts a URL, a text or an uploaded plain text file.

Text 2 Mind Map (https://www.text2mindmap.com) is a free, web-based application that converts structured lists of words or sentences into mind maps.

Textexture (http://textexture.com) is a free, web-based tool for visualizing text as a network.

TokenX (http://tokenx.unl.edu) is a free, web-based environment from the University of Nebraska, Lincoln, for visualizing, analyzing and manipulating texts.

VisuWords (http://www.visuwords.com) is a free, mind-mapping linguistic tool that shows the relationships between the queried word and related words in an interactive map with corresponding definitions.

Wordle (http://www.wordle.net) is a free, web-based, word-cloud generator with customizable font and color options.

Website Development, *See* **19. Publication and Sharing**

Notes

Preface

1   See Eileen Gardiner and Ronald G. Musto, "The Electronic Book," in *The Oxford Companion to the Book*, ed. Michael F. Suarez, SJ and H. R. Woudhuysen (Oxford: Oxford University Press, 2010), 165.
2   Cambridge, MA: Harvard Business School Press, 1997.
3   See, e.g., the discussion of the impact of the humanities in the digital era in Benjamin Alpers's review of Peter Brooks, *The Humanities and Public Life*, in "Word's Worth," The Chronicle Review, *The Chronicle of Higher Education* (April 28, 2014): http://chronicle.com/article/Word-s-Worth/146149.
4   *The Digital Sublime: Myth, Power, and Cyberspace* (Cambridge, MA: MIT Press, 2004).
5   Cambridge: Polity Press, 2005.

Chapter 1

1   Roberto Busa, SJ, "The Annals of Humanities Computing: The *Index Thomisticus*," *Computers and the Humanities* 14 (1980): 83–90.
2   "Day of DH: Defining the Digital Humanities," in *Debates in the Digital Humanities*, ed. Matthew K. Gold (Minneapolis: University of Minnesota Press, 2012), 69–71.
3   http://en.wikipedia.org/wiki/Digital_humanities.
4   Cambridge, MA: MIT Press, 2012, p. vii. Henry M. Glazdney, "Long-Term Digital Preservation: A Digital Humanities Topic?" *Historical Social Research/ Historische Sozialforschung* 37.3 (2012): 201–17, at 202–3, also highlights the vagueness of current definitions, "murky understanding" and "fuzzy boundaries" and cites several examples of similar attempts at definition.
5   *Avatars of the Word: From Papyrus to Cyberspace* (Cambridge, MA: Harvard University Press, 1998).
6   E.g., in "Humanist Learning in the Italian Renaissance," in *Renaissance Thought and the Arts* (Princeton, NJ: Princeton University Press, 1990), 1–19.

7 On the humanists both outside and inside the universities, see Paul F. Grendler, *The Universities of the Italian Renaissance* (Baltimore, MD: The Johns Hopkins University Press, 2002), 199–248.
8 https://www.nsf.gov/od/lpa/nsf50/vbush1945.htm.
9 http://content.cdlib.org/ark:/13030/hb9c6oo8sn.
10 https://www.acls.org/uploadedFiles/Publications/NEH/1964_Commission_on_the_Humanities.pdf.

Chapter 2

1 http://darwin-online.org.uk.
2 http://darwin-online.org.uk/Introduction.html.
3 The "global system of interconnected computer networks that use the standard Internet protocol suite (TCP/IP) to link several billion devices worldwide," https://en.wikipedia.org/wiki/Internet.
4 "A system of interlinked hypertext documents that are accessed via the Internet," https://en.wikipedia.org/wiki/World_Wide_Web.
5 "Software application[s] for retrieving, presenting and traversing information resources on the World Wide Web," https://en.wikipedia.org/wiki/Web_browser.
6 http://www.worldcat.org.
7 http://www.gutenberg.org.
8 http://archive.org/index.php.
9 http://www.hathitrust.org/home.
10 http://books.google.com.
11 http://www.pcworld.com/article/202803/google_129_million_different_books_have_been_published.html.
12 http://www.oac.cdlib.org.
13 https://en.wikipedia.org/wiki/List_of_digital_library_projects.
14 http://imslp.org.
15 http://www.perseus.tufts.edu/hopper.
16 http://archives.nyphil.org.
17 http://www.jfklibrary.org.
18 https://projects.gnome.org/gnumeric.
19 https://docs.google.com/spreadsheet.
20 For information on database applications, see Appendix, Section 9.
21 http://www.marenzio.org.
22 http://www.aruspix.net.
23 http://www.lazarusprojectimaging.com and http://www.honors.olemiss .edu/lazarus-project. These particular manuscripts are in the collection of the Archivio Capitolare in Vercelli, Italy.
24 Raymond G. Siemens and Susan Schreibman, eds., *A Companion to Digital Literary Studies* (Oxford: Blackwell, 2008).
25 http://www.booktraces.org.
26 http://valley.lib.virginia.edu.
27 *American Historical Review* 108.5 (2003): 1299–1307.

28 First discussed by us in "The 7 Digital Arts: Approaching Electronic Publishing," Art History and the Digital World Conference, The Getty Research Center, June 9, 2006. See https://www.getty.edu/research/exhibitions_events/events/digital_world/pdf/egardiner_rmusto.pdf.

29 http://www.vcdh.virginia.edu.

Chapter 3

1 http://www.rossettiarchive.org.

2 McGann has now presented a unified theory of such scholarship in his *A New Republic of Letters: Memory and Scholarship in the Digital Age* (Cambridge, MA: Harvard University Press, 2014).

3 http://digital.lib.ucdavis.edu/projects/bwrp.

4 http://www.nines.org.

5 http://www.18thconnect.org.

6 Suzanne Briet, Ronald E. Day, Laurent Martinet, and Hermina G. B. Anghelescu, *What Is Documentation?: English Translation of the Classic French Text* (Lanham, MD: Scarecrow Press, 2006); Roswitha Skare, Niels Windfeld Lund, and Andreas Varheim, *A Document (Re)Turn: Contributions from a Research Field in Transition* (Frankfurt am Main: Peter Lang, 2007).

7 Michael Buckland, "What Is a Digital Document?" at http://people.ischool .berkeley.edu/~buckland/digdoc.html. A Preprint of "What Is a Digital Document?" *Document Numérique* (Paris) 2.2 (1998): 221–30; and a shortened version of "What Is a 'Document'?" *Journal of the American Society for Information Science* 48.9 (September 1997): 804–9, reprinted in *Historical Studies in Information Science*, ed. T. B. Hahn and M. Buckland, (Medford, NJ: Information Today, 1998), 215–20.

8 http://chnm.gmu.edu/probateinventory/index.php.

9 http://chnm.gmu.edu.

10 http://digitalcollections.missouristate.edu/cdm4/browse.php? CISOROOT=/UnionCharter.

11 http://www.aschart.kcl.ac.uk/index.html.

12 http://www.kemble.asnc.cam.ac.uk.

13 http://www.atlanticlibrary.org/digitized_wills.

14 https://probatesearch.service.gov.uk.

15 http://www.mdlandrec.net/main.

16 http://homepages.rootsweb.ancestry.com/~surreal/NSWW/Leases/ index.html#HL.

17 http://www.territorialkansasonline.org/~imlskto/cgi-bin/index.php? SCREEN=show_document&document_id=101321.

18 http://www.londonlives.org.

19 http://www.londonlives.org/static/Project.jsp.

20 http://www.lazarusprojectimaging.com, and see also http://www.honors .olemiss.edu/lazarus-project/projects. The Vercelli team was comprised of Ken Boydston, Roger Easton, Keith Knox and Gregory Heyworth.

Chapter 4

1   Walter Benjamin, "The Work of Art in the Age of Mechanical Reproduction," in *Illuminations*, ed. Hannah Arendt (New York: Schocken Books, 1968), 214–18. Online at https://www.marxists.org/reference/subject/philosophy/works/ge/benjamin.htm.
2   Anthony Hudek, ed., *The Object* (Cambridge, MA: MIT Press, 2014).
3   http://humanorigins.si.edu/evidence/3d-collection/fossil.
4   http://www.ucl.ac.uk/3dpetriemuseum.
5   http://www.vam.ac.uk.
6   http://www.doaks.org.
7   http://visionarycross.org.
8   http://cdli.ucla.edu.
9   "Ibbi-Suen, / god of his land, / strong king, / king of Ur, / king of the four quarters: / Dān-ilī, / scribe, / is your servant."
10 https://www.english.cam.ac.uk/cmt.
11 See, e.g., Marita Sturken and Lisa Cartwright, *Practices of Looking: An Introduction to Visual Culture* (Oxford: Oxford University Press, 2001); also Edward W. Said, *Orientalism* (New York: Vintage, 1978); John Berger, *Ways of Seeing* (London: Penguin, 2008); Griselda Pollock, *Vision and Difference: Femininity, Feminism and Histories of Art* (London: Routledge, 1988).
12 As, e.g., in Bernard Frischer's *The Sculpted Word: Epicureanism and Philosophical Recruitment in Ancient Greece* (Berkeley: University of California Press, 2006). Digital version at ACLS Humanities E-Book: http://hdl.handle.net/2027/heb.90022.0001.001.
13 http://parkerweb.stanford.edu.
14 http://www.charm.rhul.ac.uk/about/about.html.
15 http://www.charm.rhul.ac.uk/index.html.
16 http://sounds.bl.uk.
17 http://www.lib.berkeley.edu/MRC/onlinemedia.html.
18 http://www.ucd.ie/irishfolklore/en/audio.
19 https://library.usu.edu/folklo/northernutahspeaks.php.
20 http://www.eviada.org/default.cfm.
21 http://library.duke.edu/digitalcollections/adviews.
22 http://www.nmnh.si.edu/naa/guide/film_toc.htm.
23 http://www.chgs.umn.edu.
24 http://www.ushmm.org/research/research-in-collections/overview/film-and-video.
25 *Space and Place: The Perspective of Experience* (Minneapolis: University of Minnesota Press, 1977), 3.
26 http://dhinitiative.org/projects/digitalmesopotamia.
27 http://bulldog2.redlands.edu/fac/wesley_bernardini/hopi.
28 http://romereborn.frischerconsulting.com.
29 http://formaurbis.stanford.edu.
30 http://www.learningsites.com.
31 http://www.metmuseum.org/exhibitions/listings/2014/assyria-to-iberia.
32 http://vwhl.clas.virginia.edu/villa.

33 http://www.cdh.ucla.edu/index.php.
34 http://www.iath.virginia.edu.
35 http://vwhl.clas.virginia.edu.
36 http://etc.ucla.edu.
37 http://paris.3ds.com/en-index.html#Heritage.
38 E.g., *Visualizing Venice* (http://visualizingvenice.org) and the *DECIMA Digital Map of Renaissance Florence* (http://decima.chass.utoronto.ca).
39 http://www.routledgeperformancearchive.com.
40 http://www.kennedy-center.org/programs/millennium/archive.html.
41 http://128.97.165.17/africa/yra.
42 See Chapter 4, note 1.
43 http://www.metmuseum.org/exhibitions/listings/2004/byzantium-faith-and-power.
44 See, e.g., his essays collected in *The Fiction of Narrative: Essays on History, Literature, and Theory, 1957–2007*, ed. Robert Doran (Baltimore, MD: The Johns Hopkins University Press, 2010).
45 James J. O'Donnell long ago pointed out this aspect of the digital in his *Avatars of the Word.*
46 See, e.g., Caroline Bruzelius and Umberto Plaja's video, "Visualizing Change," taking the spatial chronology of the church of San Lorenzo Maggiore in Naples from 500 to 1324, at http://vimeo.com/111031024.
47 Our thanks to William Tronzo for this visual comparison. See his *Petrarch's Two Gardens: Landscape and the Image of Movement* (New York: Italica Press, 2014), 164–5.
48 http://secondlife.com. See Menachem Wecker, "What Ever Happened to Second Life?," Vitae, *The Chronicle of Higher Education* (April 22, 2014) at https://chroniclevitae.com/news/456-what-ever-happened-to-second-life.
49 http://romereborn.frischerconsulting.com. See above, pp. 57–58.
50 http://www.cmrs.ucla.edu/projects/st_gall.html.
51 Stiftsbibliothek Sankt Gallen, MS 1092.
52 http://www.sundance.org/blogs/news/finding-meaning-in-virtual-reality–a-closer-look-at-new-frontier.
53 A question long ago posed by Robert Stein of the Institute for the Future of the Book. See http://www.futureofthebook.org.
54 http://www.bbc.co.uk/history/interactive/games.
55 http://www.gamesforchange.org/play/the-redistricting-game.

Chapter 5

1 Bamboo DiRT (digital research tools) was a major project (2008–12), funded by The Andrew W. Mellon Foundation, providing significant infrastructure as a "collection registry of digital research tools for scholarly use." It was extensively used in developing this chapter and the accompanying Appendix. For the newest tools available, along with licensing and platform information, readers are encouraged to consult DiRT, now an independent project, at http://dirtdirectory.org. Another registry, TaPOR

(http://tapor. ca) housed at the University of Alberta, focuses on tools used in text analysis and retrieval.
2 See Chapter 1, pp. 3, 5.
3 "As We May Think," *Atlantic Monthly*, at http://www.theatlantic.com/magazine/archive/1945/07/as-we-may-think/303881.
4 http://www.youtube.com.
5 http://www.lynda.com.
6 http://menus.nypl.org.
7 http://peasoup.typepad.com/peasoup.

Chapter 6

1 http://www.archdaily.com/84524/ad-classics-villa-savoye-le-corbusier.
2 This well-known Renaissance trope has been reapplied to the digital era most recently by Jerome McGann in his *Republic of Letters*.
3 HASTAC published a useful listing of centers and institutes at http://www.hastac.org/content/listing-digital-humanities-centers-and-institutes, although it is not totally up to date.
4 See brief discussion on p. 64.
5 We will discuss this at length in Chapter 9.
6 We will discuss this dynamic in further detail, pp. 132–4.
7 E.g., the AAA's Anthropology Resources on the Internet (http://www.aaanet.org/resources), Committee on the Future of Print and Electronic Publishing (http://www.aaanet.org/cmtes/CFPEP.cfm) and digital book review initiative (http://www.aaanet.org/issues/press/upload/Sloan-Book-Review-Prototype.pdf); AHA's published models for how to use digitized primary sources in survey courses in World History and the History of the Americas (http://www.historians.org/teaching-and-learning/classroom-content/resources/teaching-and-learning-in-the-digital-age); CAA News, which covers digital topics from "Bridging the Digital Divide" (http://www.collegeart.org/news/2013/02/05/bridging-the-digital-divide-and-so-much-more) to "Rethinking Humanities Graduate Education with Digital Humanities Centers" (http://www.collegeart.org/news/2013/04/08/rethinking-humanities-graduate-education-with-digital-humanities-centers); and MLA's Guidelines for Evaluating Work in Digital Humanities and Digital Media (http://www.mla.org/guidelines_evaluation_digital) to its biannual Prize for a Bibliography, Archive, or Digital Project.
8 http://www.humanitiesindicators.org/binaries/pdf/HI_FundingReport 2014.pdf, p. 6.

Chapter 7

1 http://opencontext.org.
2 Archivio della Latinità Italiana del Medioevo, http://alim.dfll.univr.it.
3 http://valley.lib.virginia.edu.
4 http://www.oucs.ox.ac.uk/ww1lit/gwa.
5 http://www.medici.org.

6   http://rulersofvenice.org.
7   http://plato.stanford.edu.
8   http://www.iep.utm.edu.
9   http://www.mountvernon.org/encyclopedia.
10 https://www.wikipedia.org.
11 A recent study has found Wikipedia to be more accurate than the Britannica. See http://en.wikipedia.org/wiki/Reliability_of_Wikipedia.
12 http://www.oxfordbibliographies.com.
13 http://www.getty.edu/research/tools/bha.
14 http://www.proquest.com/products-services/iba.html.
15 http://www.fordham.edu/Halsall.
16 http://www.the-orb.net.
17 http://www.hnoc.org/collections/bibliographies.html and http://historicaltextarchive.com/index.php.
18 http://www.worldcat.org.
19 http://ccat.sas.upenn.edu/nets/edition.
20 http://www.rc.umd.edu/editions/index.html.
21 http://www.nbol-19.org.
22 http://apaclassics.org/publications-and-research/digital-latin-library-project.
23 http://www.rossettiarchive.org.
24 http://etcweb.princeton.edu/dante/index.html.
25 http://www.perseus.tufts.edu/hopper.
26 http://www.jstor.org.
27 http://www.humanitiesebook.org.
28 http://muse.jhu.edu.
29 http://www.nybooks.com/articles/archives/1999/mar/18/the-new-age-of-the-book.
30 http://www.historians.org/about-aha-and-membership/aha-history-and-archives/presidential-addresses/robert-darnton.
31 *American Historical Review* 108.5 (December 2003): 1299–1307.
32 http://www2.vcdh.virginia.edu/AHR.
33 Several new journals have excelled at offering traditional book reviews online. Examples include *CAA Reviews* (http://www.caareviews.org), *Bryn Mawr Classical Review* (BMCR, http://bmcr.brynmawr.edu), *H-NET* (http://www.h-net.org), *Reviews in History* (http://www.history.ac.uk/reviews) and *The Medieval Review* or *TMR* (https://scholarworks.iu.edu/dspace/handle/2022/3631). But little has been done to move forward peer-reviewed digital articles.
34 http://rup.rice.edu.
35 http://www.publishing.umich.edu/publications/#digital-projects.
36 http://about.jstor.org/content-on-jstor-books.
37 http://about.jstor.org/content/participating-publishers-1.
38 https://www.humanitiesebook.org.
39 http://hdl.handle.net/2027/heb.90034.0001.001.
40 http://cds.library.brown.edu/projects/florentine_gazetteer.
41 http://cds.library.brown.edu/projects/catasto.

42 http://www.gutenberg-e.org/index.html.
43 http://romereborn.frischerconsulting.com.
44 http://paris.3ds.com/en-experience.html.
45 http://dlib.etc.ucla.edu/projects/Karnak/experience.

Chapter 8

1 This is not the "humanistic education" proposed from the 1960s on by such figures as Abraham Maslow, Carl Rogers or Malcolm Knowles.

2 See William Harrison Woodward, *Vittorino da Feltre and Other Humanist Educators* (New York: Columbia University Teachers College, 1964); idem, *Desiderius Erasmus Concerning the Aim and Method of Education*, foreword Craig R. Thompson (New York: Columbia University Teachers College, 1964); Marian Leona Tobriner, SNJM, *Vives' Introduction to Wisdom: A Renaissance Textbook* (New York: Columbia University Teachers College, 1968); and Pietro Paolo Vergerio, Leonardo Bruni, Aeneas Silvius Piccolomini, and Battista Guarini, *Humanist Educational Treatises*, ed. Craig Kallendorf, I Tatti Renaissance Library (Cambridge, MA: Harvard University Press, 2002) for some basic texts.

3 "Long-Term Digital Preservation: A Digital Humanities Topic?" *Historical Social Research/Historische Sozialforschung* 37.3 (2012): 201–17, at 202.

4 Ibid., 202–3.

5 Amanda Gailey and Dot Porter, "Credential Creep in the Digital Humanities," #alt-academy (May 6, 2011) at http://mediacommons.futureofthebook .org/alt-ac/pieces/credential-creep-digital-humanities.

6 http://rulersofvenice.org.

7 http://valley.lib.virginia.edu.

8 http://www.medici.org.

9 In 2007, 27.3 percent of faculty were tenured at all higher education institutions, down from 33.1 percent in 1997. See Scott Jaschik, "The Disappearing Tenure-Track Job," *Inside Higher Education* (May 12, 2009) at http://www .insidehighered.com/news/2009/05/12/workforce#sthash.8cJW6l4E .dpbs. From 1999/2000 to 2011/12, the percentage of full-time faculty with tenure decreased by 5 percent at public institutions, 4 percent at private, nonprofit institutions and 46 percent at private, for-profit institutions. See "Digest of Education Statistics," National Center for Education Statistics (http://nces.ed.gov/programs/digest/d12/tables/dt12_305.asp).

10 Recent studies of HTP practices confirm this trend. See, e.g., Leonard Cassuto, "The Rise of the Mini-Monograph," *Chronicle of Higher Education* (August 12, 2013) at http://chronicle.com/article/ The-Rise-of-the-Mini-Monograph/141007.

11 http://www.jstor.org.

12 http://muse.jhu.edu.

13 https://www.worldcat.org.

14 https://www.google.com/maps.

15 http://www.youtube.com.

16 https://www.flickr.com.

17 https://www.tumblr.com.

18 http://vimeo.com.

19 https://wordpress.org.

20 http://en.wikipedia.org/wiki/Reliability_of_Wikipedia.

21 https://www.academia.edu/about.

22 Exceptions do exist. The University of California Press has recently announced a new digital and open-access model for both monographs (Luminos) and articles (Collabra). See Rick Anderson, "University of California Press Introduces New Open Access Publishing Programs," in *The Scholarly Kitchen* (January 21, 2015) at http://scholarlykitchen.sspnet .org/2015/01/21/university-of-california-press-introduces-new-open-acc ess-publishing-programs.

23 This was first reported in 2003 in our "ACLS Humanities E-Book Project" report at the annual meeting of the Renaissance Society of America and subsequently published in revised form in William R. Bowen and Raymond G. Siemens, eds., *New Technologies and Renaissance Studies* (Tempe, AZ: ACMRS, 2008), 110–43. See also Sergey Brin and Lawrence Page, "The Anatomy of a Large-Scale Hypertextual Web Search Engine," Computer Science Department, Stanford University, at http://infolab.stanford.edu/~backrub/ google.html.

24 For an analysis of Google and its users' expectations, including the need to "temper . . . uncritical faith" and question the "illusion of precision," see Siva Vaidhyanathan, *The Googlization of Everything: (And Why We Should Worry)* (Berkeley: University of California Press, 2011), p. 3 *et passim*.

25 In April 2006, Thomas Bender surveyed this trend in the *Chronicle Review:* http://chronicle.com/article/No-Borders-Beyond-the/34180.

26 http://www.hathitrust.org.

27 https://archive.org/index.php.

28 http://www.gutenberg.org.

29 http://books.google.com.

30 Orphan works are under copyright but the current rights holder is either unclear or no longer locatable.

31 Stephen Greenblatt's *The Swerve: How the World Became Modern* (New York: W. W. Norton, 2011) on Poggio Bracciolini's discovery of Epicurus in a Swiss monastery, his copying and the work's subsequent life, offers a popular account of this endeavor.

32 Basel: Froben.

33 See, e.g., the Library of Congress News Archive on digital preservation at http://www.digitalpreservation.gov/news/index.html.

34 www.dpconline.org.

35 www.digitalpreservation.gov.

36 http://dp.la.

37 http://www.portico.org/digital-preservation.

38 http://chnm.gmu.edu/revolution/imaging/home.html.

39 http://peasoup.typepad.com.

40 http://www.neh.gov/grants/odh/digital-humanities-start-grants.

41 http://www.sloan.org/major-program-areas/digital-information-technology.

42 https://www.acls.org/programs/digital.

43 See Jennifer Howard, "At Mellon, Signs of Change," *The Chronicle of Higher Education* (June 29, 2014) at http://chronicle.com/article/At-Mellon-Signs-of-Change/147363.

44 http://www.mla.org/guidelines_evaluation_digital.

45 https://www.historians.org/publications-and-directories/perspectives-on-history/october-2001/suggested-guidelines-for-evaluating-digital-media-activities-in-tenure-review-and-promotion-an-aahc-document.

46 See, e.g., Steve Kolowich, "The Promotion that Matters," *Inside Higher Ed* (January 4, 2012), http://www.insidehighered.com/news/2012/01/04/evaluating-digital-humanities-enthusiasm-may-outpace-best-practices#sthash.gvCZTgQF.dpbs.

47 http://valley.lib.virginia.edu.

48 http://rulersofvenice.org.

49 http://cds.library.brown.edu/projects/florentine_gazetteer.

50 http://rotunda.upress.virginia.edu/dmde.

51 http://chnm.gmu.edu/revolution/imaging/home.html.

52 http://www.rossettiarchive.org.

53 http://mediacommons.futureofthebook.org/alt-ac.

54 See, e.g., their essays in *Debates in the Digital Humanities*, ed. Matthew K. Gold (Minneapolis: University of Minnesota Press, 2012), esp. Part 3: "Critiquing the Digital Humanities," 139–248.

55 These comments are based on our remarks in "Electronic Publishing and Theological Research: Some Considerations of Gender," Boston Theological Institute, Boston University, October 6, 2004.

56 Bonnie G. Smith, *The Gender of History: Men, Women and Historical Practice* (Cambridge, MA: Harvard University Press, 1998).

57 Ibid., 197.

58 London: T. Fisher Unwin, 1885, 10–23.

59 Smith, *Gender of History*, 171.

60 Ibid., 184.

61 *Chronicle of Higher Education* (January 30, 2004) at http://chronicle.com/article/The-Next-Wave-Liberation/9698.

62 Smith, *Gender of History*, 25.

63 http://en.wikipedia.org/wiki/Massive_open_online_course.

64 *Distant Reading* (London: Verso, 2013).

65 *Graphs, Maps, Trees: Abstract Models for a Literary History* (London: Verso, 2005).

66 *Computation into Criticism: A Study of Jane Austen's Novels* (Oxford: Oxford University Press, 1987).

67 Chapter 26 in *A Companion to Digital Literary Studies*, ed. Raymond George Siemens and Susan Schreibman (Oxford: Blackwell, 2008), http://www.digitalhumanities.org/companionDLS. This collection of essays is of fundamental importance as an introduction to theoretical approaches.

68 http://manovich.net/index.php/projects/cultural-analytics-visualizing-cultural-patterns.

69 softwarestudies.com/softbook/manovich_softbook_11_20_2008.pdf and *Software Takes Command* (New York: Bloomsbury, 2013).

70 "Trending: The Promises and the Challenges of Big Social Data," in Gold, *Debates*, 460–75; and http://manovich.net/index.php/projects/trending-the-promises-and-the-challenges-of-big-social-data.

71 Chicago: University of Chicago Press, 1999.

72 Cambridge, MA: MIT Press, 2002.

73 http://nkhayles.com.

74 See, e.g., her "Humanities 2.0: Promise, Perils, Predictions," in Gold, *Debates*, 476–89.

Chapter 9

1 For a good introduction see Adam D. Moore, "Concepts of Intellectual Property and Copyright," in *The Book: A Global History*, ed. Michael F. Suarez, SJ and H.R. Woudhuysen (New York: Oxford University Press, 2013), 183–96.

2 See Craig Kallendorf, "The Ancient Book," in Suarez and Woudhuysen, *The Book*, 39–53, at 44–50.

3 Translated and edited by Robert L. Martone and Valerie Martone (New York: Italica Press, 1991).

4 See David Boffa, "Sculptors' Signatures and the Construction of Identity in the Italian Renaissance," in *A Scarlet Renaissance: Essays in Honor of Sarah Blake McHam*, ed. Arnold Victor Coonin (New York: Italica Press, 2013), 35–56.

5 https://creativecommons.org.

6 See Moore, "Concepts," 193–5.

7 http://en.wikipedia.org/wiki/Google_Book_Search_Settlement_Agreement.

8 Ronald G. Musto, "Google Books Mutilates the Printed Past," The Chronicle Review, *The Chronicle of Higher Education* (June 12, 2009): B4–5 at http://chronicle.com/article/Google-Books-Mutilates-the-/44463.

9 https://authorsalliance.org/intro.html.

10 *Lives of the Painters, Sculptors and Architects*, trans. Gaston du C. de Vere (London: Everyman's Library, 1996), 1:96.

11 See, e.g., William M. Ivans, Jr., *Prints and Visual Communication* (Cambridge, MA: MIT Press, 1969).

12 "The Work of Art in the Age of Mechanical Reproduction."

13 See, e.g., the Getty Museum's Open Content Program at https://www.getty.edu/about/opencontent.html.

14 http://ohda.matrix.msu.edu.

15 http://digitalomnium.com/about.

16 http://www.fmomo.org/dedalo/pg/about.php.

17 http://www.nas.gov.sg/archivesonline/oral_history_interviews.

18 http://www.ffii.org.

19 https://creativecommons.org.

20 http://authorearnings.com/what-writers-leave-on-the-table.

21 Claire Cain Miller and Julie Bosman, "E-Books Outsell Print Books at Amazon," *New York Times* (May 19, 2011), http://www.nytimes .com/2011/05/20/technology/20amazon.html. See also Naomi Baron, *Words Onscreen: The Fate of Reading in a Digital World.* (New York: Oxford University Press, 2015).

22 Joseph Esposito, "The Digital Publishing Revolution Is Over," *The Scholarly Kitchen* (March 4, 2013), http://scholarlykitchen.sspnet.org/2013/03/04 /the-digital-publishing-revolution-is-over.

23 Craig Kallendorf, "Ancient Book," 44–9.

24 Reported by Robert Townsend in AHA's *Perspectives*: http://www.histo-rians.org/Documents/History%20and%20the%20Future%20of%20 Scholarly%20Publishing.pdf.

25 James Simpson and Sean Kelly, "The Teaching of the Arts and Humanities at Harvard College: Mapping the Future" (June 2013), 7. http://artsandhu-manities.fas.harvard.edu/humanities-project.

26 These numbers are contested. See http://chronicle.com/article/ The-Humanities-Declining-Not/140093.

27 The best guide is Peter Suber, *Open Access* (Cambridge, MA: MIT Press, 2012) at http://mitpress.mit.edu/sites/default/files/titles/content /9780262517638_Open_Access_PDF_Version.pdf.

28 *Whole Earth Review* (May 1985): 49, at http://www.wholeearth.com/ issue-electronic-edition.php?iss=2046.

29 Alice Meadows, "What Societies Really Think about Open Access," *The Scholarly Kitchen* (June 25, 2014) at http://scholarlykitchen.sspnet .org/2014/06/25/what-societies-really-think-about-open-access.

30 Rick Anderson, "Print on the Margins," *Library Journal* (June 15, 2011): 38 at http://content.lib.utah.edu/cdm/ref/collection/uspace/id/7570.

31 Suber, *Open Access*, http://mitpress.mit.edu/sites/default/files/titles/ content/openaccess/Suber_08_chap1.html#chap1.

32 Meadows, "What Societies Really Think."

33 As, e.g., in *The Literary Underground of the Old Regime* (Cambridge, MA: Harvard University Press, 1982); and Daniel Roche, *Revolution in Print: The Press in France, 1775–1800* (Berkeley: University of California Press, New York Public Library, 1989); Robert Darnton, *The Forbidden Best-Sellers of Pre-Revolutionary France* (New York: W. W. Norton, 1995).

34 See, e.g., the introduction to Adrian Johns, *The Nature of the Book: Print and Knowledge in the Making* (Chicago: University of Chicago Press, 1998), 1–57.

35 Suber, *Open Access*, 25.

36 The AHA's experience is narrated and analyzed by Robert Townsend, former AHA deputy director, in his "From Publishing to Communication: The AHA's Online Journey," http://www.historians.org/publications-and-directories/ perspectives-on-history/may-2013/from-publishing-to-communication.

37 http://www.historians.org/publications-and-directories/ perspectives-on-history/april-2005/should-historical-scholarship-be-free.

38 http://blog.historians.org/2012/09/aha-statement-on-scholarly-journ al-publishing.

39 See again Meadows, "What Societies Really Think."

Chapter 10

1 Yi-Fu Tuan, *Space and Place: The Perspective of Experience* (Minneapolis: University of Minnesota Press, 1977), 25.

2 Simon Schama, *Landscape and Memory* (New York: A. A. Knopf, 1995).

3 E.g., a search on Google Scholar for articles since 2011 on "linguistics and neuroscience" returns "about 14,900" results, including David Poeppel and David Embick, "Defining the Relation between Linguistics and Neuroscience," in *Twenty-first Century Psycholinguistics: Four Cornerstones*, ed. Anne Culter (Mahwah, NJ: Lawrence Erlbaum Associates, 2005; rpt. London Routledge, 2013), 103–18.

4 D. Shaw and C. H. Davis, "The Modern Language Association: Electronic and Paper Surveys of Computer-Based Tool Use," *Journal of the American Society for Information Science* 47.12 (1996): 932–40.

5 I.e., Edison's millions of electric lightbulbs changed society far more than his unique electronic wonder shows. See Mosco, *The Digital Sublime*, p. 121–6.

6 American Council of Learned Societies, "Our Cultural Commonwealth: The Report of the ACLS Commission on Cyberinfrastructure for the Humanities and Social Sciences," 2006 at http://www.acls.org/cyberinfrastructure/our-culturalcommonwealth.pdf.

7 http://www.acls.org/about/Default.aspx?id=598.

8 http://scholarlykitchen.sspnet.org.

9 See Chapter 8, pp. 127, 132–4.

10 "A Framework for the E-publishing Ecology," September 25, 2000, at https://www.academia.edu/174631/A_framework_for_the_e-publishing_ecology.

11 The notion of the social contract as opposed to the ecology of scholarly communication was first discussed by the authors in June 9, 2006: "The 7 Digital Arts: Approaching Electronic Publishing," Art History and the Digital World Conference, The Getty Research Center, Los Angeles. A variant of this theme appeared in 2010 in Daniel J. Cohen, "The Social Contract of Scholarly Publishing," reprinted in Gold, *Debates*, 319–21.

12 http://galileo.rice.edu.

13 http://en.wikipedia.org/wiki/Wikipedia:How_to_run_an_edit-a-thon.

Epilogue

1 http://en.wikipedia.org/wiki/Cave_of_Forgotten_Dreams.

Appendix

1 Formerly http://dirt.projectbamboo.org, currently http://dirtdirectory.org.

2 http://tapor.ca.

3 http://www.sparc.arl.org.

Glossary

The definitions in this glossary are based on current standard definitions found on the web and particularly in Wikipedia. They are confined primarily to terms used in computing and digital humanities.

.NET: a software framework, which runs primarily on Microsoft Windows, that includes a large library and provides language interoperability across several programming languages.

3D modeling: process of developing a mathematical representation of any three-dimensional surface or object (either inanimate or living) using specialized software.

3D printing or additive manufacturing (AM): a process for making three-dimensional objects from a 3D model or other electronic data through additive processes in which successive layers of material are laid down under computer control.

3D rendering: the process of automatically converting wire-frame models into 2D images.

A

ActionScript: an object-oriented language originally developed by Macromedia Inc. (now owned by Adobe Systems).

analog: a method of transmitting information by translating it into electric pulses of varying amplitude in a continuous range of values as opposed to digital technology, which translates information into binary format ("0" or "1").

Android: a Linux-based operating system designed primarily for touchscreen mobile devices, such as smartphones and tablet computers.

animation: the process of creating the illusion of continuous motion and/or shape change using the rapid display of a sequence of static images that differ minimally from each other.

annotation: metadata attached to text, image or other data. Often annotations refer to a specific part of the original data. See also MARKUP.

API, see APPLICATION PROGRAMMING INTERFACE.

application programming interface (API): an interface that specifies how some software components should interact with each other.

artificial intelligence (AI): the intelligence of machines or software; the design and study of intelligent agents.

audio, digital: technology that records, stores and reproduces sound by encoding an audio signal in digital, as opposed to analog, form.

audio recording, see DIGITAL RECORDING.

B

batch processing: the execution of a series of programs ("jobs") on a computer without manual intervention.

bibliographic management tools: tools to organize research sources and generate bibliographies in multiple citation formats (also known as citation or reference management tools).

bibliography: the organized listing of books (enumerative bibliography) or the systematic, description of books as physical objects (descriptive bibliography); as a discipline, the academic study of books as physical, cultural objects.

blog: (a contraction of the words "web log") a discussion or informational site published on the World Wide Web and consisting of discrete entries ("posts") typically displayed in reverse chronological order (the most recent post appears first).

blogging: a form of social networking that involves maintaining or adding entries to a BLOG.

bookmarking: the process of saving and annotating web pages locations.

brainstorming software: software for the development of creative ideas that may include flow charts, idea maps, word association and generative idea creation.

C

C: a general-purpose programming language and one of the most widely used.

C++: a general-purpose programming language, statically typed, free-form, multiparadigm and compiled.

cascading style sheets (CSS): a style-sheet language used for describing the look and formatting of a document written in a markup language.

charts: a graphical representation of data with the data represented by symbols, such as bars in a bar chart, lines in a line chart or slices in a pie chart.

chat, see ONLINE CHAT.

citation management software (reference management software, personal bibliographic management software): software for scholars and authors to use for recording and utilizing bibliographic citations (references).

cloud storage: large-scale networked computer data storage where data is stored in virtualized pools of storage, which are generally hosted by third parties.

clustering (or cluster analysis): grouping a set of objects in such a way that objects in the same group (cluster) are more similar (in some sense or another) to each other than to those in other groups (clusters). It is a main task of exploratory data mining and a common technique for statistical data analysis.

coding: a phase within the process of computer programming; in social sciences, an analytical process in which quantitative and qualitative data are categorized to facilitate analysis.

collation: the assembly of written information into a standard order, usually alphabetical or numeric; in textual criticism and bibliography, the process of determining the differences between two or more texts or the comparison of the physical makeup of two copies of a book.

comma-separated values or character-separated values (CSV): a file format that stores tabular data (numbers and text) in plain-text form, usually with a .csv or .txt extension.

concept map: a graphical tool that shows relationships between concepts when organizing and structuring knowledge.

content management: the set of processes and technologies that support the collection, managing and publishing of information in any form or medium.

corpus annotation: the application of a scheme to texts that may include structural MARKUP, GRAMMATICAL TAGGING, PARSING and numerous other representations.

corpus linguistics: the study of language as expressed in a sample (corpus) or samples (corpora) of "real world" text. This method represents a digestive approach to deriving a set of abstract rules by which a natural language is governed or else relates to another language. Originally done by hand, corpora are now largely derived by an automated process.

courseware: web-based software tools for managing courses that allows for grading, feedback, discussion, reply posts, files and lectures.

crowdsourcing: the practice of obtaining needed services, ideas or content by soliciting contributions from a large group of people, and especially from an online community, rather than from traditional employees, colleagues or suppliers.

CSS, see CASCADING STYLE SHEETS.

csv, see COMMA-SEPARATED VALUES.

curation, digital: the collection, archiving, maintenance and preservation of digital assets.

D

dashboard: a management information system that presents a graphical presentation of data in a convenient format, capturing and reporting specific data points from multiple entities. Dashboards can be stand-alone, web-based or desktop applications.

data: values of qualitative or quantitative variables belonging to a set of items.

data analysis: the process of inspecting, cleaning, transforming and modeling data with the goal of discovering useful information, suggesting conclusions and supporting decision making.

database: a collection of data organized to model relevant aspects in order to support processes requiring this information.

data collection: a process that ensures that data gathered are both defined and accurate and that subsequent decisions based on arguments embodied in the findings are valid.

data export/import: the automated or semiautomated input and output of data sets among different software applications.

data management: the development, execution and supervision of plans, policies, programs and practices that control, protect, deliver and enhance the value of data and information assets.

data migration: the process of transferring data between storage types, formats or computer systems.

data mining: the process of discovering patterns in large data sets involving methods at the intersection of artificial intelligence, machine learning, statistics and database systems.

data model: a description of the objects represented by a computer system together with their properties and relationships.

data modeling: the process of creating a DATA MODEL for an information system by applying formal data modeling techniques.

data sharing: the practice of making data available to other investigators.

data tree: a data structure implementing abstract data type (ADT) to simulate a hierarchical tree structure, with a root value and subtrees represented as a set of linked nodes. (See Figure 1.)

data visualization: the visual representation in abstract schematic form of data and information based on variations in attributes or characteristics. (See Figure 12.)

decision tree: a decision support tool that uses a treelike graph or model of decisions and their possible consequences, often including chance event outcomes, resource costs and utility.

DH: digital humanities.

DHCS: digital humanities and computer science.

digital asset: any item (textual, audio, visual) that has been formatted into a binary source with the right to use it.

digital asset management (DAM): tasks and decisions surrounding the ingestion, annotation, cataloguing, storage, retrieval and distribution of any DIGITAL ASSET.

digital library, see DIGITAL REPOSITORY.

digital object identifier (DOI): a character string (a "digital identifier") used to uniquely identify an object such as an electronic document.

digital preservation: strategic planning, resource allocation and conversion, reformatting and preservation activities to ensure continued access to, and usability of, digital materials.

digital recording: audio and video directly recorded to a storage device as a stream of discrete numbers representing the changes through time in air pressure (sound) for audio and chroma or luminance values for video.

digital repository: an electronic library (also referred to as a digital library) in which collections are stored in electronic media formats (as opposed to print, microform or other media) and accessible using computers.

DiRT: digital research tools.

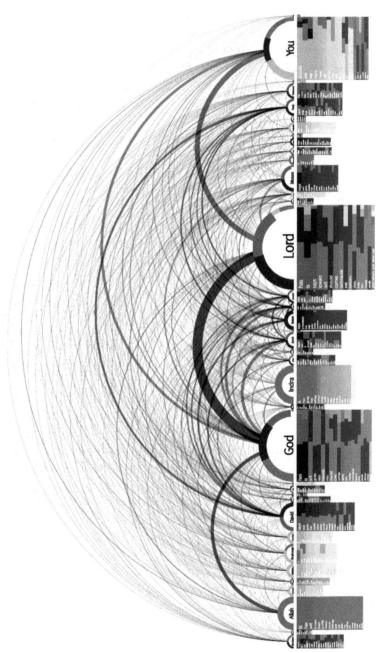

FIGURE 12. Data Visualization. The forty-one most frequently cited characters are arranged alphabetically and scaled according to how many times they are mentioned in holy texts from Buddhism, Hinduism, Islam and Judaism as well as the Bible. Philipp Steinweber and Andreas Koller. http://similardiversity.net.

doc: a filename extension for word-processing documents, particularly in Microsoft Word.

Docbook: a semantic markup language for technical documentation.

document collaboration (file collaboration): tools or systems set up to help multiple people work together on a single document or file to achieve a single final version.

document management system: a computer system or set of computer programs used to track and store electronic documents.

document sharing, see DOCUMENT COLLABORATION.

docx: a file extension for a zipped, XML-based file format developed by Microsoft for representing spreadsheets, charts, presentations and word-processing documents.

DOI, see DIGITAL OBJECT IDENTIFIER.

domain name: an identification string that defines a realm of administrative autonomy, authority or control on the INTERNET.

domain name registrar: an organization or commercial entity that manages the reservation of INTERNET DOMAIN NAMES.

downloading: transferring software, data, character sets and so forth, from a distant to a nearby computer, from a larger to a smaller computer or from a computer to a peripheral device.

Dublin Core: a set of metadata terms that describe web resources (video, images, web pages, etc.) and physical resources (books and objects like artworks) for the purposes of discovery. Named for Dublin, OH, USA, where the schema originated during the 1995 invitational OCLC/NCSA Metadata Workshop.

E

e-book (ebook, electronic book, digital book): a text-, acoustic- and image-based publication in digital form produced on, published by and readable on computers or other digital devices.

e-learning: the use of electronic media and information and communication technologies (ICT) in education.

electronic document: any electronic media content (other than computer programs or system files) that is intended to be used in either an electronic form or as printed output.

EPUB: a free and open E-BOOK standard by the International Digital Publishing Forum (IDPF). Files have the extension .epub.

eXtensible Markup Language (XML): a MARKUP LANGUAGE that defines a set of rules for encoding documents in a format that is both human-readable and machine-readable.

Extensible Stylesheet Language Transformations (XSLT): a language for transforming XML documents into other XML documents or other objects such as HTML for web pages, plain text or into XSL Formatting Objects that can then be converted into PDF, POSTSCRIPT and PNG.

F

file collaboration, see DOCUMENT COLLABORATION.

Flash: a multimedia and software platform used for authoring of VECTOR GRAPHICS, ANIMATION, GAMES and RICH INTERNET APPLICATIONS (RIAs) that can be viewed, played and executed in Adobe Flash Player.

FOSS: software that can be classified as both FREE SOFTWARE and OPEN-SOURCE SOFTWARE.

free software: computer software that is distributed along with its source code and is released under terms that guarantee users the freedom to study, adapt/modify and distribute the software.

full-text search: techniques for searching the complete text of document(s) or document collections stored in a full-text DATABASE.

G

games, digital: structured playing on a digital device, applying computer logic and real-life decision making, generally allowing multiple outcomes and players.

geocoding: the process of finding associated geographic coordinates (often expressed as latitude and longitude) from other geographic data, such as street addresses or ZIP/postal codes.

Geographic Information System (GIS): a system designed to capture, store, manipulate, analyze, manage and present all types of geographical data.

geomatics or **geomatics engineering,** see GEOSPATIAL TECHNOLOGY.

geospatial analysis, see GEOSPATIAL COMPUTING.

geospatial computing (geospatial analysis): the application of statistical analysis and other informational techniques to data that has a geographical or geospatial aspect.

geospatial technology (geomatics, geomatics engineering): the discipline of gathering, storing, processing and delivering geographic information or spatially referenced information.

GIS, see GEOGRAPHIC INFORMATION SYSTEM.

grammatical tagging (part-of-speech – POS – tagging, word-category disambiguation): the process of marking up a word in a text (corpus) as corresponding to a particular part of speech based on both its definition as well as its context – that is, relationship with adjacent and related words in a phrase, sentence or paragraph.

graph: in data structures, an abstract data type representing relationships or connections and made up of vertices or nodes and the lines (edges) that connect them.

graphics: any visual representation on a two-dimensional plane with an x and y axis; an image generated by a computer.

graph theory: the study of graphs.

H

HTML, see HYPERTEXT MARKUP LANGUAGE.

HTP: hiring, tenure and promotion within academic life.

HyperText Markup Language (HTML): the main markup language for creating web pages and other information that can be displayed in a WEB BROWSER or other HTML viewer.

I

ICT: information and computer technologies.

image: an artifact, usually a two-dimensional picture, that depicts or records a visual perception of a particular subject.

image analysis: the extraction of meaningful information from digital images by means of digital image processing techniques.

image editing: the processes of altering images, whether they are digital photographs, traditional photochemical photographs or illustrations.

image enhancement: a form of IMAGE EDITING that corrects color hue and brightness imbalances and often includes features such as red eye removal, sharpness adjustments, zooming and cropping.

image galleries: online capability provided by image hosting services that allows individuals to upload images to the service's INTERNET website and place and link to them in specific folders and locations organized by the user.

indexing: the creation of a data structure within a DATABASE to improve the speed of data retrieval operations.

information sharing: sharing information one-to-one, one-to-many, many-to-many and many-to-one using various computer technologies

including BLOGS, WIKIS, really simple syndication (RSS), TAGGING
and ONLINE CHAT.

Internet: a global system of interconnected computer networks using
the standard Internet protocol suite (TCP/IP) and linking several
billion devices worldwide.

J

Java: a computer programming language that is specifically designed to
have as few implementation dependencies as possible.

JavaScript: a computer programming language used as part of WEB
BROWSERS to allow client-side scripts to interact and communicate
with the user, control the browser and alter the displayed document
content.

K

KWiC: acronym for Key Word In Context, the most common format for
lines in a concordance.

L

language interoperability: the capability of two different computer languages to natively interact and operate on the same kind of data
structures.

linguistic annotation: any descriptive or analytic notation applied to
raw language data – textual, audio, video, physiological recordings;
may include transcriptions of all sorts (from phonetic features to
discourse structures), GRAMMATICAL TAGGING and sense tagging,
PARSING, "named entity" identification, co-reference annotation
and so forth.

linked data: a method of publishing structured data from different
sources so that it can be interlinked, connected and shared in such
a way that it can be read and queried automatically by computers.

Linux: a computer operating system that is built on a model of free and
open-source software.

M

map: a visual representation of an area; a symbolic depiction highlighting relationships between elements of that space such as objects,
regions and themes.

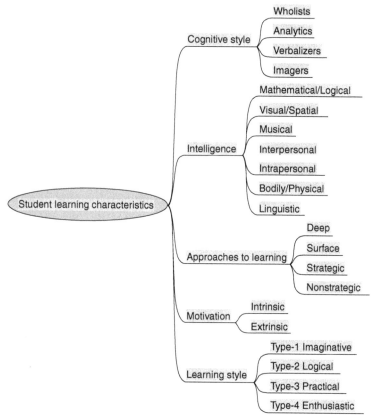

FIGURE 13. Mind Map. Student learning characteristics by Nevit Dilmen.
http://commons.wikimedia.org/wiki/File: Student_learning_charasterictics.svg.

mapping: creating graphic representations of information using spatial relationships within the graphic to represent some relationships within the data. Also data mapping or establishing a relationship between a set of inputs and a set of permissible outputs with the property that each input is related to exactly one output.

map tile: a two-dimensional array data structure or matrix that holds information on graphics and allows for simple, visual map data rendering.

markup: annotating a document's content using MARKUP LANGUAGE, which provides information regarding the structure of the text or instructions for how it is to be displayed.

markup language: a system for annotating a document in a way that is syntactically distinguishable from the text.

mashup: a web page or web application that uses content from more than one source to create a single new service displayed in a single graphical interface.

metadata (metacontent): data providing information about one or more aspects of the data, that is, data about data.

microblogging: a broadcast medium with content that is typically smaller in both actual and aggregate file size than in BLOGGING.

MIDI (Musical Instrument Digital Interface): a technical standard that describes a protocol, digital interface and connectors and allows a wide variety of electronic musical instruments, computers and other related devices to connect and communicate with one another.

mind map: a diagram used to visually outline information (see Figure 13).

morphological analysis: the analysis and description of the structure of a language's morphemes (the smallest grammatical unit in a language) and other linguistic units, such as root words, affixes, parts of speech, intonation/stress or implied context.

multimedia: media and content that uses a combination of different text, audio, still images, animation, video or interactivity content forms.

MusicXML: an XML-based file format for representing Western musical notation, which is proprietary, but fully and openly documented, and can be freely used under a public license.

N

natural language processing (NLP): a field of computer science, ARTIFICIAL INTELLIGENCE and linguistics concerned with the interactions between computers and human (natural) languages.

network analysis: the study of graphs as a representation of either symmetric relations or, more generally, of asymmetric relations between discrete objects.

Ngrams: a contiguous sequence of n items from a given sequence of text or speech. The items can be phonemes, syllables, letters, words or base pairs according to the application (see Figure 14).

notetaking: the practice of recording digital information captured from another source.

O

OA, see OPEN ACCESS.

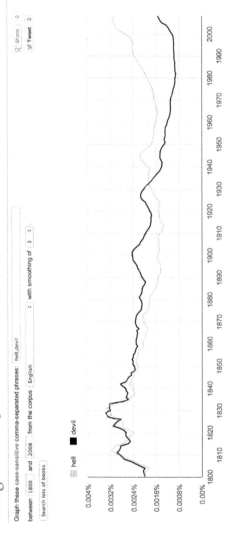

FIGURE 14. N-gram produced by the Google Books n-gram viewer querying "hell" and "devil" from 1800 to 2008. http://books.google.com/ngrams.

object-oriented language: a programming language that represents concepts as "objects" that have data fields (attributes that describe the object) and associated procedures known as methods.

OCR, see OPTICAL CHARACTER RECOGNITION.

ODT: the word processing file format of OpenDocument, an open standard for electronic documents.

online chat: communication over the INTERNET that employs real-time messaging between sender and receiver.

ontologies: (in information and computer science) the structural frameworks for organizing information and representing knowledge as a set of hierarchical concepts within a domain and representing the relationships between those concepts.

open access (OA): the practice of providing access to literature in digital form, in an online environment, free of charge to the end user and free of most copyright and licensing restrictions.

open-source software (OSS): computer software with its source code that is made available and licensed by a copyright holder who provides the rights to study, change and distribute the software to anyone and for any purpose.

opinion mining, see SENTIMENT ANALYSIS.

optical character recognition (OCR): the conversion of scanned images of handwritten, typewritten or printed text into machine-encoded text.

OSS, see OPEN-SOURCE SOFTWARE.

P

parsing (syntactic analysis): the process of analyzing a string of symbols, either in natural language or in computer languages, according to the rules of a formal grammar.

part-of-speech (POS) tagging, see GRAMMATICAL TAGGING.

PDF (Portable Document Format): a file format used to represent documents in a manner independent of application software, hardware and operating systems.

Perl: a family of high-level, general-purpose, interpreted, dynamic programming languages.

personal bibliographic management software, see CITATION MANAGEMENT SOFTWARE.

PHP: a server-side scripting language designed for web development but also used as a general-purpose programming language.

plug-in: a software component that adds a specific feature to an existing software application.

PNG, see PORTABLE NETWORK GRAPHICS.

Portable Network Graphics (PNG): a raster graphics file format that supports lossless data compression.

POS tagging, see GRAMMATICAL TAGGING.

PostScript (PS): a computer language for creating VECTOR GRAPHICS.

programming language: a formal language designed to communicate instructions to a machine, particularly a computer.

Python: a general-purpose, high-level programming language that emphasizes code readability, with a syntax that allows programmers to express concepts in fewer lines of code than would be possible in languages such as C.

Q

query language: a computer language used to make queries into DATA-BASES and information systems.

R

R: a free software environment (Windows, Mac, LINUX, web-based, iOS) for statistical computing and graphics.

rdf (Resource Description Framework): a family of World Wide Web Consortium (W3C) specifications originally designed as a METADATA DATA MODEL that is used as a general method for conceptual description or modeling of information that is implemented in web resources using a variety of syntax notations and data serialization formats.

reading: the cognitive process of decoding symbols to derive meaning from text (as in reading a book or reading music or visual objects); the act of a computer extracting data from a storage medium.

reference management software, see CITATION MANAGEMENT SOFTWARE.

relational database: a DATABASE that has a collection of tables of data items, all of which are formally described and organized according to the relational model.

repetition analysis: the process of discovering repeating patterns in large data sets involving methods at the intersection of ARTIFICIAL INTELLIGENCE, machine learning, statistics and DATABASE systems.

rich Internet application (RIA): a web application that has many of the characteristics of desktop application software, typically delivered by way of a site-specific browser, a browser PLUG-IN, an independent SANDBOX, extensive use of JAVASCRIPT or a virtual machine.

rich text format (rtf): a proprietary document file format with published specification developed by Microsoft Corporation for Microsoft products and for cross-platform document interchange.

RSS (Rich Site Summary, RDF Site Summary, Really Simple Syndication): a publication method that allows for frequently updated information: BLOG entries, news headlines, audio, video.

rtf, see RICH TEXT FORMAT.

Ruby: a dynamic, reflective, object-oriented, general-purpose programming language.

S

sandbox: in the context of software development including web development and revision control, a testing environment that isolates untested code changes and outright experimentation from the production environment or repository; also a security mechanism for separating running programs.

scalable vector graphics (SVG): an XML-based vector image format for two-dimensional graphics that has support for interactivity and animation.

scanning: an imaging technology that converts text, drawings and photographs into digital form that can be stored in a computer system and then manipulated using different software programs.

screencast: a digital recording of computer screen output, also known as a video screen capture, often containing audio narration.

semantic web: a collaborative movement led by the international standards body, the World Wide Web Consortium (W3C) to promote the computer-to-computer sharing and reuse of data across applications, enterprises and communities.

sentiment analysis (opinion mining): the use of natural language processing, text analysis and computational linguistics to identify and extract subjective information in source materials.

sequence alignment: a way of arranging sequences to identify regions of similarity that may be a consequence of functional or structural relationships between the sequences.

social media: the means of interactions among people in which they create, share and/or exchange information and ideas in virtual communities and networks.

social network: a social structure made up of a set of social actors (such as individuals or organizations) and a set of the binary ties between these actors.

social networking service: a platform to build social networks or social relations among people who, for example, share interests, activities, backgrounds or real-life connections.

spectral imaging: a branch of spectroscopy and photography in which a complete spectrum or some spectral information is collected at every location in an image plane.

spreadsheet: an interactive computer application program for the organization and analysis of data in tabular form.

SVG, see SCALABLE VECTOR GRAPHICS.

syntactic analysis, see PARSING.

T

tag cloud, see WORD CLOUD.

tagging: assigning a nonhierarchical keyword or term to a piece of information, such as an INTERNET bookmark, digital image or computer file.

TEI, see TEXT ENCODING INITIATIVE.

template: a standardized nonexecutable file format used by computer software as a preformatted example on which to base other files, especially documents.

text analytics: a set of linguistic, statistical and machine learning techniques that model and structure the information content of a textual source or sources.

Text Encoding Initiative (TEI): a text-centric community of practice across several academic fields operating continuously since the 1980s whose defining output is a set of guidelines that collectively define an XML format.

text mining (text data mining): the process of deriving high-quality information from text. See also TEXT ANALYTICS.

timelines: displaying a list of events in chronological order.

topic model: a type of statistical model for discovering abstract topics occurring within a corpus of documents.

transcription: the act or process of copying material from one medium to another.

U

Unicode: a computing industry standard for the consistent encoding, representation and handling of text expressed in most of the world's writing systems.

Unix: a family of operating systems, originally developed at Bell Labs, that are multitasking and multiuser based.

V

vector graphics: the use of geometrical primitives such as points, lines, curves and shapes or polygons – all based on mathematical expressions – to represent images in computer graphics.

video recording, see DIGITAL RECORDING.

virtual machine: a software-based, fictive computer.

virtual reality (VR): a computer environment that can simulate physical presence in places in the real world or in imagined worlds.

visualization: the visual representation of information, data or knowledge.

visual search: a computer-assisted perceptual task that scans an environment for a particular object or feature among other objects or features.

W

warping: the process of digitally manipulating an image or video to correct distortion or to morph for creative purposes.

Web 2: web sites that use technology beyond the static pages of earlier web sites.

Web 3: although definitions vary, it is generally considered to be a version of the World Wide Web that enables the use of autonomous agents to perform tasks for the user and will include TV-quality open video, 3D simulations, augmented reality, human-constructed semantic standards and pervasive broadband, wireless and sensors.

web archiving: the process of collecting portions of the WORLD WIDE WEB to ensure the information is preserved in an ARCHIVE for future researchers, historians and the public.

web browser: a software application – such as Safari, Firefox, Google Chrome, Opera and Internet Explorer – for retrieving, presenting and moving through information resources on the WORLD WIDE WEB.

web crawler: an INTERNET bot, or web robot, that systematically browses the WORLD WIDE WEB, typically for the purpose of web indexing.

web design: the production and maintenance of websites based on various skills and disciplines, such as graphic design, interface design, authoring (including standardized code and proprietary software), user-experience design and search-engine optimization.

web development: the process of developing a web site for the INTERNET (WORLD WIDE WEB) or an intranet (a private network).

web hosting: a service with INTERNET servers that allows organizations and individuals to serve content to the INTERNET.

web publishing: the process of making material available on the WORLD WIDE WEB.

weighted list, see word cloud.

wiki: a web application that allows people to add, modify or delete content in collaboration with others.

word-category disambiguation, see GRAMMATICAL TAGGING.

word cloud (tag cloud or weighted list): a visual representation for text data, typically used to depict keyword metadata (tags) in texts, often on websites, and to visualize free form text.

word frequency: the number of occurrences of words or word types in a given corpus.

word processing: the digital composition, editing, formatting and sometimes printing of any sort of written material.

World Wide Web: an information system of interlinked hypertext documents that are accessed using the INTERNET.

WYSIWYG: "what you see is what you get" display of edited material.

X

XML, see EXTENSIBLE MARKUP LANGUAGE.

XSL formatting objects: a MARKUP LANGUAGE for XML document formatting most often used to generate PDFs.

XSLT, see EXTENSIBLE STYLESHEET LANGUAGE TRANSFORMATIONS.

Z

zooming: digital, an electronic emulation of focal length change; page, the ability to magnify or shrink a portion of a page on a computer display; user interface, a graphical interface allowing for image scaling.

Bibliography on Digital Humanities

Journals

CH Working Papers (Computing in the Humanities Working Papers), http://projects.chass.utoronto.ca/chwp/titles.html (latest issue 2009).

DHCommons Journal, http://dhcommons.org/journal (forthcoming).

DHQ: Digital Humanities Quarterly, http://www.digitalhumanities.org/dhq.

Digital Medievalist, http://www.digitalmedievalist.org/journal (latest issue 2013).

Digital Studies/Le champ numérique, http://www.digitalstudies.org/ojs/index.php/digital_studies.

Electronic Book Review, http://www.electronicbookreview.com.

Journal of Digital Humanities, http://journalofdigitalhumanities.org.

Literary and Linguistic Computing, http://llc.oxfordjournals.org.

TEXT Technology: The Journal of Computer Text Processing, http://texttechnology.mcmaster.ca/home.html (latest issue 2007).

Books, Articles, Papers, etc.

American Council of Learned Societies. "Report of the Commission on the Humanities." 1964. https://www.acls.org/uploadedFiles/Publications/NEH/1964_Commission_on_the_Humanities.pdf.

"Our Cultural Commonwealth: The Report of the ACLS Commission on Cyberinfrastructure for the Humanities and Social Sciences." 2006. http://www.acls.org/cyberinfrastructure/ourculturalcommonwealth.pdf.

Andersen, Deborah Lines. *Digital Scholarship in the Tenure, Promotion, and Review Process: History, Humanities, and New Technology.* Armonk, NY: M. E. Sharpe, 2004.

Apollon, Daniel Claire Bélisle, and Philippe Régnier, eds. *Digital Critical Editions.* Urbana: University of Illinois Press, 2014.

Archer, Dawn, ed. *What's in a Word-list? Investigating Word Frequency and Keyword Extraction.* Farnham, UK: Ashgate, 2009.

Bailey, Chris, and Hazel Gardiner, eds. *Revisualizing Visual Culture.* Farnham, UK: Ashgate, 2010.

Baron, Naomi. *Words Onscreen: The Fate of Reading in a Digital World.* New York: Oxford University Press, 2015.

Bartscherer, Thomas, and Roderick Coover. *Switching Codes: Thinking through Digital Technology in the Humanities and the Arts.* Chicago: University of Chicago Press, 2011.

Benjamin, Walter. "The Work of Art in the Age of Mechanical Reproduction." In *Illuminations.* Edited by Hannah Arendt. London: Fontana, 1968, 214–18. https://www.marxists.org/reference/subject/philosophy/works/ge/benjamin.htm.

Berry, David M., ed. *Understanding Digital Humanities.* Houndsmills, UK: Palgrave Macmillan, 2012.

Bodard, Gabriel, and Simon Mahony, eds. *Digital Research in the Study of Classical Antiquity.* Farnham, UK: Ashgate, 2010.

Bodenhamer, David J., John Corrigan, and Trevor M. Harris. *The Spatial Humanities: GIS and the Future of Humanities Scholarship.* Bloomington: Indiana University Press, 2010.

Bonn, Maria, and Mike Furlough, eds. *Getting the Word Out: Academic Libraries as Scholarly Publishers.* Chicago: Association of College and Research Libraries, 2015.

Borgman, Christine L. *Scholarship in the Digital Age: Information, Infrastructure, and the Internet.* Cambridge, MA: MIT Press, 2007.

"The Digital Future Is Now: A Call to Action for the Humanities." *DHQ: Digital Humanities Quarterly* 3.4 (2009). http://digitalhumanities.org/dhq/vol/3/4/000077/000077.html.

Bourdieu, Pierre. *The Field of Cultural Production.* New York: Columbia University Press, 1993.

Bryson, Tim. *Digital Humanities.* Washington, DC: Association of Research Libraries, 2011.

Burdick, Anne, Johanna Drucker, et al. *Digital_Humanities.* Cambridge, MA: MIT Press, 2012.

Burnard, Lou, Katherine O'Brien O'Keeffe, and John Unsworth. *Electronic Textual Editing.* New York: Modern Language Association of America, 2006.

Busa, Roberto. "The Annals of Humanities Computing: The *Index Thomisticus.*" *Computers and the Humanities* 14 (1980): 83–90.

Bush, Vannevar. "As We May Think." *The Atlantic,* July 1945. http://www.theatlantic.com/magazine/archive/1945/07/as-we-may-think/303881.

California, Liaison Committee of the State Board of Education, and The Regents of the University of California, and Arthur Gardiner Coons. "A Master Plan for Higher Education in California, 1960–1975." 1960. http://content.cdlib.org/ark:/13030/hb9c6008sn.

Carter, Bryan. *Digital Humanities: Current Perspective, Practice and Research.* Cutting-Edge Technologies in Higher Education series. Bingley, UK: Emerald Group Publishing Limited, 2013.

Celentano A., A. Cortesi, and P. Mastandrea. "Informatica Umanistica: Una disciplina di confine." *Mondo Digitale* 4 (2004): 44–55.

Chatzichristodoulou, Maria, Janis Jefferies, and Rachel Zerihan, eds. *Interfaces of Performance.* Farnham, UK: Ashgate, 2009.

Classen, Christoph, Susanne Kinnebrock, and Maria Löblich, eds. "Towards Web History: Sources, Methods, and Challenges in the Digital Age." *Historical Social Research* 37.4 (2012): 97–188.

Cohen, Daniel J., and Tom Scheinfeldt. *Hacking the Academy: New Approaches to Scholarship and Teaching from Digital Humanities.* Ann Arbor: University of Michigan Press, 2013.

College Art Association. "Code for Best Practices in Fair Use for the Visual Arts." 2015. http://www.collegeart.org/pdf/fair-use/best-practices-fair-use-visual -arts.pdf.

Committee on Intellectual Property Rights and the Emerging Information Infrastructure. *The Digital Dilemma: Intellectual Property in the Information Age.* Washington, DC: National Humanities Press, 2000. http://www.nap.edu/ openbook.php?record_id=9601.

Condron Frances, Michael Fraser, and Stuart Sutherland, eds. *Oxford University Computing Services Guide to Digital Resources for the Humanities.* Morgantown: West Virginia University Press, 2001.

Council on Library and Information Resources. "Working Together or Apart: Promoting the Next Generation of Digital Scholarship." Report of a Workshop Sponsored by the Council on Library and Information Resources and the National Endowment for the Humanities. Washington, DC: Council on Library and Information Resources, 2009. http://www.clir.org/pubs/ reports/pub145/pub145.pdf.

Crawford, Tim, and Lorna Gibson, eds. *Modern Methods for Musicology: Prospects, Proposals, and Realities.* Farnham, UK: Ashgate, 2009.

Davidson, Cathy N. "Humanities 2.0: Promise, Perils, Predictions." *PMLA* 123.3 (2008): 707–17.

Deegan, Marilyn, and Willard McCarty. *Collaborative Research in the Digital Humanities.* Farnham, UK: Ashgate, 2011.

Deegan, Marilyn, and Kathryn Sutherland, eds. *Text Editing, Print and the Digital World.* Farnham, UK: Ashgate, 2009.

Delve, Janet, and David Anderson. *Preserving Complex Digital Objects.* London: Facet, 2014.

Deyrup, Marta M. *Digital Scholarship.* New York: Routledge, 2009.

Earhart, A., and A. Jewell, eds. *The American Literary Scholar in the Digital Age.* Ann Arbor: University of Michigan Press, 2009.

Fitzpatrick, Kathleen. *Planned Obsolescence: Publishing, Technology, and the Future of the Academy.* New York: New York University Press, 2011.

Flanagan, Mary. *Critical Play: Radical Game Design.* Cambridge, MA: MIT Press, 2009.

Gardiner, Eileen, and Ronald G. Musto. "The 7 Digital Arts: Approaching Electronic Publishing." Talk presented at the Getty Research Institute and College Art Forum on *Art History and the Digital World.* Los Angeles, CA, June 8–9, 2006. https://www.getty.edu/research/exhibitions_events/events/ digital_world/pdf/egardiner_rmusto.pdf.

"The Electronic Book." In *The Oxford Companion to the Book.* Edited by Michael F. Suarez, SJ and H. R. Woudhuysen. Oxford: Oxford University Press, 2010, 164–71.

Gladney, Henry M. *Preserving Digital Information*. Berlin: Springer, 2007.

Gold, Matthew K., ed. *Debates in the Digital Humanities*. Minneapolis: University of Minnesota Press, 2012.

Green, D., and M. Roy. "Things To Do While Waiting for the Future to Happen: Building Cyberinfrastructure for the Liberal Arts." *Educause Review* 43.4 (2008): 35–48.

Greengrass, Mark, and Lorna Hughes, eds. *The Virtual Representation of the Past*. Farnham, UK: Ashgate, 2008.

Hancock, B., and M. J. Giarlo. "Moving to XML: Latin Texts XML Conversion Project at the Center for Electronic Texts in the Humanities." *Library Hi Tech* 19.3 (2001): 257–64.

Hayles, N. Katherine. *My Mother Was a Computer: Digital Subjects and Literary Texts*. Chicago: University of Chicago Press, 2005.

How We Think: Digital Media and Contemporary Technogenesis. Chicago: University of Chicago Press, 2012.

Hirsch, Brett D. *Digital Humanities Pedagogy: Practices, Principles and Politics*. Cambridge: OpenBook Publishers, 2012.

Hockey, Susan. *Electronic Texts in the Humanities: Principles and Practice*. Oxford: Oxford University Press, 2000.

Honing, Henkjan. "The Role of ICT in Music Research: A Bridge Too Far?" *International Journal of Humanities and Arts Computing* 1.1 (2008): 67–75. http://dare.uva.nl/document/129927.

Inman, James, Cheryl Reed, and Peter Sands, eds. *Electronic Collaboration in the Humanities: Issues and Options*. Mahwah, NJ: Lawrence Erlbaum, 2003.

Jaschik, Scott. "Tenure in a Digital Era." *Inside Higher Ed* (May 26, 2009). http://www.insidehighered.com/news/2009/05/26/digital.

Jockers, Matthew Lee. *Macroanalysis: Digital Methods and Literary History*. Urbana: University of Illinois Press, 2013.

Jones, Steven E. *The Emergence of the Digital Humanities*. New York: Routledge, 2013.

Katz, Stanley N. "Why Technology Matters: The Humanities in the Twenty-First Century." *Interdisciplinary Science Reviews* 30.2 (2005): 105–18.

Kirschenbaum, Matthew G. *Image-Based Humanities Computing*. Dordrecht, The Netherlands: Kluwer Academic Publishers, 2001.

Mechanisms: New Media and the Forensic Imagination. Cambridge, MA: MIT Press, 2008.

Klein, Julie T. *Humanities, Culture, and Interdisciplinarity: The Changing American Academy*. Albany: State University of New York Press, 2005.

Knowles, Anne Kelly, and Amy Hillier. *Placing History: How Maps, Spatial Data, and GIS Are Changing Historical Scholarship*. Redlands, CA: Esri Press, 2008.

Lancashire, Ian. *Teaching Literature and Language Online*. New York: Modern Language Association of America, 2009.

Liu, Alan. *The Laws of Cool: Knowledge Work and the Culture of Information*. Chicago: University of Chicago Press, 2004.

"The Future of Humanities in the Digital Age." Pauley Symposium, University of Nebraska, 2006. http://digitalhistory.wordpress.com/2006/10/01/allen-liu-the-future-of-humanities-in-the-digital-age-with-roundtable-discussion.

Manovich, Lev. *Software Takes Command*. New York: Bloomsbury, 2013.

Marcum, Deanna B., ed. *Development of Digital Libraries: An American Perspective*. Westport, CT: Greenwood Press, 2001.

McCarty, Willard. *Humanities Computing*. Basingstoke, UK: Palgrave Macmillan, 2005.

McGann, Jerome. "The Future Is Digital." *Journal of Victorian Culture* 13.1 (2008): 80–8.

—— ed. *Online Humanities Scholarship: The Shape of Things to Come*. Proceedings of the Mellon Foundation Online Humanities Conference at the University of Virginia, March 26–8, 2010. Houston: Rice University Press, 2010.

—— *A New Republic of Letters*. Cambridge, MA: Harvard University Press, 2014.

McSherry, Corynne. *Who Owns Academic Work? Battling for Control of Intellectual Property*. Cambridge, MA: Harvard University Press, 2003.

Modern Language Association. "Report of the MLA Task Force on Evaluating Scholarship for Tenure and Promotion." New York: Modern Language Association, 2006. http://www.mla.org/tenure_promotion.

Moretti, Franco. *Graphs, Maps, Trees: Abstract Models for Literary History*. New York: Verso, 2007.

—— *Distant Reading*. London: Verso, 2013.

Mosco, Vincent. *The Digital Sublime: Myth, Power, and Cyberspace*. Cambridge, MA: MIT Press, 2004.

Musto, Ronald G. "Google Books Mutilates the Printed Past." The Chronicle Review, *The Chronicle of Higher Education* (June 12, 2009): B4–5. http://chronicle.com/article/Google-Books-Mutilates-the-/44463.

O'Donnell, James J. *Avatars of the Word: From Papyrus to Cyberspace*. Cambridge, MA: Harvard University Press, 1998.

O'Gorman, Marcel. *E-Crit: Digital Media, Critical Theory, and the Humanities*. Toronto: University of Toronto Press, 2007.

Peer, Willie van, Sonia Zyngier, and Vander Viana. *Literary Education and Digital Learning Methods and Technologies for Humanities Studies*. Hershey, PA: Information Science Reference, 2010.

Presner, Todd, David Shepard, and Yoh Kawano. *Hypercities: Thick Mapping in the Digital Humanities*. Cambridge, MA: Harvard University Press, 2014.

Ramsay, Stephen. *Reading Machines: Toward an Algorithmic Criticism*. Urbana: University of Illinois Press, 2011.

Rieger, Oya Y. "Framing Digital Humanities: The Role of New Media in Humanities Scholarship." *First Monday* 15.10 (2010). http://journals.uic.edu/ojs/index.php/fm/article/view/3198/2628.

Rooney, Ellen, and Elizabeth Weed, eds. "In the Shadows of the Digital Humanities." Special issue, *Differences: A Journal of Feminist Cultural Studies* 25.1 (2014).

Rosenzweig, Roy. *Clio Wired: The Future of the Past in the Digital Age*. New York: Columbia University Press, 2011.

Rydberg-Cox, Jeffrey A. *Digital Libraries and the Challenges of Digital Humanities.* Oxford: Chandos, 2006.

Schreibman, Susan, Raymond George Siemens, and John Unsworth, eds. *A Companion to Digital Humanities.* Oxford: Blackwell, 2004. http://digital humanities.org/companion.

Shaw, Deborah, and Charles H. Davis. "The Modern Language Association: Electronic and Paper Surveys of Computer-Based Tool Use." *Journal of the American Society for Information Science* 47.12 (1996): 932–40. https://scholarworks.iu.edu/dspace/handle/2022/13384.

Siemens, Raymond George, and David Moorman. *Mind Technologies: Humanities Computing and the Canadian Academic Community.* Calgary: University of Calgary Press, 2006.

Siemens, Raymond George, and Susan Schreibman. *A Companion to Digital Literary Studies.* Oxford: Blackwell, 2008. http://www.digitalhumanities .org/companionDLS.

Suber, Peter. *Open Access.* Cambridge, MA: MIT Press, 2012. http://mitpress.mit .edu/books/open-access.

Sutherland, Kathryn, ed. *Electronic Text: Investigations in Method and Theory.* Oxford: Clarendon Press, 1997.

Terras, Melissa M., Julianne Nyhan, and Edward Vanhoutte. *Defining Digital Humanities: A Reader.* Farnham, UK: Ashgate, 2013.

Thaller, Manfred, ed. "Controversies around the Digital Humanities." Special issue, *Historical Social Research* 37.3 (2012): 7–229.

Thompson, John B. *Books in the Digital Age: The Transformation of Academic and Higher Education Publishing in Britain and the United States.* Cambridge: Polity Press, 2005.

Turkel, William J. "Interchange: The Promise of Digital History." *Journal of American History* 95.2 (2008). http://www.journalofamericanhistory.org/ issues/952/interchange/index.html.

Unsworth, John. "Scholarly Primitives: What Methods Do Humanities Researchers Have in Common, and How Might Our Tools Reflect This?" Paper presented at Humanities Computing: Formal Methods, Experimental Practice. King's College, London, May 13, 2000. http://people.brandeis .edu/~unsworth/Kings.5-00/primitives.html.

"New Research Methods for the Humanities." Lecture presented at the National Humanities Center, Research Triangle Park, NC. November 11, 2005. http://people.brandeis.edu/~unsworth/lyman.htm.

Vaidhyanathan, Siva. *Copyrights and Copywrongs: The Rise of Intellectual Property and How It Threatens Creativity.* New York: New York University Press, 2001.

The Googlization of Everything: (And Why We Should Worry). Berkeley: University of California Press, 2011.

Vandendorpe, Christian. *From Papyrus to Hypertext: Toward the Universal Digital Library.* Trans. by Phyllis Aronoff and Howard Scott. Urbana: University of Illinois Press, 2009.

Warwick, Claire, Melissa M. Terras, and Julianne Nyhan. *Digital Humanities in Practice.* London: Facet Publishing in association with UCL Centre for Digital Humanities, 2012.

Williford, Christa, and Charles Henry. *One Culture: Computationally Intensive Research in the Humanities and Social Sciences.* Washington, DC: Council on Library and Information Resources, 2012.

Web Resources

Alliance of Digital Humanities Organizations, http://adho.org.

Creative Commons, http://creativecommons.org.

CUNY Digital Humanities Resource Guide, http://commons.gc.cuny.edu/wiki/index.php/The_CUNY_Digital_Humanities_Resource_Guide.

Digital Humanities and the Library, http://miriamposner.com/blog/digital-humanities-and-the-library.

Digital Humanities Bibliography, http://www.craigcarey.net/dhbibliography.

Digital Humanities Manifesto 2.0, http://manifesto.humanities.ucla.edu/2009/05/29/the-digital-humanities-manifesto-20.

Digital Research Tools (DiRT), http://dirtdirectory.org.

HASTAC: Humanities, Arts, Science, and Technology Alliance and Collaboratory, http://www.hastac.org.

Library of Congress, Office of Digital Preservation News Archive, http://www.digitalpreservation.gov/news/index.html.

Ninch Guide to Good Practice in the Digital Representation and Management of Cultural Heritage Materials, http://www.nyu.edu/its/humanities//ninchguide.

Office for Humanities Communication Publications, Kings College London, http://www.ohc.kcl.ac.uk/books.html.

Scholarly Kitchen, http://scholarlykitchen.sspnet.org.

Stanford Copyright Overview, http://fairuse.stanford.edu/Copyright_and_Fair_Use_Overview.

University of Nebraska, Lincoln, Center for Digital Research in the Humanities, http://cdrh.unl.edu/articles-resources.

Index

CPSIA information can be obtained
at www.ICGtesting.com
Printed in the USA
LVHW010349030820
662199LV00010B/187